Praise for *D. L. Moody—A Life*

Kevin Belmonte's *D. L. Moody* revitalizes the story of the nineteenth century's greatest evangelist. This book is an absolute tour de force and will serve as important reading for general audiences and scholars alike.

> DR. D. MICHAEL LINDSAY
> *President of Gordon College, author of the Pulitzer*
> *Prize–nominated book* Faith in the Halls of Power

After his exhilarating work on Wilberforce, Kevin Belmonte has produced another gripping biography of a great individual who helped to turn the tide of his time rather than just drift with it. Belmonte's sweeping narrative, which takes Moody from the poverty and meagre education of his childhood to his role as a passionate speaker, educator, and philanthropist, never loses track of a central theme: that our circumstances, or the climates of opinion in which we are born, do not have to determine our views or restrict our hope. He shows how Moody stood firm on the rock of his moral and spiritual convictions and was enabled to change the world for the better.

> THE REVEREND DR. MALCOLM GUITE
> *Chaplain of Girton College, Cambridge University, England*

Kevin Belmonte has written a book very much in the spirit of his previous work on William Wilberforce. It is a book to be read by all of us, as the model of D. L. Moody should be utilized in all of our lives.

> PHILIP ANSCHUTZ
> *Founder and CEO of The Anschutz Corporation*

I'm not sure what I'm loving more, the surprising story of D. L. Moody, or Kevin Belmonte's terrific telling of it—makes me want to be a better person, and a better writer.

> STEVE BELL
> *Juno Award winning singer/songwriter,*
> *creator of the album "Keening for the Dawn"*

A fascinating and inspiring account of the life of an extraordinary man, skillfully told. *D. L. Moody—A Life*, by Kevin Belmonte, will introduce a new generation to an often-overlooked hero whose love for Christ and the poor changed the world.

> CHERIE HARDER
> *President of The Trinity Forum, Washington, D.C.*

A long overdue reminder of one of the nineteenth century's great luminaries. Kevin Belmonte has written an extraordinary account of D. L. Moody's life journey. What an important work.

> CHARLES OLCOTT
> *Former President and CEO of Burger King Corporation*

This is a robust and engaging biography of a man who changed his world. The worth of this book is not only embedded in the text, but also in the endnotes —which will rightly send you and me racing elsewhere to dig deeper and find out more about the great D. L Moody.

> CANON DAVID ISHERWOOD
> *Rector of Holy Trinity Church, Clapham (William Wilberforce's church)*
> *Vicar of St Peter Prescott Place*

The story of D. L. Moody must be told, and I am overjoyed that acclaimed author Kevin Belmonte has done so. The nineteenth century experienced the influence of Moody's life and work. Now, thankfully, twenty-first-century readers can reap the benefits.

> MARK RIVERA
> *Pastor of Bethany Church, Raymond, New Hampshire*

Kevin Belmonte traces the life of D. L. Moody from cradle to grave, displaying how God miraculously transforms the ordinary into the extraordinary. He plainly captures how the mundane course of life, when placed under the hand of God, can result in a life of immeasurable impact.

> TOMMY MCCLAM
> *Youth Pastor, and Director of Mentoring, YouthBuild USA*

No living person knows D. L. Moody more intimately than Kevin Belmonte, a biographer without peer when it comes to the uneducated farm boy from Northfield, Massachusetts, who became the most recognized global evangelist of his day, and a champion of Christian education whose legacy even now is being revived.

> F. LaGard SMITH
> *Visiting Professor of Law, Faulkner University*

I can't imagine any follower of Jesus not finding something to admire about D. L. Moody by reading this book. I'm grateful for the privilege of reading it.

> THE REVEREND JUDSON STONE
> *Chaplain, First Rate, Inc.*

Kevin Belmonte reminds us that D. L. Moody was revolutionary in his own time—an innovator, evangelist, and world-changer.

CATHERINE BLAKE
Adjunct professor, Peter T. Paul College of Business & Economics
The University of New Hampshire

I thought I knew William Wilberforce and G. K. Chesterton, until I read Kevin Belmonte's brilliant books, and saw them from a completely new perspective. Now Kevin has done it again with D. L. Moody. *D. L. Moody—A Life* will not only reveal the remarkable story of a man who changed the world, but inspire you to change yours.

PHIL COOKE
Filmmaker, media consultant, and author of Unique: Telling Your Story in the Age of Brands and Social Media

After his marvelous work on Wilberforce and Chesterton, Kevin Belmonte has given us a portrait of D. L. Moody so rich, so eloquently presented, and so detailed that Moody becomes nearly a living figure as you read through these pages. This is literary portraiture at its finest.

LANCIA E. SMITH
Author and photographer

Moody's character and life were God's template for present-day evangelism, Christian education, and the philanthropic means to subsidize every vision God gave him. Trusting God's faithfulness, these visions and plans were surmountable and completed. Throughout the world today, D.L. Moody's legacy is resplendent!

—DELLA JANE BROOKS-HEALEY
Author and great-granddaughter of President John Adams

D. L. Moody.

A LIFE

Innovator | Evangelist | World-Changer

KEVIN BELMONTE

MOODY PUBLISHERS

CHICAGO

All Scripture quotations are taken from the King James Version.

Published in association with the literary agency of Books & Such Agency.

PHOTO CREDITS: Page 246 courtesy of David Powell; page 270 courtesy of Kevin Belmonte. Photos chapters 4, 6, 20, and page 269 from Moody Bible Institute archives folder "Moody Family"; photos chapter 9 from MBI archives folder "Campaigns: Scotland" and "Campaigns British Isles"; photo chapter 21 from MBI archives folder "Campaigns: Kansas." All other photos courtesy of MBI archives and part of the Moodyana Collection.

Edited by James Vincent
Interior design: Ragont Design
Cover design: Erik M. Peterson
Cover photo courtesy of Moody Bible Institute archive folder
    "D.L.M. Life-Ministry/40-50 years of age folder 1"

Library of Congress Cataloging-in-Publication Data

Belmonte, Kevin Charles.
  D. L. Moody : a life : innovator evangelist world-changer / Kevin Belmonte.
    pages cm
  Includes bibliographical references and index.
  ISBN 978-0-8024-1204-1
  1. Moody, Dwight Lyman, 1837-1899. 2. Evangelists—United States—Biography. I. Title.
  BV3785.M7B343 2014

269'.2092—dc23
[B]
                                    2014001658

We hope you enjoy this book from Moody Publishers. Our goal is to provide high-quality, thought-provoking books and products that connect truth to your real needs and challenges. For more information on other books and products written and produced from a biblical perspective, go to www.moodypublishers.com or write to:

Moody Publishers
820 N. LaSalle Boulevard
Chicago, IL 60610

3 5 7 9 10 8 6 4 2

Printed in the United States of America

To the students, faculty, staff, and alumni
of Northfield Mount Hermon—in gratitude
for the life and legacy of your founder.

CONTENTS

Foreword

O n my journey to help define, preserve, and make accessible the legacy of my great-grandfather, Dwight L. Moody, and to assure his rightful place in American history, I had the pleasure of meeting Kevin Belmonte while he was in Northfield, Massachusetts, doing research about Mr. Moody.

I was impressed with his enthusiasm to learn about my great-grandfather, and his interest in sharing that knowledge with others via seminars, lectures, and articles. Upon learning about his authorship of books written about other famous people, I read several of them. I was impressed by Kevin's thorough knowledge of subject matter, but even more pleased with his literary style that makes reading enjoyable and easy to comprehend.

Needless to say, I was surprised and pleased when Kevin told me he had written a book about my great-grandfather, and asked me if I would like to review an early draft. I accepted that offer. My reaction: Kevin's thorough knowledge of subject matter and his user-friendly literary style are also clearly reflected in *D. L. Moody—A Life*.

During my journey mentioned above, I have met and come in contact with people from all over the United States and several foreign countries. I am continually amazed at how these people from different religious, nationality, age, gender, economic and geographical backgrounds still love and respect Dwight L. Moody. Reading Kevin Belmonte's book will help you understand why "Moody Still Lives" today!

It is clearly evident Kevin has absorbed the Moody Spirit, and is anxious to do all he can to preserve the Moody Legacy. I heartily recommend *D. L. Moody—A Life*.

DAVID S. POWELL

Mount Hermon, Class of 1948

Yale University, Class of 1952

*I got a treat last night. Moody sat up alone with
me till near 1 o'clock telling me the story of his life.
He told me the whole thing. A reporter might have
made a fortune out of it.*

*I hope you will see something of Moody. . . . My
admiration of him has increased a hundredfold.
I had no idea before of the moral size of the man,
and I think very few know what he really is.[1]*

—Henry Drummond

Preface

MCKINLEY, T. R., AND WILSON

Revivals are, as we read elsewhere, cyclonic. They recur. Possibly, one is due. If so, society will have reason to be grateful if there arises a revivalist so sound in himself, so true to his faith, so human in his contacts, so consecrated in his loyalties, as Dwight L. Moody.[1]

—*The New York Times*

It is rare to find a man given homage by three presidents, let alone three in succession. Yet such was D. L. Moody. The presidents who praised him understood that he had shaped their time. And if the visage of Theodore Roosevelt would one day be set on Mount Rushmore, Moody gained a kind of immortality only presidents can bestow: their genuine respect.

We can read the words they wrote about Moody, and what they said of him.

Following the death of D. L. Moody in late December 1899, William McKinley sent a moving letter of condolence to Moody's widow.

There was a sequel. Several months later, Moody's son Will called at the White House. Ushered to an inner room, he was given preference over other callers. When taken to see the president, Will's intention was to extend an invitation for the president to come to Northfield, Massachusetts, home to three schools D. L. Moody had established. This done, Will had no wish to trespass on the president's time. He would extend the invitation, offer thanks, and leave. There were many other callers that day.

But McKinley was in no hurry. He bade Will sit down, saying, "I want to talk with you, Mr. Moody." He paused for a moment, then said, "Do you realize that your father was a very great man?"

Will was circumspect in his reply. "I am sure he was a *good* man," he said.

McKinley grew insistent. Will Moody never forgot the words that came next.

"But your father was a great man too," the president said, "and when greatness and goodness are combined, you have a rare character."[2]

———⟨⟨⟨⟩⟩⟩———

By mid-September 1901, President McKinley had met a tragic death, taken too soon by an assassin's bullet. One year later his successor, Theodore Roosevelt, would journey to Northfield. This set the stage for a meeting no less memorable than Will Moody's White House interview.

The Pioneer Valley had never seen anything quite like it. The finest carriage in town was sent to meet the president's entourage at the Mount Hermon Station. Will Moody and T. R. stepped inside it, and began the short drive to the Auditorium of the Northfield Seminary for Young Women, the first school Moody built. A guard of honor, comprised of local town officials, went before them on horseback.

Unintentionally, a comic air pervaded this brief transit. The guard of honor, it soon became apparent, was filled with men "who had not ridden astride for many a moon." They had to help each other onto their horses, and it was all rather awkwardly done. They were no Rough Riders. Both Will Moody and the president had to hide their amusement.

When Roosevelt alighted from the carriage and stepped inside the Auditorium, Will Moody brought him over to Emma Moody, D. L.'s widow. Time slowed, chastened by courtliness. The president took Mrs. Moody's hand and spoke to her with great kindness, telling her what a deep respect he had for her husband.[3] For a few moments, perhaps, Emma Moody could forget her grief. Rightly honored, she became, if only for a day, the president's lady.

———⟨⟨⟨⟩⟩⟩———

Twelve years later, in mid-November 1914, readers of the *Congregationalist* magazine were treated to a rare event: a letter from the White House. The magazine's editor had written to ask Woodrow Wilson if he had, as rumored, once met D. L. Moody.

Wilson's reply offers one of history's best introductions to Moody. For on October 26, 1914, Wilson had written: "My dear Dr. Bridgman, this is not a legend; it is a fact, and I am perfectly willing that you should publish it. My admiration and esteem for Mr. Moody was very deep indeed." Then, following Wilson's signature, his description of the famous meeting appeared.

"I was," he remembered,

in a very plebeian place. I was in a barbershop, sitting in a chair, when I became aware that a personality had entered the room. A man had come quietly in upon the same errand as myself, and sat in the chair next to me. Every word that he uttered, though it was not in the least didactic, showed a personal interest in the man who was serving him; and before I got through with what was being done for me, I was aware that I had attended an evangelistic service, because Mr. Moody was in the next chair. I purposely lingered in the room after he left and noted the singular effect his visit had upon the barbers in that shop. They talked in undertones. They did not know his name, but they knew that something had elevated their thought. And I felt that I left that place as I should have left a place of worship.[4]

When President Wilson wrote his letter, D. L. Moody had been dead fifteen years. We are nearly one hundred years removed from that time. Yet Moody's legacy as an author, educator, philanthropist, and preacher remains vibrantly alive. He was one of the great souls of history, as the following pages attest.

FROM HOME TO BOSTON

*The first meeting I ever saw [Moody] was in a little old
shanty abandoned by a saloon-keeper . . . I saw a man
standing up, with a few tallow candles around him, holding
a negro boy, and trying to read him the story of the Prodigal
Son. A great many of the words he could not make out,
and had to skip. I thought: "If the Lord can ever use such
an instrument as that . . . it will astonish me." After that
meeting was over, Moody said, "Reynolds, I have got only
one talent: I have no education, but I love the Lord Jesus
Christ, and I want to do something for Him."[1]*

—William Reynolds

From the vantage point of history, 1837 was a year of portents. Queen Victoria ascended the throne of Britain. Charles Dickens began publishing *Oliver Twist* (in serial form). Across the ocean in America, an aspiring lawyer named Abraham Lincoln was admitted to the bar.

The world took little note that Dwight Lyman Moody was born on February 5, 1837, in Northfield, Massachusetts. But there were points of connection with the lives of his more famous contemporaries. For a start, his years on earth almost precisely mirrored the span of Victoria's reign. In his youth, Moody knew hardship on a Dickensian scale, and he knew the slums of the great city of the west: Chicago. It was here that Moody, when twenty-three, met Abraham Lincoln.

Still, when it came to his origins, Moody was in later life self-deprecating, and once marshaled a quip Mark Twain would have envied, protesting that his ancestry was of little importance. "Never mind the ancestry!" he said. "A man

I once heard of was ambitious to trace his family to *The Mayflower*—and he stumbled over a horse-thief! Never mind a man's ancestry."[2]

This flash of wit aside, Moody's family ties included some noteworthy relations. Among them were Jonathan Edwards, Harriet Beecher Stowe, Oliver Wendell Holmes, and President Grover Cleveland. Moody was also related to Franklin Roosevelt—a descendant, as Moody was, of William Holton, who settled in Northfield in 1672.[3]

Moody was likely unaware of his kinship with these famous figures; yet it is certain that his origins, and the town of his birth, were in many ways the making of him. They are profoundly important. Before middle age, he would know international fame. But no one could have predicted that, given his start in life. It was anything but promising.

Dwight Moody was the sixth child of a large and growing family. His mother, Betsy Holton Moody, was a capable, caring woman descended from Puritan forbears who settled in Northfield in the late 1600s. His father, Edwin, was a tradesman skilled in masonry.

Family lore held that Edwin Moody was something of a rough, ready, loveable rogue. Tall and stocky, he had a strong physique that suited the mason's trade. He was genial, devoted to his wife, and said to be dashing.

Still, there were worrisome traits. By turns, Edwin was called a "shiftless, lazy fellow"—though one honestly adored by his wife, children, and neighbors. He was more fond of whiskey than was good for him. And he had little money saved at the time of his marriage. This meant he had to borrow money to buy a house and small parcel of land. Betsy's relations were none too impressed with what they considered a poor farm on "a regular sand heap," but it was a place the newlyweds could call their own and start a family.[4]

During their first ten years of marriage, Edwin's load of debt increased, and it was said he was "never more than a few steps away from his creditors." Still, by all accounts, his marriage was considered a happy union.[5]

Certainly, it was a fruitful one. For by 1841, when four-year-old Dwight began attending school, he was one of seven children in school, or soon to start. And at this time, his mother was once again pregnant.

⊸⟐⟐⊷

The Moody family endured heartrending tragedy on May 28, 1841. Dwight was in the local schoolhouse with some of his siblings when a neighbor put his head in at the window, asking if any of Ed Moody's children were there. He bore terrible news: their father had just died.[6] He was only forty-one.

We have only a bare recital of how it all happened. An early biographer, W. H. Daniels, reports that on the morning of May 28, Edwin Moody was hard at work, "but feeling a pain in his side, caused by over-exertion, he went home to rest. At about one o'clock in the afternoon he felt the pain suddenly increasing, staggered to the bed, fell upon his knees beside it, and, in this posture, death seized him."[7] All circumstances pointed to a massive heart attack.

Little Dwight retained no memory of his father's funeral. But he did remember the desperate struggle that followed for his mother, left a widow with seven children. "It brings the tears to my eyes every time I think of it," he later said. "My father died before I can remember. There was a large family of us. Twins came after his death [now there were] nine of us in all. He died a bankrupt, and the creditors came in and took everything—as far as the law allowed. We had a hard struggle. Thank God for my mother! She never lost hope."[8]

Betsy Moody now had virtually no means of support. The family homestead was encumbered with a mortgage, and only "the merciful provision of the law securing dower rights" saved her from loss of the family home. As it was, she was left with only the roof over her head and her now fatherless children. The creditors had been heartless in the extreme, taking everything they could, even the kindling wood in the shed.[9]

One scene from this desperate time stayed with Dwight Moody all his life. Since the family's supply of firewood was now gone, Betsy told her children "they must stay in bed till school-time to keep warm." It was the only thing she could think of. Her relief must have been overwhelming when, soon after, she saw her brother Cyrus Holton drive up with a wagonload of wood, which he sawed and split for immediate use.

"I remember," said Moody later, "just as vividly as if it were yesterday, how I heard the sound of chips flying. I knew someone was chopping wood in our woodshed, and that we should soon have a fire. I shall never forget Uncle Cyrus coming with what seemed to me the biggest pile of wood I ever saw in my life." Such memories, Moody's son Will would later say, "always made Father's heart vibrate with sympathy for those who were in want."[10]

———◈◈◈———

Welcome as Cyrus Holton's kindness was, the pressures on Betsy Moody mounted steadily. She had two newborn children and seven others to try and provide for. In the face of such overwhelming odds, some of her neighbors pleaded with her to break up her home and place the older children in families where they might be better cared for.[11]

Betsy would have none of it. "Not as long as I have these two hands," she vowed.

Such resolve, her well-meaning neighbors felt, was foolhardy in the extreme. "You know," they insisted, "one woman can't bring up seven boys. They'll turn up in jail, or with a rope around their necks."[12]

This tough love, if what these neighbors intended, only burdened Betsy Moody further, as she later told Dwight. Through each day, she did everything she could to offer a brave face for her children, but "she cried herself to sleep at night." Looking back, Moody said: "We didn't know that, or it would have broken our hearts. We didn't know what trouble our mother was passing through."[13]

At times, Betsy was cruelly treated. Four days after she gave birth to the twins she'd been carrying, Ezra Purple, the wealthy landowner who held the mortgage on the Moody farm, came to collect his yearly payment. Betsy, still recovering, had to receive her insistent creditor in her bedroom. She said the only thing she could: she didn't have money just then, but would get it as soon as she might. With a severity Scrooge would have admired, Ezra Purple castigated Betsy in coarse language and stormed from the house. Getting into his carriage and setting the whip to his horse, the sudden jolt broke the harness, and he was pitched headlong to the ground, though he escaped injury. Outraged neighbors, when they heard of this, said: "A pity he didn't break his neck."

After the event, Uncle Cyrus and another Holton brother pooled their money and covered the mortgage. For one more year, at least, Betsy would be able to stay in her home. Years later, D. L. Moody would turn the tables on the family of Ezra Purple—but for very different reasons.[14]

—◁◦◦◦▷—

Betsy Moody might have despaired, but an unlooked-for mercy arrived in the person of the Reverend Oliver Everett, the aging minister of the First Congregational Church.

His kindness was a sunshine of hope. Materially, he brought the Moody family food and other staples from his own home. He offered to help with the children's schooling and urged Betsy to keep the family together.[15] Aging though he was, he wasn't daunted by the prospect of spending hours in a home filled with active, energetic children. Some clergymen, as they grow older, become more quiet and retiring. Everett had a rare gift for expressing genuine, if modestly expressed, affection. Betsy Moody's children warmed to him. Young Dwight never forgot Everett's habit of placing an affectionate hand on his head, or saying a kind word.

For a fatherless boy, such things loom large, and linger in the memory. Dwight always recalled Everett's gift for homespun, simple kindness. His pastoral visits were frequent and welcomed. In addition to discreetly given gifts of money, he would very helpfully settle quarrels among the Moody boys. It was his habit as well "to give the little ones a bright piece of silver all round" and to encourage Betsy Moody by "telling her God would never forget her labor of love." At one time, he took young Dwight into his family "to do errands, and go to school."

This was saying something, for as Dwight grew older, he increasingly showed himself a headstrong, wild colt of a boy. As an old New England phrase had it, "no one could slap a saddle on him." More than once, Everett would scratch his head in perplexity. He meant to correct Dwight more often than he actually did. But the boy's pranks were disarmingly funny.[16]

Reverend Everett was singular in his kindness and singular in his faith commitment. The First Congregational Church may have turned Unitarian, as many Congregational churches throughout New England had done at this time, but Everett remained within a more orthodox wing of that body. He believed in the Bible as the inspired Word of God, in Christ as Savior, and in the church and her sacraments.[17]

So it was that in 1842, he "baptized the Moodys in one batch," invoking the ancient—and Trinitarian—phrase, "in the name of the Father, Son, and Holy Ghost."[18] It was an earnest of his ministry among them. Coming alongside this needy family, the hope of heaven had drawn near, for hope was not least among the gifts Oliver Everett shared with them.

———◦◈◦———

Surviving accounts indicate that from his earliest years, Dwight Moody was headstrong, resolute, and not easily turned from something once he'd set his mind on it.

Around harvesttime, Dwight once wished to visit his grandmother Holton, who lived about four miles away. He was just five years old, and so long a journey seemed insurmountable.

Someone had given him five cents earlier, half the required amount for a child's fare to cover that distance. Still, he refused to admit defeat. When the passing stage stopped, he pleaded with the driver to accept the five cents for his fare.

The stage was already full inside, but at last, the driver consented "to take him as baggage" and placed him on top of the coach, within the rack that guarded the trunks.

So it was that he arrived at his grandmother's, to everyone's great surprise, and spent much of the day at their old farm. His relatives thoroughly enjoyed his visit but urged him to make an early start for home. They thought he would have to walk the distance, but Dwight had other ideas. A coach ride would do, and nothing else.

So he went out into the fields, picked a clutch of wildflowers, another of caraway, and once more hailed the coach—offering the flowers and caraway in exchange for a return fare. Something about the little boy's sturdy determination won the driver over again, and Dwight returned home in triumph perched on the stage box.[19]

Other Tom Sawyer-like incidents took place in Moody's younger years. One was an instance of Yankee grit and shrewd dealing, if not stubborn determination. At the close of one summer's work, when Dwight was perhaps ten or twelve years old, he found an old horse on the home farm, which his elder brother thought not worth keeping over winter, as he had no use for him. All attempts to sell the poor creature had proved fruitless.

"I can sell that horse," said Dwight confidently. With that, he mounted the horse, and set off to find a buyer.

After a while he came upon an old farmer who, unknown to Dwight, was fond of a joke. It tickled the farmer's fancy to see "such a little chap peddling a horse." So the farmer said he would trade for the horse and, in return, give Dwight a sleigh and a wagon.

Dwight couldn't believe his good fortune, and quickly dismounted to go see what he'd acquired. Soon enough, he found the sleigh and wagon—buried under a mountain of hay in the mow of the farmer's barn. One can well imagine the farmer saying with a laugh, "Good luck, son," and handing him a pitchfork.

But Dwight refused to be beat. With boyish bravado, he said he thought the whole thing a bargain and set to work removing the huge pile of hay, one pitchfork-full at a time.

It took him two days to finish. But when he did, he had a sleigh and wagon to take home to his family. It was hard to say who was more surprised—the farmer or the rest of the Moody family.[20]

"In those younger days," Will Moody would say of his father, "he seemed to love the excitement of a crowd." One uneventful winter prompted a decision that "something must be done" to liven things up.

So telling no one, Dwight took great pains to write out an announcement for a temperance meeting, "to be addressed by an out-of-town lecturer," and posted it on the district schoolhouse door. On the evening announced, a large crowd gathered in the schoolhouse, which was warmed and lighted for the occasion.

But no speaker came, and Dwight was first among those who roundly condemned the practical joker who put over the hoax. Years went by before anyone discovered it was he.[21]

The district schoolhouse was the setting for more than one well-remembered Moody prank. As it happened, local citizens set great store by the "Closing Exercises" held at the school each year. For younger students especially, it was a chance to show what they'd learned in a public setting. Parents had a chance to be proud of their children.

One year, Dwight, already a town character, had been asked to give a recitation—some lines from Mark Antony's oration over Julius Caesar. Given prior behavior, he was an unlikely choice. Nevertheless, to heighten the dramatic effect, a small box, representing a coffin, was placed on the teacher's desk, which became a makeshift funeral bier.

How Dwight managed to smuggle a tomcat into that small box, much less keep it quiet, remains a mystery. But as he reached the close of his recitation, he knocked the lid off the box, and out jumped one very loud and very frightened cat. The cat's cries weren't the only screams that followed. One can only imagine what Betsy Moody thought.[22]

<hr />

Meanwhile, notwithstanding Reverend Everett's assistance early on, provision for the Moody family remained a continuing challenge. Dwight, as he grew older, often found temporary employment, as his elder brothers did, in neighboring towns.

He never forgot his first experience of this, which dates to 1847: "There were nine of us children," he said, "and my mother had great difficulty in keeping the wolf from the door. My next older brother, Luther, had found a place for me to work during the winter months in Greenfield, a neighboring village about thirteen miles away, and early one November morning we started out together on our dismal journey.

"Do you know, November has been a dreary month to me ever since. As we passed over the river and up the opposite side of the valley, we turned to look back for a last view of home. It was to be my last, for weeks, for months perhaps, and my heart well nigh broke at the thought. That was the longest journey I ever took, for thirteen miles was more to me at ten years old than the world's circumference."[23]

How vivid this memory was can be seen in the balance of Moody's recollection. Fifty years on, it still held power and meaning.

"When at last we arrived in the town," he remembered, "I had hard work to keep back my tears, and my brother had to do his best to cheer me. Suddenly he pointed to someone and said: 'There's a man that'll give you a cent; he gives one to every new boy that comes to town.'

"He was a feeble, old, white-haired man, and I was so afraid that he would pass me by that I planted myself directly in his path. As he came up to us, my brother spoke to him, and he stopped and looked at me.

"'Why, I've never seen you before. You must be a new boy,' he said.

"He asked me about my home, and then, laying his trembling hand upon my head, he told me that, although I had no earthly father, my Heavenly Father loved me, and then he gave me a bright new cent."

Dwight concluded: "I don't remember what became of that cent, but that old man's blessing has followed me for over fifty years; and to my dying day I shall feel the kindly pressure of that hand upon my head."[24]

The place of that penny in Moody's young life has a more somber counterpart. For bright as the close of that memory was, another memory associated with the earning of a penny showed just how vital his childhood earnings were for his needy family. Well before he was ten years old, he went to work. That memory lingered too and was one Moody shared at his mother's funeral.

"I recall when I first earned any money," he said then. "It was one cent a week for tending cows. It went into the common treasury. Every penny was needed, and was put to the best purpose."[25]

With what free time he had, Dwight seemed always on the move, whether swimming in the Connecticut River or running in the hills around his home. "And I could run like a deer," he remembered.[26]

One can well understand why he loved to run the hills around his home. Northfield is one of the most beautiful rural towns in New England, with mountains and wooded ridges that ring the fertile Connecticut River Valley. In all seasons of the year, especially autumn, the countryside is stunning, particularly when morning mist gilds the mountains, and they seem crowned with an otherworldly beauty.

And what of his education? Always, it had to be balanced with the need for him to generate income, however slight. The vignettes given above show that he was bright, resourceful, and determined—yet when it came to his schooling, the stories become haphazard and worrisome.

It wasn't that he hadn't the capacity to have been a good student. Subsequent events in Moody's life would show he had a keen intellect, and that he, like Abraham Lincoln, had many of the gifts of one both self-taught and independent. Yet, in his youth, the ungovernable sides of his nature, coupled with sporadic attendance at school, militated against his success as a student.

The limited time of his formal education was notably described by W. H. Daniels, who learned firsthand from Betsy Moody what those years were like. "Dwight," Daniels wrote, "went through as many as a dozen terms at the little district schoolhouse; but very little of the schools ever went through him."[27]

Moody would soon leave Northfield to make a life for himself. But before he did, and before his days at school were over, the picture that emerges is that of a hard-to-handle young man chafing to get away—with only his mother's most earnest pleas to keep him from giving free rein to the roustabout sides of his nature.

Though he did attend church with his siblings when a youngster, and was grateful in later life for Oliver Everett's example, as he grew older, Moody eventually came to resent going to church. The departure of Everett—as much of a surrogate father as he ever had, or might have accepted—was marked by the arrival of a pastor whose cold indifference sapped any appeal there might have been for Sunday services.

This new pastor was a forbidding man personally and had a dour pulpit presence. When Sunday in those less happy days arrived, and the Moody children, tired from a week's work, filed into their pew, little that was desirable awaited them.

"I don't know that the new minister ever said a kind thing to me," Moody remembered, "or even once put his hand on my head. I don't know that he ever noticed me, unless it was when I was asleep in the gallery, and he woke me up. That kind of thing won't do; we must make Sunday the most attractive day of the week; not a day to be dreaded, but a day of happiness."[28]

One reads Moody's last recollections of this dour clergyman with real regret. "When I was a boy," he said, "I used to look upon Sunday with a kind of dread. Very few kind words were associated with that day."[29]

Absent the fatherly presence of someone like Oliver Everett, Dwight would now barely brook authority. In four sentences, Daniels described the teen Moody had become: "His pride," Daniels wrote, "was all the time leading him to undertake things far beyond his years. His mother said, 'He used to think himself a man when he was only a boy.' The fatherly authority was wanting, and he soon came to feel himself his own master. Anything was easier than submission."[30]

Coarse habits began to rear their head. "I'm ashamed to tell it," Moody later remembered, "but I got so I could swear, and it didn't trouble my conscience."[31] To the dismay of family and friends, "passionate outbursts of temper," and fistfights with other boys became common.[32]

Instances of delinquency began to occur. Dwight thought nothing of leading a group of boys in stampeding a neighbor's cattle, done by quietly climbing into the empty rafters of the man's barn, then suddenly raising loud whoops and yells, while jumping about on the loose planks. Frightened young steers broke through barnyard fences and scattered to the winds.

That someone could have been seriously hurt seems to have escaped him, even as he'd crossed the line over into vandalism and could have been prosecuted for damages (worse yet, his mother might have been), had he and his friends been caught.

Given all this, it's not surprising that during the limited time of Moody's formal schooling, battles with his teacher were common. In speaking of it, he recalled: "At the school I used to go to when I was a boy, we had a teacher who used to keep a rattan in his desk." Just the thought of it, he said, brought memories of painful punishment. "My back tingles now as I think of it."[33]

In such circumstances, "a smattering of 'the three R's,' a little geography, and the practice of declamation" were the sum of Dwight's learning. His reading was described as "outlandish beyond description." He never stopped to spell out an unfamiliar word "but mouthed his sense of it," or made up a new word that sounded to his ear as suitable as the original.[34]

"How do you spell 'Philadelphia?'" he once asked, wishing to post a letter;

but before anyone had time to answer his question, he gave two options: "F-i-l, or F-e-l? Well, never mind; I'll write it so that they can't tell which it is—*e* or *i*."[35]

As for Moody's handwriting, or tendency to scrawl across a page, hieroglyphics might have proved more legible to his early correspondents. Punctuation was optional, and his letters were full of words creatively rendered. "Sure" was spelled *shure*, "believe," *beleave*, and "clerk" was closer to "cluck," spelled *clurk*.

Well into his forties, such phonetic spelling persisted. A letter to his mother, written in 1879, presented the word "bed" as though it were the word "bread" with the "r" left out. Asked about this time why he did not write letters more often himself, rather than use a stenographer, he offered a one-word explanation: *spelling*. Perhaps laughing a bit at himself, he continued, "but I'm getting over the difficulty. I'm always sure of the first letter, and the last—and anywhere between may be upstairs or downstairs!"[36]

❦

Dwight's last term of school was in the winter of his seventeenth year. He was then a student in name only, leading other boys into so much trouble that at length his teacher was in despair and threatened to turn him out.

At this, Betsy Moody was sorely grieved. She was ashamed that one of her sons might be turned out of school. For once, Dwight was contrite over his behavior and heeded his mother's wish that he go to the teacher, ask forgiveness for bad conduct, and "try to be a credit to his mother, rather than a disgrace." This he did and for the rest of the term, to everyone's surprise, applied himself faithfully to study. But in truth it was too late, really, to make up for lost ground,[37] biographer Daniels concludes. Soon after, this new resolve was followed by an attempt to strike out on his own.

It was then Dwight left the family farm for a job in Clinton, Massachusetts, finding work with a printer. Newly hired, his first task was to address by hand, from a mailing list, the wrappers of a local paper. As a country boy who knew nothing of crowded streets or houses containing several tenements, the half-numbers of some of the addresses had no meaning, and such a street address he set down to the next number beyond. This naturally caused great confusion, and when the mistake was traced to him, he was fired.[38]

—◦/◦/◦—

Returning home, he worked for a time on neighboring farms. But his ambition had been roused. He could only think of greater possibilities and opportunities beyond Northfield. He would bide his time.[39]

It came one day in the early spring of 1854. Dwight had just turned seventeen and was cutting and hauling logs on a mountainside with his brother Edwin. Suddenly he stopped and said with loud frustration: *"I'm tired of this! I'm not going to stay here, I'm going to the city."*

His family naturally objected and used every reason they knew of to get him to stay. He had no qualification for a career in the city, they said. The cities were full of young men looking for work. In Northfield, at least, he could find steady work on the farms.

But Dwight was adamant. He was certain the one thing for him to do was to go to Boston. So, saying goodbye to his mother and the rest of the family, he started from home—though he had no definite plans for how to get to Boston. He didn't care. He would go, even if he had to walk every step of the one hundred miles.

Then, halfway between his home and the train depot, he met his elder brother George, who hadn't been home for several days.

"Where are you going?" George asked.

"Boston," Dwight said, "to make my living in whatever business I can find."

Straightaway, George could see that it was useless to try and dissuade him. And with a brotherly kindness Dwight never forgot, George handed him five dollars, just enough for a one-way trip to Boston. What he would do when he got there, no one knew.[40]

YOUNG MAN ABOUT TOWN

When I first went to Boston I was what you might call a
tramp; I was in that city without a place to lay my head.[1]

—*Echoes from the Pulpit*

Boston was a city of 160,000 people when D. L. Moody arrived there in early spring 1854.[2] Franklin Pierce, from neighboring New Hampshire, was president of the United States. Harvard College was two years from its 220th anniversary.

Three years before, in 1851, Herman Melville published *Moby Dick*—the same year of Nathaniel Hawthorne's *House of Seven Gables*. And in 1852, Harriet Beecher Stowe published *Uncle Tom's Cabin*. But certainly Moody knew nothing of these wider currents of culture. Indeed, Boston was a world away from anything he'd ever known.

Stepping down from his train, he did have a destination in mind. But more than once, he must have stopped just to take everything in. And since he looked every inch the country novice, it's possible that more than once, people in Boston stopped—just to take him in.

As for that destination, Samuel Socrates Holton was unaware of it, but his sister's son Dwight had it in mind to join the staff of his prosperous boot and shoe store on the corner of Court Street and Brattle Street.[3] Industrious, circumspect, and pious, the thirty-seven-year-old Holton was just twenty years older than his restive, enterprising nephew. Young D. L. meant to make his fortune in Boston.[4] Uncle Samuel, he was certain, would set him on his way.

But that's not the way it happened. One of the best accounts of Moody's arrival in Boston comes to us from the pages of *The Saturday Evening Post*. In

1900, Will Moody, D. L.'s eldest son, published a nationally syndicated series of essays recounting key moments in his father's life. His first experiences in Boston were among them.

For a start, the *Post's* readers learned, young Moody was woefully unprepared. He'd come to a strange city, "with no money to live on while he was looking for work."[5] What's more, when he strode through the door of Uncle Samuel's store, he did so unannounced. Neither Uncle Samuel, nor another uncle, Lemuel, had any idea he was coming. And his plan, if it could be called that, completely unraveled when Uncle Samuel asked within minutes "how he expected to get a living."[6] This wasn't how it was supposed to be. Why wasn't he immediately offered a position? Pride kept young Moody from making an outright request, and Uncle Samuel wasn't about to tender an offer.

There was a context for this. Uncle Samuel had come to Northfield for Thanksgiving 1853. During this visit, sixteen-year-old D. L. expressed a wish to come to Boston and work. Samuel was wisely noncommittal and said nothing of any misgivings he had about his headstrong nephew. Later, however, he asked D. L.'s older brother George about the idea. The answer he received was blunt enough: "Don't take him on," George said, "for in a short time, he'll want to run the store."[7]

Fast-forward to the spring of 1854, and little had changed. Uncle Samuel had enough on his hands trying to run a busy store. He didn't need a hard-to-handle nephew into the bargain. He had no wish to be cruel, but it seems he reasoned that experience might prove a very effective teacher. Should D. L. find a position, why then, he would soon learn that he had to go along to get along. If not, he would return to the farm in Northfield chastened—not a bad thing in itself.

So, after a few moments of asking after the family, and how everyone was, Uncle Samuel said that he really ought to get back to work.[8] In a thrice, young Moody was back on the street, with no job and no clear idea of what had just taken place.

—————

Uncle Lemuel Holton, however, had witnessed this exchange. Taking D. L. aside, he said, "You can stay with me until you find something."[9]

Any thought of this being a hopeful sign was too quickly dispelled. Those first days in Boston were a trial young Moody never forgot. "I remember how I walked up and down the street trying to get a situation . . . when they answered me roughly, their treatment would chill my soul . . . It seemed then that there was a place for everyone else in the world, but not for me. For about two days I had that awful feeling that nobody wanted me. I have never had it since, and I never want it again."[10]

Moody then tried the city of Lowell, again without success. His feelings were a mixture of wounded pride, embarrassment, and stubborn resolve. Returning to Uncle Lemuel's home, he stated a rash determination "to travel on foot to New York City."[11] Lemuel then took the dispirited boy aside and sought to turn him to a better course.

"Why don't you ask your uncle Samuel for a situation?" he suggested.

Stubbornness persisted. "He can ask *me*," D. L. said, "he knows how I want work."[12]

"But if the job's worth having," Lemuel countered, "it's worth asking for. Go talk to him."[13]

D. L. may have protested a little further, but not much. Uncle Lemuel's wise counsel won out. He swallowed his pride, went to Uncle Samuel's store, and asked for a job.

Samuel Holton was frank. He didn't refuse his chastened nephew outright, but some straight talk came before any thought of taking him on. If he were going to entertain the idea at all, there would have to be conditions.

"Well, Dwight," he said, "I'm afraid you'll want to run this store yourself if you come into it. Now, that won't do at all—men who work for me have to do just as I say: not as they like. But, if you are willing to do the best you can, and do it just as I say—and if you will ask about things when you don't understand them, and promise to go to church—and if you won't do anything or go anywhere that you wouldn't want your mother to know about, we'll see. I'll give you till Monday to think it over."

"I don't need to wait till Monday," D. L. said quickly; "I'll promise now."[14]

It was as "a boy of all work"[15] that Moody began employment in Samuel Holton's boot and shoe store. In short, he did anything that needed doing—

sweeping, moving stock about, and learning all about the wares the store traded in. Eventually, he became a salesman too, with ever-increasing success. Say what one would about his rough edges—and there were many—he worked hard, didn't make the same mistake twice, and kept to the agreement he'd struck with Uncle Samuel. He may have chafed under its restrictions, but at least he had work. That was something he never forgot.

We know this because some twenty-four years later, in 1878, Uncle Samuel suffered reverses that placed him in "great necessity." D. L. was famous by this time on both sides of the Atlantic and well established financially. He lost no time in writing to his uncle. "You gave me work & good advice & I look back to that hour as the turning point in my life & I feel as if I owe you a debt I can never pay, so the money I send you is not a loan but a part payment of what I owe you."[16]

Meanwhile, throughout the spring and summer of 1854, Moody began to make his way. His letters, though often puzzle-like in their phonetic spelling, are nonetheless the best window we have on this time of his life. By any measure, it was colorful.

"I have a room up in the third story," he wrote home, "and I can open my winder and there is 3 grat buildings full of girls—the handsomest there is in the city. They swar like parrats [pirates]."[17] Other people around him, then, had rough edges too.

Heeding Uncle Samuel's counsel to seek the right kind of company, and in part because he was genuinely lonely, D. L. told his family that he'd decided to join "the Christian saciation," by which he meant the Young Men's Christian Association of Boston.

Membership cost a dollar a year, and it offered a great deal for a young man hungry to get ahead in life. "I can have all the books I want to read free of expense," he told his family back in Northfield, "they have a large room and the smart men of Boston lecter to them for nothing and they get up a question."[18]

Moody wished to be a successful clerk in Uncle Samuel's store, and to do that he needed to be a smart clerk. He began to go to some of these lectures. The speakers he may have heard were a who's who of literary Boston at that time, among them Oliver Wendell Holmes and Henry Wadsworth Longfellow. Moody drank in all that he could and remembered what he heard.

Not that all of his time in Boston was so staid, or so respectable an affair. Moody had an alarming brush with the law, for in late May 1854 he joined the abolitionist riots that broke out over the pending extradition of a fugitive slave named Anthony Burns. Moody "took part in the attack on the old court-house to free Burns." He used to tell how the crowd "took great planks to stave in the door, but when the soldiers fired and the crowd smelt powder," they backed away.[19] Moody wrote a letter describing it all, the roiling mobs, threats of violence, and an escape from companies of police patrolling the streets, when Dwight and a fellow demonstrator climbed above an awning and stayed for five hours in an attempt to wait out the police:

> I got up in to the secont story, right over our shade [i.e., awning], and thare I stade un till it was over with . . . all the compineys was out and thare was 35 difrent compineys. George Beans and my self got up there about 10 aclock and thare we sat un till 3 in the afternoon. Thay took [Burns] out a bout 2 ½ [2:30] to such groaning and hising you never hird.
>
> I was all burnt up in the son [sun]. The polis came up to the store when he was clearing the street and told us to com down, but we was up so he could not reach us, and he told us to come down the secont time, but we would not com—so he at to let us be—and so I see it all.[20]

Such scenes are things we know too little of about Moody's early years. So easily, this letter might not have survived all the years from 1854 to the present. But it did, and there is little else like it among his papers.

Other vignettes survived as well. Moody had scant leisure time, but such time as he had he seized with both hands. He ran about in the open spaces of Boston Common, and he grew to know the passageways and gangplanks leading down to Braman's Baths—a basin on Chestnut Street where he could swim in the Charles River and, once dry, eat handfuls of cheap snacks then popular:

black mince "slugs," and apple doughbats. In winter there were toboggan runs, spills, and inevitable fights. Preliminaries involved a fair bit of cussing. "I used to have a terrible habit of swearing," he would later say. "I would get mad, out would come the oaths."[21] Punches and scraps weren't far behind.

For very likely the first time, he had his picture taken too. He was proud of his rising success and wanted to show his family back home that he was making good.

He cut quite a figure. History remembers Moody as always wearing a beard, and true enough, he was typically Victorian in that way. But at seventeen he was clean-shaven, and the strong, husky boy who'd known farm life in Northfield is readily seen.

Clearly, too, he was on his best behavior. One had to stand still for several seconds in those days to create a good picture. So, although his mouth is set, there's a hint of a smile about his eyes. Notwithstanding his roustabout ways, there is kindness written in those eyes too—something latent, perhaps, but it's there. It's an intelligent face as well, with a subtle, yet discernible grit and determination. The photographer, likely plying his trade in a storefront studio, had done his task well.

Still, the visored black cap Moody wore was ill fitting and awkward. It looked as though he'd pilfered the cap from an absentminded train conductor. The overcoat he wore—collar up, and buttoned to the top—looks out of place, as though it's too big for him and he has some growing to do. But on the whole, there's something appealing about this image—he was a young man worth keeping an eye on.

Jokes and ribbing would always be arrows in Moody's quiver, and throughout his life, he gave as good as he got. Not surprisingly, they were never far away during his time in Uncle Samuel's store. As he remembered, "I was full of animal life and shut up in the store through the day, and sleeping there at night, I had to have some vent, and used to lie awake at nights to think of some new joke to play on somebody. My first victim was the cobbler employed in the store. He was an Italian however, and although he liked me, he had such an awful temper that my joking him came near costing my life."[22]

In his youth, Moody was quite capable of playing jokes beyond the point of vexation. Fashioning shoes by hand is painstaking, labor-intensive work. Repairing them is often no less difficult. So, when Moody let loose a prank in the midst of a repair, the infuriated cobbler cut the shoe he'd been mending to pieces in frustration.

The final trick Moody played on the poor man brought a vivid object lesson. We don't know quite what the trick was, but it proved the straw that broke the camel's back. The cobbler quickly grabbed his knife and sprang at Moody. "For a few minutes," Moody remembered, "I had all I could do to keep out of his reach."[23]

Goading the cobbler aside, Moody became a valued employee. He'd inherited his father's roguish charm, and what might have been off-putting persistence in most people somehow proved quicksilver for him. Most often, he persuaded people, and he sought every opportunity to make a sale. He worked hard.

What's more, he genuinely liked people, and they found themselves smiling at this colorful young man's tenacity. They not only bought staple items from the store, they began to buy costlier shoes from him. Within three months of coming to Boston, he was the leading salesman in the store.[24]

No one was more surprised than Uncle Samuel, but he couldn't argue with the figures D. L. tallied. Moody reveled in his success. "I never enjoyed myself more," he wrote home, "the time goes by like a whirl wind."[25]

Soon Moody began sending money home, along with boots and shoes for his family.[26] At such times, he would tell them of his feats of salesmanship: "I took as much as any one last Saturday," or, "I am giting a long as fast as most of them."[27]

The only complaint he had was a wish for more news from home. To his brother George, he wrote: "I wish the duse you would some of you write to me . . . what in thunder the reason was I did not get a letter this morning I could not make out."[28] He concluded by saying he hoped for a visit home soon but wasn't sure if he could get away.

⸻◈◈◈⸻

In his move to Boston, Moody experienced another kind of homecoming, one that changed the course of his life. "The way home" was his description for the hope of heaven held out by the gospel. This is what he found in Boston.[29]

True to his word, Moody had begun attending church upon taking a position in the shoe store. Writing home to his mother, he said, "I go to meating at Mount Vernon Str. Orthedx. I don't know how it is spelt, but you will know what I mean."[30]

Dr. Edward Norris Kirk, educated at Princeton, was pastor of Mount Vernon Congregational Church, and under his ministry, it became a center for cultured, ardent faith. Uncle Samuel had been wise in his choice of a house of worship. Mount Vernon was a place where his nephew had every chance of finding good role models.

Still, it took some getting used to. Moody felt like a fish out of water, once telling a friend that his fellow parishioners "seemed to live in a world almost out of his sight."[31] Most were well dressed and affluent. Yet they were genuinely caring, and Moody later admitted he was sensitive about his own humble origins. Still in his teens, he was at sea about a lot of things. Gradually, these insecurities subsided.

One might have thought Dr. Kirk would influence Moody, but in truth, Dwight found Kirk's sermons hard to understand. Also, because he worked so much during the six days preceding Sunday, he sometimes fell asleep during the church service.[32] It was hard to take in much of anything.

Instead, Sunday school was where Moody's real connection to the things of God began, and it had everything to do with his teacher, Edward Kimball. A man of tact and sensitivity, Kimball stood out from the first Sunday they met. As Moody remembered, "I was assigned to a Bible class with some students from Harvard College . . . They said the lesson was in John, and they handed me a Bible. What did I know about John?"

Taking the Bible he'd been given, Moody started looking through its first pages, instead of the New Testament. "Those Harvard students," Moody said, "began to nudge one another and whisper—*greenhorn from the country*." Moody thought: "What a fool I am to be caught in this scrape."[33]

Kimball saw what was going on and gave the boys a hasty glance of reproof. "That was enough," the wise teacher remembered. "I quietly handed Moody my own Bible, open at the right place, and took his." Moody, in gratitude, said he would "stick by the fellow who had stood by him, and had done him a turn like that."[34]

At other times, Moody's naïveté must have charmed Kimball and prompted a smile. One Sunday, the life of Moses was under discussion. For young Moody, there was one word, and one word only, to express the newfound respect he felt for this leader of biblical times. So as soon as Kimball finished his lesson, Moody exclaimed: "Say, Mr. Kimball, that man Moses must have been *smart!*"[35]

So it went for the first year of Moody's time in Boston. He attended church, grew to know Edward Kimball better, and grew to trust the friendship he was shown. The year 1854 passed into 1855. At work, and in church, Moody kept learning. He saved money and sent money home to his family. He began to carve out a life for himself.

As for matters of faith, D. L. had pretty firm ideas about that. He was grateful enough to learn about the Bible; he knew any well-read person ought to know something about it. But this business of becoming a Christian—well, that was another thing altogether. "I thought," he said later, "I would wait till I died, and then become a Christian. I thought if I had the consumption, or some lingering disease, I would have plenty of time to become one, and in the meantime, I would enjoy the best pleasures of the world."[36]

But something more was unfolding. To all appearances, Moody's coworkers saw the same roustabout, get-ahead, hardworking eighteen-year-old they'd come to know. But "an inward struggle had developed."[37]

When Mr. Kimball taught elements of biblical literacy, Moody listened and learned. But Kimball spoke also of a glad surrender of faith, one centered on the forgiveness of sin and the acceptance of Christ as one's Savior.

Surrender, submission. Moody balked at that. He thought himself the master of his fate. Mr. Kimball was asking him, asking all of the students, to let God pilot them through their journey in life. The hope of heaven beckoned, but he wrestled with the cost it called for.

Moody's struggle with this persisted. Forty years later, it remained a vivid memory. "I had a terrible battle to surrender my will," he said, "and take God's will."[38]

It reached a point of climax on April 21, 1855. That morning, Edward Kimball resolved to "speak to Moody about Christ, and about his soul."[39]

Kimball's memories of that morning stayed with him the rest of his life. "I started downtown to Holton's shoe store," he recalled. "When I was nearly there, I began to wonder whether I ought to go just then, during business hours . . . I thought maybe my mission might embarrass the boy—that when I went away, the other clerks . . . might taunt Moody and ask if I was trying to make 'a good boy' out of him."

Lost in thought, Kimball walked right past Holton's shoe store. "When I found I had gone by the door," he said, "I determined to make a dash for it, and have it over at once."[40] Once inside, he asked for Moody and was told he was in the back part of the store, wrapping up shoes in paper and putting them on shelves.

"I went up to him," Kimball remembered, "and put my hand on his shoulder. As I leaned over, I placed my foot upon a shoebox. Then I made my plea." He told Moody "of Christ's love for him, and the love Christ wanted in return." He spoke from the heart. Moody said after there were tears in Kimball's eyes.[41]

Something of eternal moment kindled. And there, in the back of the shoe store, Moody "gave himself, and his life, to Christ."[42]

Years later, Moody said, "One day my teacher came around behind the counter of the shop I was at work in, put his hand upon my shoulder, and talked to me about Christ . . . I was brought into the Kingdom of God."[43]

Moody could not have known it, but years later, his conversion would be considered so seminal an event in the religious history of America that the city of Boston honored it with a bronze memorial plaque. Visitors to Court Street may see it still. Its text reads:

D. L. MOODY
CHRISTIAN EVANGELIST,
FRIEND OF MAN,
FOUNDER OF THE NORTHFIELD SCHOOLS,
WAS CONVERTED TO GOD
IN A SHOE STORE ON
THIS SITE
APRIL 21ST, 1855

The morning star had risen in his heart. Moody never forgot the day that followed. Lines from his memory touch on poetry: "it seemed to me that the sun was shining brighter than ever before . . . the birds were singing for my benefit . . . the old elms waved their branches for joy . . . all nature was at peace."[44]

Something so simple as the desire to get away and seek a fortune can lead to unexpected things. Moody was an at-risk youth. His early life could have been a spiral downward. It could have unfolded very differently than it did. He knew that, and he would have been the first to affirm how truth gilds the phrase: "a gracious hand leads us in ways we know not, and blesses us."[45]

3

WEST TO THE WINDY CITY

Moody went down into the slums of Chicago,
to people never seen inside the churches.[1]

—*The New York Times*

Moody worked for two years in Boston. It proved a turning point in his life. He'd discovered a natural aptitude for business. And though some days were marked by trial and error—common enough for someone in their late teens, especially for someone as headstrong as he was—his great desire to get ahead, and willingness to work hard, made him a highly successful clerk in his uncle's boot and shoe store. He also began to display elements of a teachable heart.

Boston was a time of beginnings for Moody—never more so than in his decision to become a Christian. For this, he owed a lifelong debt to the caring, patient witness of Edward Kimball. In the months after his conversion, Kimball and other parishioners at Mount Vernon Congregational Church mentored him. This training, along with time among other young people at the Boston YMCA, proved invaluable. He began to see what it was like to serve others—to help others, as Uncle Samuel and Edward Kimball had helped him. That desire to serve, and give back, began to grow.

Many rough edges had fallen away. But it was another city, another setting where that work would continue. For in the early autumn of 1856, Moody suddenly left Boston for Chicago.

The reason can be traced partly to some remaining rough edges. He'd heard there were tremendous opportunities to get ahead in Chicago, the great boomtown of America. "The height of my ambition," he remembered, "had been to be a successful merchant."[2] More and more, he spoke of going west.

That put Uncle Samuel in a trying position. He felt a responsibility for his nephew, and however grateful he was for young Moody's embrace of faith and his undoubted success as a clerk, he was still a minor (two years from age twenty-one). He still had some learning to do.

It was a difficult problem. Holton regretted the thought of losing such a valued employee—Moody now managed a newly opened branch of the store farther up Court Street—and he seems to have honestly believed that if his restive nephew would just settle in for two more years of training and steady growth, it would do him a world of good.

Moody may well have demanded a raise, but biographer John C. Pollock has speculated that, most likely, Uncle Samuel issued an ultimatum Moody refused: that he sign an agreement not to go west.

Evidence from surviving letters supports this idea. After his arrival in Chicago (he hadn't told anyone he was leaving), Moody told his mother, "Uncle Samuel objected to my goin." He told his younger brother Warren, "I hope you will never have anyone to cross your path as they have mine, and blast your hopes." One last line captured everything he felt: "I thought the quicker I went and got out of [Uncle Samuel's] way the better . . . I lov Boston and have got some warm friends there, but as I was situated there, it was not very pleasant."[3]

Moody's son Will confirmed much of this. As things stood in Boston, they "seemed to offer little promise for the future." Uncle Samuel was a man of "extremely conservative methods" and "did not feel the same enthusiasm" that drove young Moody. Chicago had an undeniable allure as "the new city of the Western prairies." Moody could be his own man there. That desire trumped everything else.[4]

He left Boston without so much as a word to his family back home in Northfield. It's possible there was one final argument over the ultimatum and young D. L. was fired—a conclusion drawn by Pollock. Will Moody was somewhat coy about this, writing with typical Victorian reserve that "a crisis finally came in his relations with his employer."[5]

We do know, however, that on the afternoon of Monday, September 15, 1856, nineteen-year-old D. L. Moody purchased a through ticket on an immigrant train from Boston to Chicago for five dollars. When he left the Causeway Street depot at 4 p.m., he'd spent what money he had. There hadn't been enough for a return fare.[6]

———⌘———

Chicago was a thousand miles away. In 1850, six years before Moody arrived, it was home to nearly 30,000 people. By 1860, its population would triple, to 109,000. In 1855, seventy trains a day entered or departed from Chicago. By 1860, eleven different railroads would serve the city.[7]

The train Moody arrived in was lost among so many others. He'd grown used to Boston, but Chicago was another thing altogether. This city wasn't like anything he'd ever seen.

It was home to once and future titans of industry. In 1847, Cyrus McCormick, inventor of the mechanical reaper, had established his first factory there. In 1851, just four years later, he was an international sensation, winning the Gold Medal at the London Crystal Palace Exposition. From there McCormick toured the continent, captivating audiences in Hamburg, Vienna, and Paris. The capstone was his election to the French Academy of Sciences, "as having done more for agriculture than any other living man."[8]

Chicago was also home to Marshall Field, creator of the famous department store empire. In the 1850s, Field wasn't so different from Moody himself, a newcomer to Chicago from the family farm, with a great capacity for hard work. Before the close of his career, he would command an annual income of 40 million dollars. Yet he was different from the more notorious robber barons of what would become the Gilded Age. Field's business was noted for its sterling emphasis on quality and customer service, while he had an all too rare reputation for honest and good character.[9]

In the early days of his career, Marshall Field worked with John Farwell, who made a fortune selling dry goods. Farwell arrived in Chicago in 1845, and by 1870, annual sales at John V. Farwell & Co. had reached nearly 10 million dollars. By the close of the 1880s, Farwell was ranked as one of the top three wholesalers in the United States. His company flourished well into the twentieth century.[10]

Clearly, there were fortunes to be made in Chicago, and Moody was bent on making one. "I was very ambitious to get rich," he would say later, "one hundred thousand dollars: that was my aim."[11] It was a lofty goal, for one hundred thousand dollars in 1856 would be worth much more than one million dollars today.

Moody was anything but a titan of industry when he arrived in the Windy City. Indeed, for two days he experienced a reprisal of going from street to street looking for work, much as he'd done when he came to Boston.

This time, however, there was a difference. He'd thought to secure and bring with him a letter of recommendation from Mount Vernon Congregational Church. That letter, along with help given by another Holton relative, Uncle Calvin Holton, resulted in both a job and a circle of new friends within a week of his arrival in Chicago.

As for his job, Uncle Calvin lived a few miles outside the city, in Des Plaines. He knew Charles and Augustus Wiswall, two brothers who had emigrated from Massachusetts and opened a shoe store on Lake Street.[12] From the first, one clerk recalled, "Moody was a first-rate salesman." Described as "zealous and tireless," he took pride "to make his column foot . . . the largest of any on the book, not only in the way of sales, but also of profits."[13]

Moody was twice-blessed for he found a ready-made set of friends at the Plymouth Congregational Church. His letter provided an entrée, and the members took to him quickly. One parishioner recalled Moody as "one of the happiest looking" young men he'd ever seen. "His cheeks were then full . . . and he possessed such a pleasant smile and look that he attracted much attention." He "soon became a general favorite . . . notwithstanding his very limited education."[14]

Moody had stepped aboard the train from Boston on September 15. Ten days later, he wrote the first of his letters home to Northfield, telling his mother: "I reached this far-famed city of the West one week ago tonight." Knowing she would worry over whether he was among good folk, he was quick to write: "I went into a prayer-meeting last night, and as soon as I made myself known, I had friends enough. After meeting they came to me and seemed to be as glad to see me as if I were their earthly brother. God is the same here as He was in Boston, and in Him I can find peace."[15]

Moody left Boston under circumstances that were less than ideal, but the gifts of family and faith were with him now in a way they hadn't been when he left home at seventeen. That counted for something. What's more, he was really on his own now. The Wiswall brothers placed no restrictions on him in the way Uncle Samuel had. So long as he did his work, they had no quarrel with him. Indeed, he proved himself a model employee. His tenacity and industry resulted in "a steady increase in responsibility and income."[16]

Nor was his burgeoning desire to serve others forgotten. D. L. knew he wouldn't be where he was in life without the kindness he'd been shown from the time of his leaving Northfield to the present. He'd been given a helping hand. He would give that gift, so far as he was able, to others. He'd seen that modeled in the faith of Edward Kimball and others in Boston. It was something that had drawn him to belief and brought good things in its train. If Kimball had been an agent of grace, he could be too.

———

Moody set about Christian service as though he were acting on a business plan. First step: hire a pew. Second: fill it every Sunday. And so he set out to do just that. He would "hail young men on the street corners, visit their boarding-houses, or even call them out of saloons."[17]

This was commending the faith in a way few people had seen, but it was natural enough to Moody. He knew few people who were unchurched would attend Sunday services all on their own. He would go to where they were, just as Edward Kimball had sought him out in the shoe store back in Boston. In this, he had a model that meant everything to him. He would follow it in Chicago.

There was something novel and engaging about it all. For many in the city, it was a new home, just as it was for Moody. He brought with him an earnest, cordial greeting. If the folk he met were friendless in Chicago, he would be their friend—he would take them to where they would be welcomed: the church setting he now called home.

The model Kimball had shown him, in concert with his genuine regard for others, produced results. And as a storyteller in the time-honored New England tradition, what he shared of his own story may have appealed to the people he met. What is known for certain is that "before long he was renting four pews, which he filled every Sunday" with guests of every description.[18]

As yet, however, there was no thought of devoting himself solely to "Christian work," as he would have called it. He drove his concern for others in double harness with his keen desire to make his fortune. And in that regard, he soon made tremendous strides.

Say what one might about Moody's lack of education, he was a quick study. In Boston, he had constantly learned all he could about business, and there had been many successful people there for him to ask questions of and learn. Before leaving, he was managing a store all on his own. He took all that he'd learned, brought it to Chicago, and built upon it.

One of his employers, Charles Wiswall, took note. "His ambition made him anxious to lay up money," Wiswall remembered, "his personal habits made him exact and economical."[19] Moody saved everything he could, and he clearly had "a head for business," in the parlance of the time.

He invested his savings in land, which he sold at a profit. He made loans at high rates and was ever devising plans to increase his income and capital. And, when the Wiswalls' store started a "jobbing department," he became their point man. His gift for innovation showed itself: he carefully watched the train depots and scanned hotel registers for possible customers from neighboring towns. Deploying the roguish charm that was his stock-in-trade, in tandem with a thorough knowledge of the Wiswalls' fine product line, he was soon "making better and larger sales than his fellow-clerks."[20] If Chicago was the Windy City, Moody was a one-man cyclone of industry. He was scrupulously honest as well, as his mother had taught him to be. Little wonder, then, that the Wiswall brothers had reason to be grateful.

———⁙———

Moody's early days in Chicago were not without their share of adventure. He was, after all, only nineteen—and his new home, with its outlying towns, was a rough-hewn setting indeed. He was rough-hewn himself, and that stood him in good stead.

Sent out to represent Wiswalls' store as a commercial traveler, Moody once hired a pair of livery horses for a trip to a newly settled frontier town. While driving down a steep hill, he discovered the holdback straps were too loose. The wheels of the carriage began to strike the horses' heels.

Frightened by this unseen source of pain, the team immediately became unmanageable and bolted. They ran out of the roadway into a tract recently cleared of heavy timber. It took every ounce of nerve, and sheer physical strength, to guide them safely back onto the road. "It was the most exciting ride I ever had," Moody remembered, "standing up in the buggy with my hat gone and my hair on end, I was just able to dodge the huge stumps and get my team back into the road." Several minutes later, where the road rose to meet another large hill, the steep incline slowed the fast-tiring horses enough for Moody to get them under control.[21]

When in Wiswalls' store, Moody's fellow employees were no more immune to his pranks than the cobbler in Holton's store had been. Indeed, it was the cobbler at Wiswalls' that he most frequently chose to torment.

The best joke required no little amount of stealth. While the cobbler was away from his low stool, Moody made an undetectable slit in its leather seat and set a full pail of water directly underneath so as to be hidden from view. When the unsuspecting cobbler returned and sat down, he jumped up with a cry as Moody watched from a safe distance helpless with silent laughter. Wiping the seat, the hapless man sat down once more, only to wet his britches further. Once more, he wiped the seat and sat down again. Twice, maybe three times, this happened before the cobbler discovered the bucket of water.[22] History is silent as to whether he set out after Moody, spluttering curses, the cobbler's knife in hand. He must have been tempted.

Meantime, Moody had taken to visiting several different churches in the precincts of Chicago. On any given Sunday, he had three opportunities to do so, as services were held morning, noon, and night. He attended the Methodist Episcopal Church, visited the Presbyterian house of worship, and heard sermons at the First Baptist Church. This last was particularly important, as it was there he first set eyes on the pretty and demure teenager who would one day become his wife: Emma Revell. He wasn't introduced to her the first Sunday he attended, but he remembered her face. In later years, both would count it blessing beyond price that their shared faith brought them together.[23]

As 1857 drew to a close, twenty-year-old D. L. Moody left Wiswalls to become a traveling salesman and debt collector for the wholesale boot and shoe store run by C. H. Henderson. It was a sign of the steady rise in his fortunes. While working for Wiswalls, he had slept on the premises.[24] It was a measure of thrift and canny necessity: it allowed him to pocket money as quickly as he could. This was the more important as he'd already begun to send money home to his mother. Driven as he was to make his mark, he'd never forgotten that charity begins at home.

By winter 1858, working for Henderson, Moody took up residence in the fine boardinghouse on Michigan Avenue run by Mrs. Herbert Phillips for "the smart bachelors of Chicago." Fellow boarders included two future millionaires: Levi Leiter (later father-in-law to Britain's Lord Curzon) and Marshall Field. Remembering those competitive days, Moody would say he could have beat the lot—except Marshall Field.[25]

Mrs. Phillips was "Mother Phillips" to one and all. Aside from Leiter and Field, there were several other boarders "whose names became prominent, not only as foremost citizens of Chicago, but as some of the most successful men of the country."[26] These included Edward Isham, Norman Williams, and General John L. Thompson.

Isham, a graduate of Harvard Law, became a prominent Chicago attorney. After the great Chicago Fire of 1871, Isham and Robert Todd Lincoln (son of President Lincoln) formed the law firm known as Isham, Lincoln, and Beal.[27] Norman Williams also became a prominent lawyer in Chicago, a director of the Commercial National Bank, the Chicago and Central Union Telephone Company, the Western Electric Company, and the Pullman Palace Car Company. When he died in June 1899, he was eulogized in *The New York Times*.[28]

A native of New Hampshire, Thompson was a lawyer in the law offices of Scammon, McCagg & Fuller when the Civil War began. Noted for his bravery as a leader of men, by war's end Thompson was brevetted a brigadier general. In 1866, he partnered with Norman Williams to found the firm of Thompson and Williams.[29]

After Moody's death in 1899, Isham remembered him as "an exceedingly earnest, active, and forceful man, strenuous in all his activities." At the same time, he was popular among the boarders at Mother Phillips's house, Isham saying he was "a broad-minded, generous-hearted, affectionate man, dear to all who knew him." Mindful of Moody's later celebrity as a prominent Christian leader, Isham concluded with these words: "He was the same in early days as later, and everyone of the circle remained fond of him to the very end, no matter how much he differed from him in opinion." In sum, Moody could commend the faith without being censorious or hypocritical. He knew how to seek friendship and be a friend. This was a telling tribute, especially from an early friend who did not share his religious views. Moody left a lasting impression.

Posterity has Mother Phillips to thank for setting Moody on the road to becoming a trailblazer in mission work among the slums of Chicago. When he expressed interest in volunteering for service work, she suggested he try the Wells Street Mission Sunday school, which bordered the North Side of the city. There were many poor folk there, many in need, she said.

So one Sunday morning Moody walked to the little mission school on the corner of Chicago Avenue and Wells Street. He offered to lead a class. The superintendent there said he had twelve teachers already and only sixteen students, but if Moody "could work up a class of his own," he would be welcome.

That was all Moody needed to hear.

The next Sunday, he appeared with eighteen ragged and dirty children, gathered off the streets. Turning them over to some of the other teachers, he sought out more children, until the school was full to overflowing. He had no thought of teaching the children himself but saw it as his place to "drum up" recruits for the school.[30] When he saw these poor children, he remembered the poverty of his youth. He'd known what it was for hope to be a stranger. A flame of compassion flared within him. This was work he could give himself to.

In the fall of 1858, notwithstanding the fine assistance he'd given the Wells Street Mission Sunday school, Moody and his friend J. B. Stillson decided to go where no one went and start a Sunday school, a slum in Chicago known as Little Hell.

As described by W. H. Daniels, an early Moody biographer, it was "a section on the Lake shore, north of the river, which was to Chicago what the Five Points were to New York, Old Ann Street to Boston, or St. Giles's to London. It was a moral lazaretto, a place socially quarantined by its squalor and crime. Picture scenes from the Martin Scorsese film *The Gangs of New York*. To see the squalor, abuse, violence, and abject poverty depicted there is to catch a glimpse of what it was Moody and Stillson found. Here they planned to start their school in an abandoned freight car on North State Street. No decent person, it was said, walked those streets after nightfall. Few would have dared during the day.[31]

The two men (and another friend, T. B. Carter, who could sing) made that abandoned freight car come alive with youthful zeal. Its sides fairly shook with noise—shouts, whoops, and cheers. It was a hive of activity, for the gang of street boys who first joined Moody, Stillson, and Carter couldn't bear standing still. Indeed, they were rousingly told to "Stand Up, Stand Up for Jesus," and that hymn was never sung as it was then. After, the boys might allow a few moments of relative silence, where Stillson might tell a story from Scripture, but for no more than a minute or two. Then it was back to the shouts, whoops, cheers, and raucous singing.

Moody and his friends plied the undernourished boys with food, ran races, and did anything they could to capture and hold their attention. It was often bedlam by another name, but for the first time in their lives, those boys knew they had a friend who asked nothing but their company. Raucous it may have been, but it was safe. And the truth was, Moody wasn't much older than they were. He and his friends seemed like older brothers. If this is what faith looked like—head, hand, and heart for God—the boys wanted more of it. They knew nothing of church and few of them could read. But that freight car was the nearest thing they knew to heaven. They kept coming.[32]

A SUNDAY SCHOOL DRUMMER

In the fall of 1858, Mr. Moody started a Sabbath
school of his own in a vacant saloon, his helpers
being Mr. Stillson and a Mr. Carter . . . Seeking
out some of the street [children] who did not like
the Wells Street mission school and had therefore
dropped out, Mr. Moody invited them to "assist"
him in his new venture. The boys were pleased
to become "partners," and willingly entered upon
the work. One of those boys subsequently became
postmaster of Chicago, and Commander-In-Chief
of the Grand Army of the Republic.[1]

—The Shorter Life of D. L. Moody, vol. 1

These words were written by Paul Dwight Moody, president of Middlebury College, and his brother-in-law, A. P. Fitt. During President Moody's tenure, Middlebury was one of America's premier colleges. It remains so. To walk its grounds is to be reminded of much that culture and wise investment can provide.

Yet it is also true that schools that exert a life-changing influence may have a far humbler origin. Paul Moody, the youngest son of D. L. Moody, knew this firsthand, and spoke of it at length in the two-volume memoir he cowrote about his father.

Indeed, Paul's father had aided a boy of the streets who later rose to become a hero of the Civil War—and commander in chief of the Grand Army of the Republic—Jimmy Sexton.

Sexton first met Moody as "a stalwart young man about twenty years of age . . . dressed in a checkered suit of gray clothes." He had "close-cropped hair, a muscular frame," and was "easy though awkward in manner."

Moody greeted Sexton and his friends in a "familiar and friendly way" and asked: "Boys, don't you want to go with me to Sunday school?"

Sexton and his gang cared more about the prospect of food. "Would there be anything to eat?" they asked, partly in challenge.

"Come along," Moody said, "we'll find out."[2]

Moody knew from personal experience how to talk to boys with rough edges. Exchange Chicago for Northfield, and there wasn't a great world of difference between the boy he'd been, with a gang of poor boys at his side, and this gang of street boys in Chicago, led by Jimmy Sexton.

Like recognized like, and friendship was born. "We became at once close friends," Sexton recalled in a letter of 1892. And sure enough, Moody hunted them up the following week, along with others. They all trooped along to the derelict saloon. As promised, Sexton and his friends helped out. Food was supplied, word got round in Little Hell. An unlikely school began to grow.

Other things about Moody stood out in Sexton's memory. True, he had a "crude and somewhat uncouth appearance," but Sexton and his friends found him "simple, unaffected and kind." Though "awkward in the selection of his words," he had a ready and ample fund of wit. Immediately, Sexton recalled, "we all swore allegiance to our new-found stranger friend. His earnestness and sincerity gave us confidence in his loyalty, and soon made us feel that we stood upon an equality with a good fellow." Then came a true test: despite a steady barrage, no amount of hectoring or ribbing seemed to bother Moody. Quite the reverse. "Our chaffing pleased rather than annoyed him," Sexton wrote.[3]

Jimmy Sexton's debt to Moody was vividly described in the book *Early Recollections of Dwight L. Moody*. Little Hell was perhaps the last place someone might think to hold "a little house prayer meeting," but for Moody it was the best place. No one needed prayer more than the folk who lived there, if he could help bring spiritual comfort, in addition to the food, firewood, and other staples he carried with him as well, he would do what he could.

Moody remembered, from boyhood, how important the meeting of physical needs was. He remembered Uncle Cyrus Holton's gift of firewood when

John V. Farwell (top hat) and D. L. Moody pose with Moody's "bodyguard," part of Moody's Sunday school class.

creditors had come after his father's death and taken everything, including his family's firewood. He could do what Uncle Cyrus had done and be to others what Uncle Cyrus had been to him and his fatherless family. He could also be like Oliver Everett, bringing the consolation of faith, even as he brought food, clothes, gifts of money, coal, or wood. And he could bring the hope of heaven to people—right where they were—as Edward Kimball had done for him by coming to Uncle Samuel's shoe store to tell him of Christ. He understood that he couldn't expect people to go to church if they didn't speak English, as many recent immigrants to Chicago didn't—or that, if their clothes were threadbare, shame might keep them from a sanctuary door.

Further, why would they go to church if they had no reason to think it had anything to offer them? He knew what faith had done in his life. But if others had no idea what faith was, he could share his story with them and meet them where they were. In time, they might wish to join him in church and so learn more of the many good things he had learned about. But even if they never did, he could bring faith and hope to them, with a love that put food on the table, or wood in a battered old stove or tumbledown fireplace.

As for the "little house prayer meetings," Moody's gift for them was a natural insight gleaned from a once meager, but now steadily growing, knowledge of the Bible. As he read, he discovered many short prayers in Scripture: "Lord, help me" was one he always remembered. Even people who knew little English could be taught that prayer. He could teach that.

❧❧❧

One Saturday night, after one of those house prayer meetings in Little Hell, Moody was returning home. A violent storm broke over the city, and he took shelter under a wooden shed. A sudden flash of lightning revealed that someone else had taken shelter there too: Jimmy Sexton, whom Moody hadn't seen in his school for quite some time.

Till the storm abated, Moody talked with the boy. It was then he learned Jimmy's father had thrashed him severely for attending Moody's Sunday school. Whiskey made a demanding father an abusive one.

This couldn't continue, and Moody went to intercede with Jimmy's father. The old man was not impressed by Moody, only a few years older than his own son.

"What do you believe?" the old man wanted to know. Moody told him. Talk continued; more questions were asked. Try as he might, the old man could find no fault with Moody's creed, such as it was. Jimmy would be allowed to return to Moody's mission school. It was some time more before the father's battle with whiskey was won, but by all accounts, it was.

Moody's intercession made all the difference in Jimmy Sexton's life. By the outbreak of the Civil War, little more two years later, the young man's life had turned around. And it was his association with Moody, of which more will be said, that continued to guide the course of his young life to the path of a distinguished career that followed.

This story of Moody and Jimmy Sexton comes from J. V. Farwell, better known as John Farwell, the future merchant prince of Chicago. Farwell had become a coworker with Moody, of which more will be said. And it is from Farwell's pen that we have a sequel to the story of Jimmy Sexton just told.

When the Civil War began, Farwell wrote, Sexton was elected captain of one of the Board of Trade Regiment's companies. But the adjutant general learned he was not yet eighteen, and no eighteen-year-old boy, he stoutly insisted, could command a company.

Whereupon Sexton, and the young men of his would-be command, protested so strongly that the general said to him,

"Who do you know in Chicago?"

"J. V. Farwell and D. L. Moody." The general said he knew Farwell and had a great respect for him. "You get a letter from Mr. Farwell," he told Sexton, "and perhaps I won't ask how old you are."

Sexton got the letter, and the adjutant general agreed to the highly unusual step of allowing him to take command of a company of Union soldiers.[4] A storied career followed, one that led in time to Sexton's becoming postmaster of Chicago, and later commander in chief of the Grand Army of the Republic. Moody and Farwell had changed this young man's life, and with it, hundreds of other lives.

As for John Farwell himself, the story of his meeting with Moody is memorable. "Any description of Mr. Moody's work," Farwell wrote in 1907, "should begin where he began."[5] They met when Moody was "a Sunday School drummer," that is, when he was just beginning to bring children from Chicago's streets to church.

"My first acquaintance with Mr. Moody," Farwell remembered, "was as a young man, and a late attendant of a nine o'clock morning class meeting in the old Clark Street Methodist Episcopal Church, coming in a little before ten o'clock."[6]

Farwell was irritated that someone looking so disheveled should arrive late and disrupt the morning service. That Moody fell asleep, well before the service ended, bothered Farwell even more. But he had reason to regret that hasty surmise, once they were actually introduced. As Farwell explained: "The recollection that I then thought him a very lazy Christian haunts me still, for I ascertained afterwards that he came in after spending all morning in getting poor children into a Mission Sunday School."[7] Moody, in essence, had been up at first light and done a day's work before attending service at the Methodist Episcopal Church. Little wonder he was late or so tired.

D. L. Moody rides down Wells St. in Chicago gathering boys and girls for his Sunday school. It grew, and one day President-Elect Abraham Lincoln visited.

Caught in an impromptu moment during his visit to Moody's Sunday school, President-Elect Abraham Lincoln encourages students before departing to Washington, D.C.

Farwell realized his mistake and soon embarked on a philanthropic partnership with Moody for which many in the nineteenth century had cause to be thankful. No, Moody was not at all what he seemed.

———⦿⦿⦿———

John Farwell and Moody forged a great friendship. One reason this was true was that Moody had Farwell to thank for the day he met President-Elect Abraham Lincoln—Sunday, November 25, 1860.

Some years after Moody's death, Farwell told the story of this meeting. "At Mr. Lincoln's first visit to Chicago after his election," Farwell remembered, "he was an invited guest of [Mr. Moody's] school, then grown to fifteen hundred children."

Lincoln had agreed to come, on the condition that "he was not to be asked for a speech." So it was that Lincoln arrived and got a firsthand view of the mission work Moody and Farwell were doing in Chicago's slums. He thought, perhaps, to stay a few minutes, then leave—as he had another pressing engagement. But Farwell never forgot what took place next.

"As Mr. Lincoln was about to leave," Moody quickly stepped forward and said: "If Mr. Lincoln desires to say a word as he goes out, of course all ears will be open."

When Moody said this, Lincoln had reached the center of the hall, well on his way to the door. Suddenly he stopped, and then, as Farwell wrote, "he made a most appropriate Sunday School address, in which he referred to his own humble origin, and closed by saying, 'With close attention to your teachers, and hard work to put into practice what you learn from them, some one of you may also become president of the United States in due time—for you have had better opportunities than I had.'"[8]

CAMPS AND BATTLEFIELDS

*Little did we know that our nation was soon to be
baptized in blood, and that we would soon hear
the tramp of a million men, that hundreds and
thousands of our young men, the flower of our
nation, would soon be lying in a soldier's grave.*[1]

—D. L. Moody

In the days following the firing on Fort Sumter and the start of the Civil War, Chicago, like all other cities of the Union, was galvanized into action. Camp Douglas was formed near the southern limits of the city, "and there recruits were massed and instructed." Among these new soldiers were a large number of "Moody's boys," former students from the mission school he'd established in the North Market Hall. A company was also raised among his friends and former associates in business. On all sides, Moody "was urged to enter the service of his country."[2]

He held deeply to the cause of the Union. Moreover, the traditions of his home, and his New England origins, had fostered strong abolitionist views. Soon after coming to Chicago, and getting a job in Wiswalls' boot and shoe store, Moody joined a lyceum, a popular nineteenth-century forum for public discussion. This lyceum comprised clerks from neighboring merchant houses. They met frequently, and points of political difference between the North and South were warmly discussed by members on either side. Moody's involvement in the lyceum says much for the fervency of his views.[3]

Yet in spite of all this, he could not conscientiously enlist. "There has never been a time in my life," he would later say, "when I felt that I could take a gun and shoot down a fellow-being. In this respect I am a Quaker."[4]

Still, Moody was determined to take part in war relief work. That was something he could, and did, give himself to unstintingly. He immediately "assisted in forming an Army and Navy Committee of the Young Men's Christian Association," consisting of J. V. Farwell, B. F. Jacobs, and himself.

The first work undertaken by the commission was to hold religious services for the soldiers who passed through Chicago. On the forming of Camp Douglas, Moody and his coworkers built a small temporary chapel in which over fifteen hundred meetings were held.[5]

Edgar Hawley, one of Moody's oldest Chicago associates, long remembered those early days of the war. Moody's outside-the-box approach to ministry figured prominently.

"At one time," Hawley remembered, "there were about twelve thousand men there. Regiments were coming in, and others going to the front all the time. The Young Men's Christian Association had a chapel for the use of the men, where frequent meetings were held. The Western Branch of the Christian Commission included among its members J. V. Farwell, B. F. Jacobs, D. L. Moody, and several others. We issued an *Army Hymn Book*, with an American flag on the front page, and it was distributed freely among the soldiers."[6]

Moody and his coworkers constantly visited the tents and barracks. In June 1861, he wrote about it all to his mother in Northfield. "I am all taken up with this," he told her, "I am drove more now than ever in my life."[7]

A little more than six months later, another sphere of service opened. On February 16, 1862, General Ulysses S. Grant and Union troops took the Confederate Fort Donelson. They captured ten thousand Confederate soldiers, of whom about nine thousand were sent to Chicago and placed in Camp Douglas.

Within a week of the Confederate prisoners' arrival, Moody wanted to reach them for Christ. As Edgar Hawley remembered, Moody simply said: "Hawley, let's go down and hold a meeting there in the chapel with the prisoners."[8] He'd scarcely given the matter any thought; he was just acting on the impulse to do what he could.

As Hawley recalled, it was about five miles down to the camp. As they got near the entrance, Moody said: "Hawley, here is a ministerial pass—take it."

Hawley stopped in his tracks. "But how will *you* get in past the guard?" he asked.

"In some way!" Moody said confidently. Hawley was dubious and said so.

Hawley passed the guard without any trouble. Moody wasn't so lucky. He was ordered to halt at the point of fixed bayonets.

"Stand back!" the head guard bellowed.

Moody hadn't counted on this. "But I'm Moody," he protested, "president of the Young Men's Christian Association."

"I don't care who you are; you can't get in here!"

Moody was stymied. But at just that moment, a captain who was passing by stepped forward. He'd recognized Moody.

The man was heaven-sent. Moody asked him to intercede.

"Let me in," he pleaded, "if only for the work's sake."

The officer nodded, then turned to the guard, saying: "Let one of your men take Mr. Moody to headquarters; I'll be responsible."

So it was that Moody was taken into the prisoner holding area—under military guard. Once the matter was explained at camp headquarters, the officer in charge said: "Well, seeing you're here, and considering your reason, you may stay, but don't repeat it. And, if you're not out of here by eight p.m., you'll go into the guard-house for the night."

Having got past the sentries, Moody now seemed unconcerned. He and Hawley went to the Camp Douglas chapel, arranged things, and invited the men. It was soon packed full.

Moody chose that moment to turn to Hawley with a twinkle in his eye, and say: "Now, Hawley, *you* preach."

Hawley was incredulous. "But I'm not a minister," he objected. Moody was unmoved. "But *you* came in on a ministerial pass," he said innocently, "and I didn't."

There was little else for Hawley to do but deliver an impromptu sermon. "*We had an interesting service,*" he remembered. "Moody took charge, and it seemed as though the Spirit of the Lord came down upon these men with great power. They came forward to the altar twenty, thirty, forty at a time. We closed the meeting and began inquiry work. Moody had the platform, and God used him wonderfully. The whole audience melted, and we saw strong men in tears."

Overwhelmed by the incredible response of the prisoners, Moody could only whisper in amazement to his friend, "God is here!" They ministered for a few minutes more and closed the service.

Then they looked at their watches. "It was but a few seconds to eight," Hawley remembered, "and we had to run to get out of camp." They'd only narrowly missed a night's confinement in the guardhouse. But however haphazard at the outset, Hawley concluded his story by saying those prisoner meetings were "kept up two or three weeks." Many were converted.

Biographer J. C. Pollock wrote of those early days of wartime work: "Camp Douglas, especially when casualty lists began to appear, and the war ceased to resemble a picnic, burned into Moody the sacredness of the individual; each one mattered; each of these [men] might soon be a sprawling corpse in some Southern wood or wheat field, each needed the gift and assurance of eternal life."[9]

Yet Moody, just twenty-four at the outset of the Civil War, was still painfully aware of his shortcomings. He had grown used to talking to poor boys from Chicago's slums, with little or no education, like himself. Although deeply committed to his relief work, he had some knowledge of the Bible, but far too little, he thought, to talk with young men his own age, or older, in any meaningful way about faith.

Up to now, he'd been able to get along by asking Hawley, B. F. Jacobs, or some other YMCA friend to preach. Were it not for Hawley's willingness to step up at the last minute to give a message to the prisoners, Moody would have had to address them himself. That thought bothered him more than being confronted with fixed bayonets. History remembers Moody as a preeminent preacher. But there was a time when he dreaded the thought of preaching.[10]

───────⟨ ⊙/⊙/⊙ ⟩───────

Another of Moody's friends, Daniel McWilliams, was present at a dinner held several months before Grant captured Fort Donelson. It was the summer of 1861, and Moody was also a guest. McWilliams and his fellow guests came away with a lasting impression of Moody. Undeniably, he had an "earnestness in seeking to lead persons to the Savior, and an intense thirst for knowledge of the Bible."

But, as McWilliams remembered, "The entire dinner time was taken by

Mr. Moody in quoting verses, and in asking the ministers [there] to tell him: 'What does this verse mean?'"[11]

The upshot of it all was this: the Civil War was D. L. Moody's training ground—not for combat—but for learning about key facets of relief work and Christian service. His business background had honed his gifts for administration and start-up initiatives. His peers recognized he clearly had a talent for those things. Now, the onset of war was forcing him, of necessity, to speak in settings that lay outside his comfort zone and to do all he could to enhance his knowledge of the Scriptures. He wished to help others become followers of Christ. He still had much to learn of what it meant to be a follower himself.

And here it may be said that sometimes the steepest learning curve is the best. Moody hadn't time to grow too introspective about his shortcomings. Fair enough, he had some. But there was still much work to do. He was willing, he was dedicated, and he was teachable. He had strong reserves of stamina, and his relief work was a great help in fostering good morale and offering support for soldiers confronting the specter of war. By the autumn of 1861, Moody's qualities and potential had been noticed. He received an invitation from the chaplain of an Illinois regiment of Zouaves to visit their camp at Elizabethtown in Kentucky, not far from Abraham Lincoln's birthplace.[12]

We can track Moody's activities at this time through the regiment's newspaper. Calling him "the active missionary," the reporter wrote that Chaplain Moody had "labored unceasingly both day and night in distributing books, papers, tracts."[13]

Moody had looked to the physical needs of the soldiers as well. In a letter written in January 1862, Moody told his brother Samuel, "I have some 500 or 800 people that are dependent on me for their daily food, & new ones coming all the time. I keep a sadall horse to ride around with . . . & then I keep a nother horse & man to carry around the things with . . . I have to go into the countrey about every week to buy wood & provisions . . . also coal, wheet meal & corn."[14]

He was trying also, as best he might, to study. But it proved a very steep challenge: "I do not get 5 minuets a day to study," he told Samuel, "so I have to talk just as it happens."[15]

One year later, in January 1863, the war took on a wholly different character for Moody. He came under fire while rendering aid to the wounded during the Battle of Murfreesboro (Tennessee). Afterward, in the small hours of the morning, he came upon one soldier who hadn't long to live.

"I asked what I could do for him," Moody remembered.

"Chaplain," he said, "help me to die."

Moody's heart went to the man at once. "I told him I would bear him in my arms into the Kingdom of God if I could, but I couldn't." He spoke a few words of the gospel, as best he understood it. The soldier shook his head, saying, "God can't save me; I've sinned all my life."

Moody was heartbroken: "Nothing I said seemed to help him." Promises from Scripture, prayerful words—all to no avail. Peace seemed beyond the soldier's grasp.

Finally, Moody thought to read a story about Christ, and how the wise man Nicodemus came at night with questions about eternity. It was a story from the third chapter of John's gospel.

As Moody began to read, something changed. The soldier's eyes never left him as he spoke. "He seemed to drink in every syllable," Moody said.

Then came the verse that read "As Moses lifted up the serpent in the wilderness, even so must the Son of man be lifted up: that whosoever believeth in him should not perish, but have eternal life" (John 3:14–15). On hearing this, the soldier stopped him, and asked:

"Is that there?"

"Yes," Moody said.

"I never knew *that* was in the Bible," the soldier said wonderingly, "please—read it again."

Moody did so. Weak as he was, the soldier leaned over on his elbow at the side of his cot. He brought his hands together tightly. When Moody finished, he said:

"That's good. Won't you read it again?"

Slowly, Moody repeated the passage the third time. When he finished he saw the soldier's eyes were closed. The troubled expression on his face had given way to a peaceful smile.

Soon after, it seemed he began to speak to himself. His lips moved, almost without a sound. Moody bent over him to catch what he was saying and heard a faint whisper:

"As Moses lifted up—the serpent—in the wilderness,—even so—must the Son of man be lifted up:—that whosoever—believeth in him—should not perish,—but have eternal life."

He opened his eyes and said: "That's enough; don't read any more." Quietly, Moody stepped away to snatch a few hours' sleep.

Early the next morning, he came again to the soldier's cot, but it was empty. The attendant in charge told him the young man had died peacefully. "After your visit," the attendant said, "he rested quietly, repeating to himself, now and then, 'Whosoever believeth in him should not perish, but have eternal life.'"[16]

In all, Moody went to the front nine times during the Civil War.[17] In many ways, his relief work in wartime was the making of him. His prior work in Chicago's slums acquainted him with grief. He knew what it was to find hopelessness and squalor there. But the suffering he saw during the war, among soldiers on both sides of the conflict, brought a sad and singular wisdom to his heart.

He also discovered a rare gift for coming alongside people in need. Sometimes, it was bathing a fevered brow for a man who never recovered consciousness. Sometimes, it was sharing words of solace from Scripture. Sometimes, he held a soldier's hand and offered a heartfelt prayer as the man slipped away to eternity.

Working through these years, amid so many scenes of extremity, Moody discovered the truth behind words spoken long years before by George Whitefield: "In the place of sorrow, news of Christ can refresh the soul. And though the interval may be brief, that news can bring peace at the last."[18]

For the rest of Moody's life, scenes of the war, and the faces of men, came to his memory. The ways that dying men found heaven's hope stayed with him. He could honor their memory by sharing that hope, by telling their stories. For the rest of his life, he did.

The Civil War brought Moody together with a man who would later become one of his most celebrated coworkers, D. W. Whittle. During the siege of Vicksburg, which lasted from late spring to midsummer 1863, Whittle, a lieutenant in the Seventy-Second Illinois, was severely wounded and sent home.

Whittle's popularity in Chicago was such that he was given a heartwarming reception on his return home. The American Express Company, his prewar employer, sent company friends, with a band of music and wagons, to escort him from the station. A few days later, Lieutenant Whittle was asked to make a speech at a patriotic rally. Other prominent men had also been asked to speak. As Whittle recalled:

> I, a boy of twenty-one, was put forward to speak, with Bishop Simpson on the platform behind me, waiting to give his address. I was weak from my wound, and felt foolish at being in such a position. Directly in front of me, in the center of the hall, a sturdy young man jumped to his feet and cried:
>
> "Give him three cheers!"
>
> I recognized the face of Mr. Moody, as he led the cheering with great earnestness. This manifestation of sympathy nerved me for the few words that followed, and I have often thought it was a specimen of what his courage, faith, and example have been to me all through his life. When I told him some time afterward of how much good his sympathy had done me that night, and how vividly I remembered his earnest, determined look as he led the crowd, I was rewarded by his reply:
>
> "I took you to my heart that night, and you have been there ever since!"[19]

In April 1864, Moody's relief work brought him in close association with General Oliver Otis Howard, later a founder of Howard University, one of America's finest historically African-American schools. General Howard "was in thorough sympathy" with Moody's work and later recounted what those days were like:

Moody and I met for the first time in Cleveland, East Tennessee. It was about the middle of April 1864. I was bringing together my Fourth Army Corps. Two divisions had already arrived, and were encamped in and near the village. Moody was then fresh and hearty, full of enthusiasm for the Master's work. Our soldiers were just about to set out on what we all felt promised to be a hard and bloody campaign, and I think we were especially desirous of strong preaching. Crowds and crowds turned out to hear him. He showed them how a soldier could give his heart to God. His preaching was direct and effective, and multitudes responded with a promise to follow Christ.[20]

Moody and President-Elect Abraham Lincoln had met briefly on Lincoln's trip to Washington. Unknown to either, it was the eve of the Civil War. Moody's friend J. V. Farwell would connect their lives once more at its close. In his Harvard University Press study, *Lincoln's Last Months*, scholar William Harris wrote of what transpired on Sunday, January 29, 1865. "The president," said Harris, "along with Mrs. Lincoln and numerous national leaders, attended the final session of The Christian Commission convention. Presided over by Secretary of State Seward, the meeting was held in the House of Representatives, which was packed with hundreds of people; many others were turned away. A spirit of religious revivalism prevailed in the chamber."[21]

Here Moody's friend and coworker John Farwell continued the story. "At the close of the war," Farwell recalled, "the Christian Commission, which had first begun work in Chicago under Mr. Moody, held a convention in Washington. At one of the meetings . . . . President Lincoln and his cabinet were present." At one point, the singer Philip Phillips gave a stirring performance of the song, "Your Mission." Its closing verse was—

> *If you cannot in the conflict prove yourself a soldier true—*
> *If where fire and smoke are thickest, there's no work for you to do,*
> *When the battlefield is silent, you can go with careful tread,*
> *You can bear away the wounded, you can cover up the dead.*

As Phillips sang, Farwell couldn't help but watch President Lincoln, who sat "wiping tears from his eyes." Lincoln was so deeply moved that he "sent up a request that this song be repeated at the close of the service." It was. Farwell closed his recollection with an arresting thought. That last verse, he said, "described Mr. Moody's work on many a battlefield, when the fight was over."[22]

———❦———

Moody was present for two other seminal events close to the end of the war. The first was the so-called Hampton Roads Peace Conference, held on February 3, 1865. Though his recollection of that event was brief, it revealed his longing for a terrible war to end.

"I remember," Moody said, "the excitement when Lincoln and Grant and Stephens (vice-president of the Confederacy) and one or two others met on the James River at the close of the war to agree on terms. I was nearby at the time. The whole nation was breathless to hear the results of that conference, which would mean so much to a country that had already been wasted with years of bloodshed. Every newspaper was eager to find out what was to be the outcome."[23]

Moody's eyewitness-to-history account of General Grant's entry into Richmond, Virginia, on April 3, 1865 began: "It was my privilege to go to Richmond with General Grant's army."

This was the opening sentence for what later became one of Moody's finest and most oft-repeated sermons. It bears reading in full. He hadn't been in Richmond long, he would tell audiences,

> before it was announced that the negroes were going to have a jubilee meeting . . . Their chains were falling off, and they were just awakening to the fact that they were free.
>
> I thought it would be a great event, and I went down to the African Church, one of the largest in the South, and found it crowded. One of the colored chaplains, of a northern regiment, had offered to speak.
>
> I have heard many eloquent men in Europe and in America, but I do not think I ever heard eloquence such as I heard that day. He said,

"Mothers! you rejoice today; you are forever free! That little child has been torn from your embrace, and sold off to some distant state for the last time. Your hearts are never to be broken again in that way; you are free."

The women clapped their hands and shouted at the top of their voices, "Glory, glory to God!" It was good news to them, and they believed it. It filled them full of joy.

Then he turned to the young men, and said, "Young men! You rejoice today; you have heard the crack of the slave-driver's whip for the last time; your posterity shall be free; young men rejoice today, you are forever free!" And they clapped their hands, and shouted, "Glory to God!" They believed the good tidings.

"Young maidens!" he said, "you rejoice today. You have been put on the auction-block and sold for the last time; you are free—forever free!"

They believed it, and lifting up their voices, shouted, "Glory be to God!" I never was in such a meeting.[24]

6

EMMA

From the day I became engaged to Emma Revell,
I have been a better man.[1]

—D. L. Moody

A mid the incessant relief work that marked his Christian service during the Civil War, D. L. Moody got married. His bride was Emma Revell, the girl he'd seen briefly just after he first arrived in Chicago. The date was Thursday, August 28, 1862. She was nineteen, he twenty-five.

By that time, they'd known each other for four years. How they met can be traced directly to Moody's pioneering work among the children of Chicago's slums. In 1858, Moody had been asked to speak at the Baptist church Emma's family attended. As he spoke, fifteen-year-old Emma saw "a tall, slender young man of five feet ten." At twenty-one, he was a strong, "Simon Peter sort of man," with "clear and frank" eyes, she would recall. He had thick, dark brown hair. His speech leaned unmistakably toward the rustic side, but he was, in a word, handsome.[2]

Dwight seems to have been captivated by her from the start. "I saw her first," he later told a friend, "when she was in a Sunday school class with her two sisters, and I learned to love her then."[3]

To look at pictures of Emma Revell in her youth was to see a slim, pretty girl with her dark hair gathered at the back, like many a cameo carving of the day. She had dark, expressive eyes. One could easily imagine them flashing when she smiled or laughed. That she must have done so often rests in the fact that she was her father's favorite. Her family had emigrated from England when she was a small child, and Emma was the apple of her father Fleming Revell's eye.[4]

When young D. L. Moody had spoken before the Sunday school class that Emma and her sisters attended, he told them of his "Sunday work." During the week, he was out of town as a commercial traveler, selling boots and shoes. Each Saturday night, he returned to his boardinghouse room in Chicago and was up by six on Sunday morning. Then it was over to the North Market Hall as early as he could get there, rolling out beer kegs, and sweeping up sawdust. For each Saturday night, dances were held there. Cigar stubs and other kinds of rubbish had to be cleared away. He cleaned everything as quickly as he could, for so soon as he finished, his "scholars" would begin to arrive—scores of poor children from the inner city, among them the members of his "bodyguard"— Red Eye, Smikes, Jackey Candles, Giberick, Billy Blucannon, and all the rest.

"Someday," Moody told Emma and the other members of her class, "I hope to have hundreds of children in my Sunday school. If I do, I hope some of you will come down to North Market Hall and help us out. We need you."[5]

Emma was one of those who took Moody up on his offer. As their grand-daughter would one day write, after Emma became a volunteer at Moody's North Market Hall mission school, "many changes began to take place in the young man's plans and dreams for the future."[6]

Moody began to escort Emma home, which was already a meeting place of sorts for young people. Emma's little brother, nine-year-old Fleming Revell Jr., was witness to their growing fondness for one another. Like many a little brother, he did things like crouch behind the stove on winter nights "to listen to the conversation of this young man who came to the house to see one of my sisters—in a very democratic company, and a very democratic sort of courting, because I think I never remember his ever coming alone. Around that little sheet-iron stove there was always a circle of young men . . . because there were *three* girls."[7]

There were good reasons why Emma's parents did not object to young Moody's courtship of their daughter. One, church leaders, including their pastor, held him in high regard. Two, they got to know him well in visits to their home and saw the rough-hewn quality in him. He was a young man of character—good, kind, and winning in his ways. And from a background of childhood poverty, he'd made himself something. Three, Moody was widely known to be an extremely capable and fast-prospering young businessman. His employers, first the Wiswall brothers, then C. H. Henderson, reposed great trust in his acumen, industry, and integrity. He already had a substantial income and significant funds in the bank. Countrified speech and sometimes rustic habits notwithstanding, he was a good catch. Last of all, Emma was very clearly taken with him.

Emma Moody, nineteen. D. L. Moody, age twenty-five; their wedding year [1862]

We know little of how Moody asked Emma to marry him, but we do know how he let people know of her consent to his proposal. As family lore in subsequent generations had it, suddenly, in 1860, "without much warning," Moody rose one night in a church service and announced that he'd just become engaged "to Miss Emma Revell, and therefore cannot be depended upon to see the other girls home from meeting."[8] Whether he told Emma he was going to say this isn't known. But if he hadn't, it would not have been out of character. Rope and knot, as he so often said, he was ever a man to do things spontaneously. "I have always been a man of impulse. Almost everything I ever did in my life that was a success was done on the impulse."[9] One exception was his proposal to Emma. He waited four years to ask her to marry.

Asking Emma Revell to marry him was the best thing he ever did, and he knew it. Who could blame him for blurting out the news for sheer happiness. He had news worth talking about.

All may have been well enough when Moody and Emma were engaged. But by the time they married, a special circumstance had arisen that placed Moody's finances in serious question.

His finances could not have been better at the start of 1860. He was then working for the merchant firm of Buell, Hill, & Granger, and he'd saved $7,000 toward the $100,000 that had always been his goal. For one year alone, he'd made by special commissions, above his regular salary, over $5,000, an unusually large sum for a young man under twenty-four.[10]

Indeed, the $7,000 Moody had set aside in savings would be worth $150,000 in today's dollars. Moody's annual salary at Buell, Hill & Granger was $5,000, and given the special commissions he'd earned during one banner year, he'd earned $5,000 more.[11] Thus the $10,000 between salary and commissions for that one year would be worth well over $200,000 today. By any measure, Moody was a highly successful young businessman—funds worth $150,000 today in the bank, and yearly earnings exceeding $200,000 in modern currency.[12]

By the close of the year, however, Moody walked away from a career that would undoubtedly have made him an even wealthier man.

Not that it was easily done. He cast his decision in one memorable phrase: "The greatest struggle I ever had in my life was when I gave up business."[13]

He told the story himself. "I had never," he said, "lost sight of Jesus Christ since the first time I met Him in the store in Boston. But for years, I really believed that I could not work for God. *No one had ever asked me to do anything.*"[14]

Once he'd traveled out west, nothing was different. As he remembered:

When I went to Chicago, I hired four pews in a church, and used to go out on the street and [recruit] young men and fill these pews. I never spoke to the young men about their souls; that was the work of the elders, I thought.

After working for some time like that, I started a mission Sunday-school. I thought numbers were everything, and so I worked for numbers. When the attendance ran below one thousand, it troubled me, and when it ran to twelve or fifteen hundred, I was elated. Still, none were converted; there was no harvest.[15]

All this changed following a remarkable series of events. For Moody, they led to an epiphany that he described by saying: "Then God opened my eyes."[16] In the North Market Hall mission school Moody had started, one class had proven especially troublesome. One might have thought a boy's class, full of young toughs, was the root of the problem.

But it wasn't. The problem was "a class of young ladies," as Moody recalled. Despite the best efforts of their teacher, they remained supremely indifferent, even hostile, to any talk of religion. It's hard to see why they kept coming, but they did. Perhaps the time-honored allure of young men in the same building was part of it. No one knew for sure.

One Sunday, their usual teacher was ill. Out of kindness, Moody took the class. They laughed in his face. He later said: "I felt like opening the door . . . telling them all to go out, and never come back."[17]

Things came to a head on the day when their teacher came to the store where Moody worked. "He was pale and looked very ill," Moody remembered.

"What's the trouble?" he asked.

"I've had another hemorrhage from the lungs," the young man said. "The doctor says I cannot live on Lake Michigan, so I'm going back to New York state. I suppose I'm going to die."

This was terrible news, but soon Moody thought he saw another source of deep concern. He asked the reason.

"I've never led any of my class to Christ," his young friend said. "I really believe I've done the girls more harm than good."

"I'd never heard anyone talk like that before," Moody remembered. "It set me thinking."

Several moments passed, then Moody spoke.

"Suppose you go and tell them how you feel. I'll go with you, if you want to go."

And so they harnessed a carriage and went.

Moody would say in retrospect: "It was one of the best journeys I ever had. We went to the house of one of the girls, called for her, and the teacher talked to her about her soul. There was no laughing [in our face] then. Tears stood in her eyes."

After Moody's friend "had explained the way of life," he suggested a word of prayer. He asked Moody to pray. "I'd never done such a thing," Moody remembered, "as to pray to God to convert someone. But we prayed, and God answered our prayer."

Moody and his friend went to other houses, to see the other members of the class. Moody could see how much this effort was weakening his friend, but the young man was resolute. He could only admire his friend's determination.

"He would go upstairs and be all out of breath," Moody said, "and he would tell each girl what he'd come for. It wasn't long before they broke down . . . They sought for salvation."

They continued on, but Moody could see that this effort was fast going beyond his friend's strength. "When his strength gave out," Moody said, "I took him back to his lodgings. The next day we went out again." So it was that, at the end of ten days, he came again to the store where Moody worked, "his face was literally shining."

"Moody," he said, "the last one of my class has yielded herself to Christ."

All his life, Moody could never remember such a time of joy. The store became a sudden cathedral.

Just one night later, Moody's friend had to leave for New York state. Moody thought to show him one last kindness. He called his friend's class together for a prayer meeting. When they all met, Moody recalled: "God kindled a fire in my soul that has never gone out."[18]

His memories of that meeting, and the unlooked-for gift it brought, always remained vivid. As it began, Moody said, his friend:

sat in the midst of his class, and talked with them, and read the fourteenth chapter of John. We tried to sing *Blest Be The Tie That Binds*, after which we knelt to pray.

I was just rising from my knees, when one of the class began to pray for her dying teacher. Another prayed, and another, and before we rose the whole class had prayed. As I went out I said to myself: "O God, let me die rather than lose the blessing I have received tonight!"

Just before the train started, one of the class came, and before long, without any pre-arrangement, they were all there. What a meeting that was! We tried to sing, but we broke down. The last we saw of the teacher, he was standing on the platform of the rear car, his finger pointing upward, telling that class to meet him in Heaven.[19]

"Then God opened my eyes."

For Moody, these events brought a moment of epiphany. But they also ushered in a deeply trying transformation. After bidding farewell to his dying friend, he felt he never wanted to do anything other than what he had done over the last few days: tell others of "the way of life." But then, so much of his identity was wrapped up in what he'd achieved in business, all in the face of such odds. He felt himself in a terrible quandary.

"The height of my ambition had been to be a successful merchant," he remembered, "and if I'd known that meeting was going to take that ambition out of me, *I might not have gone.*"[20]

One only has to consider what it was Moody was giving up. All his life, his driving purpose had been to forever erase the poverty of his youth. Nothing was going to keep him from becoming a wealthy businessman.

He had done that, or at least he was certainly well on his way. And he was engaged to wonderful young woman. How could he even consider setting this source of security aside? Yet that's what he did. The experience of being with his teacher friend and seeing young people transformed—that had transformed him.

Consider as well how history would have been different had Moody not resolved to step away from his business career. The Northfield schools, Moody Bible Institute, millions of conversions throughout Britain, Canada, and

America—none of these things would ever have happened.

Of course, Moody knew nothing of these things. They lay in the future. But we may, with hindsight, see all that hinged on his decision. As it was, he would live long enough to see many of these things unfold. And so he could say: "How many times I have thanked God since for that meeting!"[21]

But just what had Emma Revell gotten herself in for? As the biographer John C. Pollock put it so memorably, speaking of her marriage in 1862, she'd "fallen in love with a prosperous shoe salesman, become engaged to a children's missioner, and was now about to marry a six-horse Jehu." She very rightly must have wondered where it would end.[22]

As it was, by the start of the Civil War, she saw little of her newlywed husband. He was making daily forays from Chicago to Camp Douglas and out all hours of the day, sometimes going as far as Kentucky for extended periods. To make matters worse, at least in one sense, it seemed for a time there was a very real possibility Emma would lose him to enlistment as a noncombatant army chaplain.

A letter Moody wrote to his mother at this time showed how real that possibility was. "I am now at work among the soldiers a good deal," he told her. "I had a good time in Kentucky. The boys wanted to have me become their chaplain, but my friends would not let me go, so I shall remain in the city."

This was saying a great deal. Moody's friend John Farwell was almost certainly among those who put their foot down at the thought of Moody's enlisting. Others who worked with Moody at the YMCA likely added their voices, and Emma would not have been silent.

They feared that in this instance, Moody's heart had run ahead of him. Farwell asked him to take a salary, and the strong implication is that Farwell himself would have supplied it. But Moody refused his friend's advice, because it would impede his freedom.[23]

Many would call this a reckless step, and to many, perhaps even Emma herself for a time, it may have seemed so. She believed in her husband and knew his ability and industry, but what could be done in the meantime?

We do know that his savings dwindled fast, and for the first year after leaving business, his income was only $150, or about $3,200. It was a drastic change. Yet, providentially speaking, it was necessary. For, as J. C. Pollock has also observed, Moody was forced to take on a new role—that of a fund-raiser. He needed money to support his relief work during the Civil War. Beyond that, funds were needed to help with his work for the YMCA, indeed, to support the YMCA chapter in Chicago itself.

If necessity is the mother of invention, it was in this case the parent that gave rise to one of Moody's most celebrated and long-lasting achievements: he became one of the late nineteenth-century's most successful fund-raisers and philanthropists—securing and channeling millions of dollars—in nineteenth-century dollars—into a wide array of good causes. These included orphanages, schools, chapters of the YMCA, inner-city missions, church building projects, and other initiatives.[24] His start down that road may have been shaky at the outset, but he was born to do it.

Still, it all took a lot of getting used to. Some wives, perhaps many, would not have stood for it. Emma Moody did, and this speaks volumes of the depth of her love, her character, her capacity for faith, and her willingness to make sacrifices. Nor should it be forgotten that she was a missionary herself. She'd answered his challenge to serve as a teacher in the North Market mission school. She continued in that role after their marriage.

At one time, Emma was teaching a class of forty middle-aged men from some of the roughest places in Chicago. Though young, she was neither intimidated by nor incapable of teaching the large company of older men.

Moody knew Emma was a gifted teacher, and she had "pluck," a Victorian word rich in meaning. As the dictionary has it, pluck refers to a "courageous readiness to fight or continue against odds: dogged resolution."[25] Emma Moody certainly had that, and she respected it in her husband. They were well suited to one another.

By 1864, the Moody family finances were on a more stable footing (thanks to the generosity of friends like John Farwell), and their family began to grow.

Mr. and Mrs. D. L. Moody in 1864 and 1869

On October 24, they welcomed their first child—a daughter, whom they called Emma. "The baby is cunning," Moody told his mother. "I love it dearly."[26]

The Civil War had not yet ended, but it would within six months of this time. When it did, Moody was able to be home more often to do his work for the YMCA, and Emma rejoiced in that. As she wrote to Moody's youngest brother, Sam: "I have been staying with my mother . . . until a little while ago,

[when] I came to Hyde Park with my baby. We are only one and half miles from Chicago, so Mr. Moody can come down every night and return every morning. The trains run often through the day. I have a very pleasant boarding place. It is a building used for a young ladies' seminary but open through the warm weather for a boarding house. My room looks out on the lake, and it is always pleasant. The baby is much better here than in Chicago. It is much cooler also. Emma is enjoying it here very much and is beginning to talk quite plainly."[27]

In October 1866, Emma wrote again to Sam Moody, saying that her two-year-old daughter was her father all over again. "Little Emma is very well," she said. "She is growing so fast that you would scarcely know her, and so full of mischief. You would certainly think she was a second edition of D. L. Moody in his childhood. She is trying to talk, and I can understand most everything she says. She can speak her name quite plainly. She is a good deal of care now; but she pays as she goes, for she is so loving and so cunning. I suppose by the time she pays you another visit, she will be a big girl, for she grows so fast."[28]

In the meantime, Moody's work for the YMCA was flourishing. It will be remembered that at the outset of the Civil War, Moody had "assisted in forming an Army and Navy Committee of the Young Men's Christian Association."[29] Now that the war was over, he transitioned to active involvement with the Chicago YMCA once more. "I believe in the Young Men's Christian Association with all my heart," he would say years later. "Under God it has done more in developing me for Christian work than any other agency."[30]

From the autumn of 1860, when he'd given up business to devote himself solely to Christian work, Moody was deeply committed to the work of the Chicago YMCA. As secretary of the Chicago YMCA, and for several years as its president, he worked earnestly to build up the organization in every department.[31] His experiences during the Civil War with his Christian Commission work and the Army and Navy Committee of the Young Men's Christian Association that formed at that time drove his involvement.

Under Moody's leadership, the Chicago YMCA prospered greatly and was soon in need of a larger facility to meet. Its board of managers "had thought, planned, and prayed for a building of their own, but with little or no practical result." Finally, it was proposed that Moody, so "recently successful in erecting the Illinois Street Church," should be elected president, with John Farwell for vice president. However, in a rather odd sequel, it was thought Moody might not be quite respectable enough to serve as president. He and Farwell, therefore, switched places on the proposed election ticket.

While that election was in process, Moody did what he did best: tirelessly solicit financial pledges. The object was to secure funds sufficient to build a YMCA hall "with a seating capacity for three thousand people, as well as rooms for smaller meetings and offices."

Businesslike as he was, Moody also felt the need for prayer over this great venture. His friends B. F. Jacobs and J. W. Dean became "prayer partners," and they often met to ask that "the way might be opened for such a building."

This done, and "believing that his prayer would be answered," Moody lost no time in obtaining a charter from the state of Illinois, exempting the Young Men's Christian Association's real estate from taxation.

John Farwell donated valuable land to the YMCA. It was a handsome bequest, as the lot was then valued at $40,000.[32] In today's currency, that amount would be equal to approximately $627,000.

From here on, the YMCA project gained momentum. Its first cash subscription of $10,000 was secured from Cyrus H. McCormick, the Moody friend who had prospered in founding the company we know today as International Harvester. McCormick's gift was a sum equal to $150,000 today. Others generously gave too, until a sufficient fund was secured for "the first hall ever erected in America for Christian Association work," a pioneering distinction in the annals of nineteenth-century philanthropy.

The new YMCA building was dedicated on Sunday, September 29, 1867. An overflow audience was present for the occasion and "taxed the utmost capacity of the hall," as many visitors had come from distant cities.

Moody gave a memorable speech on this occasion; he "recounted the blessings the Association had received, and how God had led them from small beginnings to their present position of influence." He expressed his belief that by the Lord's blessing, a religious influence was to go out from this association that "should extend to every county in the State, to every State in the Union, and finally crossing the waters, should help to bring the whole world to God."[33]

It is also interesting to note that a plan had been under way "by some of the subscribers to the Association building fund" that it should be named after Moody. This was the more fitting, as the new hall owed so much of its existence "to his vigorous efforts."

Moody learned of this at the dedication ceremony and took to the platform to protest. Grateful as he was for the gesture intended to honor him, he gave "a short and vigorous appeal" asking the audience to name it Farwell Hall, "in honor of the man who was chairman of the building committee, and had been so liberal a giver."

Moody's proposal "was carried by acclamation." However, John Farwell insisted on having a last word, even as he accepted the honor given him. After the dedication ceremony, he stoutly maintained that "the audience had acceded to the only mistake Mr. Moody ever made in connection with this enterprise." For Farwell, the new YMCA building should have been called Moody Hall. There were many who agreed.

————◦∕◦∕◦————

In all Moody's Christian ministry—from being a Civil War chaplain away from home to raising funds for the YMCA and later still as a traveling evangelist—his marriage to Emma thrived. Words Moody's eldest son, Will, wrote to his mother just after Moody's death are a moving tribute to the happiness they knew in marriage. "He owed so much to you," Will wrote. "He himself often said he owed more to you than to anyone else, and how much you had done for him since you first 'took him in hand.' To you he owed such an education as no one else could have given him; and he alone realized fully what we all know in part—how great a part of the success he achieved in God's service was due to your counsel and help. . . . Father often spoke of it to us. . . . He always held you up as a model wife, and said if we children did as well as he did in marriage, how rejoiced he would be."[34]

THE PICKPOCKET'S GIFT

Love comes into a man's heart from God . . . love is the lever with which Christ lifts the world. He came down into the world because he loved it.[1]

D. L. Moody

Moody's ministry was always marked by a remarkable degree of candor and humility. Many times he publicly confessed a fault or shortcoming. Within his family, he often regretted a flash of ill temper or a display of poor judgment. But little time passed, often just a few minutes, before he asked forgiveness.

Not long after marrying, Moody began to reproach himself for not being able to do more for God—this after he'd already completed a hard day's work. Soon, he saw what folly it was. "I thought it was because I wasn't spiritual," he said. "It was because I was a fool. The Lord isn't a hard taskmaster. I was nearly killing myself by foolishly working day and night, and going without meals. I have learned since then that if I am to do my best for God, I must use sense."[2]

To read of such *mea culpas* is refreshing. They underscore Moody's humanity. He accomplished great things in his life, but he was far from perfect. He knew that better than anyone else.

Perhaps Moody's most famous and most instructive *mea culpa* appeared during his friendship with a former pickpocket turned preacher, Henry ("Harry") Moorhouse. When they met, Moody made a snap judgment and decided he wanted little or nothing to do with Moorhouse. For a time, he treated the young man with studied indifference.

But God had something else in store. Though he resisted Moorhouse's first overtures of friendship, that friendship would bring something far better than Moody could have imagined. He was the last to see it. But when he did, it changed the course of his ministry.

Moody met Harry Moorhouse in Dublin, Ireland, in 1867, toward the close of a trip he had taken to the British Isles for the sake of his wife Emma's health. Before he and Emma arrived in Dublin, however, there were some colorful happenings along the way.

=====◦/◦/◦=====

That the Moodys were in the British Isles at all was owing to a doctor's counsel. In 1867, their family physician suggested a sea voyage for Emma, who had "a harassing cough." Moody had been worried about his wife and quickly booked passage for England, where Emma had close relations. They left America's shores on February 22.

Aside from this, Moody also had "an earnest desire" to hear and meet C. H. Spurgeon and George Müller, two leaders in Britain he much admired. Spurgeon was famous as the gifted and eloquent pastor of London's Metropolitan Tabernacle. Müller's faith-based work in founding orphanages had saved hundreds of lives throughout England. Moody deeply admired their good works, but he admired their sense of consecration and spiritual vitality no less.

When Moody arrived in port, he was unknown in England, save to such British friends as had visited America. One of them was Fountain J. Hartley, secretary of the London Sabbath School Union. Hartley invited Moody, soon after his arrival, to speak at an anniversary meeting in Exeter Hall.

It was then customary in England for a speaker on such an occasion "to be connected with a formal resolution, as its mover or seconder, in order to give him a right to the floor." So Moody was asked to offer a motion of thanks to the chairman of the evening meeting—in this instance none other than Lord Shaftesbury, then the most famous social reformer in the world.[3]

Toward the close of the meeting, the vice-chairman stood and said he was glad to welcome "an American cousin, the Reverend Mr. Moody, of Chicago," who would now "move a vote of thanks to the noble Earl."

Moody had never done anything like this, of course. Now, with "refreshing frankness, and an utter disregard of conventionalities," he stood and said to the audience:

> The chairman has made two mistakes. To begin with, I'm not the "Reverend" Mr. Moody at all. I'm plain D. L. Moody, a Sabbath-school worker. And then, I'm not your "American cousin." By the grace of God I'm your brother, who's interested, with you, in our Father's work for His children.
>
> And now, about this vote of thanks to "the noble Earl" for being our chairman this evening. I don't see why we should thank him— any more than he should thank us. When at one time they offered to thank our Mr. Lincoln for presiding over a meeting in Illinois, he stopped it. He said he'd tried to do his duty, and they'd tried to do theirs. He thought it was an even thing all round.

That opening "fairly took the breath away from the audience," dispelling any doubt this august gathering had a colorful New England Yankee in their midst.

But no one was offended. Everyone there thought Moody's "novelty was delightful." He won them over, Lord Shaftesbury included, and the story of "Moody's motion" soon spread far and wide.

After this, Moody visited the YMCA in Aldersgate Street, describing his gospel work in Chicago "with a freshness and vigor that captivated all who heard him." His British friends took particular interest in his work among the children of Little Hell and other slums.

And true to his stated ambition, Moody secured an interview with Charles Spurgeon. It was the first meeting of a friendship both men came to treasure. Moody also traveled to Bristol—the place, as he told his mother by letter, "of George Müller's great orphan schools."

Moody was deeply moved by what he saw. "Müller has 1,150 children in his house," he told his mother, "but never asks a man for a cent of money to support them. He calls on God, and God sends the money to him. It is wonderful to see what God can do with a man of prayer."

While Moody was traveling about and meeting people he'd long wanted to see, Emma had several visits with relatives in England. During one short trip, she had a bizarre experience that might well have claimed her life.

Stepping into what she thought was an empty railway carriage, Emma anticipated a quiet trip. But after the train started, she realized that "a strange bundle of clothing, propped up against one corner of the car" was really a dirty and derelict man who'd hidden himself there. But Emma couldn't leave. An unobservant train conductor had locked the door of her compartment, common practice as a safety measure. There was no other way out. She was trapped until the train arrived at the next depot on the line.

The man suddenly sat up and slid across the seat next to Emma, who was "huddled in her corner next to the car door." Then he spoke. "Do you know what I would have done with my wives if I had been Henry the Eighth?"

Terribly frightened, Emma summoned great courage and pluck. She quickly reasoned she had to humor this man. So she said:

"No, do tell me."

Then followed a deranged litany, lasting several minutes. The crazed passenger graphically described how he would have gotten rid of each wife, some by drowning, others by beheading. Finally, "he stopped to see the effect of his words."

Knowing she had to keep this man occupied until the train drew up to the next station, Emma began to spin horrid yarns of her own. She "outdid him on every score" and kept him talking "until the train came to a standstill."

When it did and the door to her compartment opened, she quickly stepped out and told the conductor "in whispers" of the condition of the man she'd left behind her in the carriage. Emma's quick thinking, and remarkable courage likely saved her life.[4]

During their stay, the Moodys had been encouraged to visit Scotland and Ireland. So, while in Dublin, they attended a church service held by the Plymouth Brethren. Afterward, Moody finally met Harry Moorhouse. A boyish-looking former pickpocket, Harry had spent time in prison before being converted.

Moorhouse introduced himself to Moody, and as they chatted, he said in his thick accent: "I'd like to come to America and preach."

Henry (Harry) Moorhouse, a great Moody friend and a gifted preacher

Moody wasn't impressed. Taking time to exchange a few pleasantries was one thing, but this young man looked to have more rough edges than Moody himself once had. As he later recalled: "I looked at him. He was a beardless boy—didn't look as if he was more than seventeen [though he was really in his twenties]. I said to myself: 'He can't preach.'"

Harry Moorhouse was unaware of this silent surmise, and he was nothing if not persistent. He asked Moody what ship he was taking to return to America. "I'd like to go there with you," he said.

Moody was looking at a young man not unlike a mirror image of himself at seventeen, but the evangelist apparently did not recognize that reality. He only knew he now wished to be rid of this young man who was fast becoming a nuisance. He said something vague and noncommittal about the time and place of his return to America and said goodbye.

Once home in Chicago, Moody had forgotten about Harry Moorhouse. Then he got a letter from the young man, saying he'd arrived in America and "would come to Chicago and preach for me if I wanted him."

Moody must have shaken his head. "I sat down," he said, "and wrote a very cold letter." In it, he told Moorhouse, "If you come west, call on me." There was no invitation to preach, nothing more of encouragement than to say he *might* see Moorhouse.

"I thought that would be the last I should hear of him," Moody remembered, "but soon I got another letter, saying that he was still in this country, and would come on if I wanted him."

Moody wrote another letter, telling Moorhouse to "drop in" if he came west. A few days later, Moorhouse sent a third letter, "stating that next Thursday, he would be in Chicago."

Moody was stymied. "What to do with him I didn't know. I'd made up my mind he couldn't preach. [As it was,] I was going to be out of town Thursday and Friday."

So, prior to leaving, Moody told the officers of his church: "There's a man coming here Thursday and Friday who wants to preach. I don't know whether he can or not. You'd better let him try. I'll be back Saturday."

The church officers weren't thrilled with the idea. "They said [Moorhouse] was a stranger," Moody remembered, "and might do more harm than good."

Again, Moody advised, "You'd better try him. Let him preach two nights." Finally, they agreed. [5]

When Moody returned the following Saturday morning, he wasted little time in asking his wife, Emma, how young Moorhouse had done:

"How's that young Irishman coming along? Do people like him?"

That question showed how little interest Moody had really taken in Moorhouse. He was *English*, not Irish. To this, Emma replied:

"They like him very much."

"Did you hear him?" Moody asked.

"Yes."

"Did you like him?"

"Yes," Emma said, "very much. He preached two sermons . . . I think you'll like him—although he preaches a little differently than you do. He tells sinners God *loves* them."

Moody wanted none of that. Heretofore, he'd dealt often in fire-and-brimstonish sermon fare—insisting that "God was behind the sinner with a double-edged sword, ready to hew him down." He told Emma flatly:

"Moorhouse is wrong."

Emma could give as good as she got. She said: "I think you'll agree with him when you hear him. He backs everything he says with the Word of God. *You* think if a man doesn't preach as you do, he's wrong."

"We'll see!" Moody said, and he went that very night to hear Moorhouse for himself.

As Moody took his seat for the service, he noticed everyone had brought their Bibles. As the service started, Moorhouse stood and walked to the pulpit.

"My friends," he began, "if you'll turn to the third chapter of John, and the sixteenth verse, you'll find my text." As Moorhouse said this, Moody noticed that people around him had begun to smile. What, he wondered, was going on?

He soon found out.

"[Harry] preached a most extraordinary sermon from that verse," Moody recalled. "He didn't divide the text into 'secondly' and 'thirdly' and 'fourthly'—he just took it as a whole, and then went through the Bible, from Genesis to Revelation, showing that in all ages, God loved the world; that He'd sent prophets and patriarchs and holy men to warn people, and last of all, God sent His Son. And after they murdered Him, He sent the Holy Ghost."

Moody was cut to the heart. "I never knew up to that time," he recalled later, "that God loved us so much . . . I could not keep back the tears. It was like news from a far country. I just drank it in."

The next night, Moody was again among the great crowd who'd come to hear Moorhouse. The young Englishman stood as before and said: "My friends, please turn in your Bible to the third chapter of John, and the sixteenth verse. There, you'll find my text."

Then, as Moody remembered, "he preached another extraordinary sermon from that wonderful verse . . . proving God's love again, from Genesis to Revelation. He could turn to almost any part of the Bible, and prove it . . . He struck a higher chord . . . it was sweet to my soul to hear it."[6]

For an entire week, Harry Moorhouse kept preaching from John 3:16. On the seventh consecutive night, he went into the pulpit. Every eye was upon him, all wondering what he was going to preach about. He said: "My friends, I've been hunting all day for a new text, but I can't find one as good as the old one. So we'll go back to the third chapter of John." People long remembered the close of his sermon. "My friends," he said:

> for a whole week, I've been trying to tell you how much God loves you, but I can't do it with this poor, stammering tongue. If I could borrow Jacob's ladder, climb up to heaven, and ask Gabriel, who stands in the presence of God—if he could tell me how much love the Father has for the world—all he could say would be: *God so loved the world, that He gave His only begotten Son, that whosoever believeth in Him should not perish, but have eternal life.*[7]

It was a revelation. Moody had never known anything like this "inexhaustibility of Scripture." He'd never, he said later, "dreamed of anything like it."

Once a thorough skeptic, he now became a student. He asked Moorhouse how to study, and together, they invited friends to his Chicago home for the first of the "Bible readings" that would become famous as a part of his ministry.

"I've never forgotten those nights," Moody confessed with profound gratitude. "I've preached a different gospel since."[8]

THE CHICAGO FIRE

*When I was burned out in the great fire, and was left perfectly
destitute, I received a letter with some money from this young man
in Boston, who said: "You helped me, and took me in your home,
keeping me six weeks—and refused to take anything for it . . .
I have never forgotten your kindness."*[1]

D. L. Moody

Moody described his family's escape from the great Chicago Fire many times throughout his life. Scattered over many books, there are literally dozens of recollections.

But the financial aid a Boston man gave Moody and his family is especially telling. Moody and his family escaped the Chicago Fire with the clothes on their backs and little more. They were homeless. The letter and money Moody received after the fire must have meant all the world to him.

He'd probably forgotten once hosting the young man who'd sent these gifts in his Chicago home, the home he'd now lost. But the young man had always remembered: *"You . . . took me in your home, keeping me six weeks—and refused to take anything for it."*

Now that kindness came back to Moody, when he needed it most.

Two weeks after the fire, he returned home and tried to find something, anything, that could be saved.

One thing only was found. As his daughter, Emma, remembered, her father drove the family to the site of their former house: "Father got down in the ruins, going over everything with a cane. The only thing of value that he found was a little toy iron stove."[2]

The fire had claimed everything else. "Chicago was laid in ashes," Moody's son Will would later write. "The great fire swept out of existence both Farwell Hall and the Illinois Street Church . . . Everything was scattered."[3]

Before the inferno swept Chicago's streets with such destruction, Moody had been working at a breakneck pace. "Before the fire," he said, "I was on some ten or twelve committees. My hands were full. If a man came to me to talk about his soul, I would say: 'I haven't time; I've got a committee to attend to.'"[4]

Clearly, he'd been working too hard. It had been that way for years. After the fire, the fallout of that overwork and unacknowledged worry caught up with him.

＝＝

The first news of the fire reached Moody while he was preaching a sermon before a capacity crowd at the second Farwell Hall, the YMCA facility he'd worked tirelessly to create.

It was a tragic source of irony that the first Farwell Hall was lost to fire within four months of its dedication in 1867. That loss had been catastrophic, as the building was only partly insured. Then, as was his wont, Moody "took matters in his own hands." He acted so quickly it was said "he had secured subscriptions for the new hall before the old one ceased burning."

The ruins of the old hall "were still smoldering when he received a telegram from J. D. Blake, of Rochester, Minnesota, an early friend of the general Association work, offering to take $500 worth of stock in the new building."[5]

In this fund-raising effort, Moody was at the center of what was then called "the lightning Christianity of Chicago," a vivid description of the city's reputation for rapid-response charity. As a local clergyman, the Reverend Macrae, remembered:

When the costly hall of the Young Men's Christian Association took fire in 1867, the secretary and other officials, as soon as they found the building was doomed, ran about among the merchants in the city for subscriptions. "Our hall is burning, Sir; the engines are at work, but there is no hope. We shall [need] a new one. Let us have money enough to begin at once!" Thousands upon thousands of dollars were subscribed . . . and it is said that before the fire was out, money enough had been raised to build a new hall.[6]

On the night of Sunday, October 8, 1871, Moody was preaching in the new Farwell Hall when the courthouse bell sounded an alarm. But he and the audience initially paid it little heed. "They were accustomed to hear the fire-bell often," one account said, "and it did not disturb them much when it sounded."[7]

The gifted young composer and soloist Ira Sankey, who had just begun his work alongside Moody, was also there, and his recollections bring that harrowing night to life. "At the close of his address," Sankey wrote,

> Mr. Moody asked me to sing a solo . . . Standing by the great organ at the rear of the platform I began the old, familiar hymn, "Today the Saviour Calls." By the time I had reached the third verse, my voice was drowned by the loud noise of the fire engines rushing past the hall, and the tolling of bells . . . we could hear . . . the deep, sullen tones of the great city bell, in the steeple of the old court-house . . . ringing out a general alarm.[8]

By now, Sankey wrote, the audience was understandably "restless and alarmed." The sound of "tremendous confusion was heard in the streets." Moody closed the meeting at once.

As the people left, Sankey and Moody descended the small back stairway to emerge on Arcade Court. "From our position there, we watched the reflection of the fire, half a mile away, on the west side of the city . . . After a few moments, we separated, I to go over the river to where the fire was raging, and he to his home on the North Side. We did not meet again for more than two months."[9]

As Sankey made his way, he was nearly caught up in one of the most horrific parts of a great urban inferno: a firestorm. He'd come upon a block of small frame buildings burning fiercely and stopped to give whatever help he could. "I assisted in tearing down some board fences," he wrote,

> to try to keep the fire from spreading to the adjoining territory. While thus engaged, the wind from the southwest had risen almost to a

hurricane, and the flying embers from the falling buildings were quickly caught up and carried high upon the roofs of the houses adjoining, which were soon in flames ... The fire spread from building to building, and from block to block, until it seemed evident that the city was doomed. All this time, the fire was moving towards Farwell Hall and the business center of the city.[10]

Meanwhile, as Moody made his way home, he'd seen "a great flare in one section of the city"; he knew then that this was an inferno of tremendous size. He stopped and took a quick look back at his church, the Illinois Street Church, then started running in the direction of his home and family. He then had no way of knowing, but soon after midnight, the church would be gone.[11]

The scene that met Moody's eyes, when he reached his home on State Street, was one of pell-mell confusion. The fire was fast approaching, and there was just time for him and Emma to dress their children warmly, gather what they could, and flee.

The first thing was to see to their children's safety. As Moody's daughter (also named Emma) later wrote in her memoirs: "When the fire had come almost to our door, a neighbor took my brother and me with his children out north to the suburb Buena Park, to the Spaffords' house. They were friends of [my] mother, who had the tragic experience, a few years later, of losing their four little girls in the sinking of the *Ville de Havre*. It went down in mid-Atlantic. Only the mother was saved ... [As for the night of the fire,] my mother did not know for twenty-four hours whether or not we had been trapped by the flames. Her hair began to turn white that terrible night."[12]

Sometimes, history converges in unforgettable ways. Emma Moody's allusion was to the terrible sea disaster that would become the inspiration for Horatio Spafford to share his enduring faith by writing "It Is Well with My Soul," the now classic hymn. It staggers the imagination to think that the Spaffords were able to help save the Moody children but would later suffer the loss of their own four little daughters.

But all this lay in the future. Now that Moody and his wife had safely seen their children away, they remained as long as possible to help others. Then they sought refuge on the west side of the city with her sister Sarah.

Emma Moody rescued this portrait of her husband during the Chicago Fire, painted by artist G. P. A. Healy in 1867.

Before taking flight, however, Emma Moody was able to save something that her husband strongly admonished her to leave behind. As their daughter recalled, "When mother and father were thinking what was the one thing each prized most and wanted to save, mother chose a painting of father, which had been done by a well-known artist . . . named G. P. A. Healy [who] usually received about $2,000 for his portraits. He had given this painting to mother a few years before, when we moved into our home on State Street. It was his gift toward furnishing the house, which was entirely done by friends."[13]

Once the painting had been secured, Emma Moody asked her husband to carry it. He refused. "Wouldn't it look nice," he said, "if any one of my friends met me carrying away a painting of myself, instead of some other valuables!"

So it was that Emma Moody carried away that painting herself. "We still have it in our family," her daughter would write. "In later years, I felt that that home in Chicago meant more to Mother than any other she ever had. I was about seven years old the year of the fire, and my brother Willie, two and a half."

How Emma Moody got the painting out of its heavy gold frame was a story in itself. Just as she was saying she wanted to take it, "robbers entered the house to plunder and steal." But on entering, one of them became suddenly conscience-stricken. He turned to Emma Moody "and asked her if there was anything he could do for her." She asked him to kick the heavy gilt frame from the painting, so that she could carry the painting more easily. He did. Then, just as quickly, he was gone.[14]

This bizarre bit of gallantry aside, Emma Moody paid a price for her resolve. As the would-be thief kicked away the heavy gilt frame, part of it broke away so quickly that she hadn't time to get out of the way. It hit her hard, giving her a black eye and bruised face.[15] Still, she was undeterred. Injured, but grimly determined, she went out on the street to leave, painting in hand. Her husband soon joined her, carrying a few things and filling a baby carriage "with such clothing and articles as there was room for." No other conveyance, a wagon or handcart, was to be had. All they'd been able to rescue were "a few cherished tokens," among them, the family Bible.[16]

Though he and his family were safe, Moody seemed overwhelmed for a time by a numbing sense of loss. He felt himself a man adrift. Moody's son-in-law, A. P. Fitt, rightly said that the Chicago Fire brought a "night of fiery ordeal that tried many a man's soul."[17]

Still, Moody felt duty bound to do what he could to help others. He also wanted to help the church he'd founded, the Illinois Street Church, now nothing but ashes. Leaving Emma and their two children in the care of friends, he now devoted himself to relief work.

Moody soon left for the East "to raise money for the homeless, and also for a new church." Friends rallied to his side as well. George H. Stuart and John Wanamaker, of Philadelphia, along with other friends raised three thousand dollars. In weeks, a temporary building, seventy-five by one hundred feet, was built on a lot not far from the site of the former church. On Christmas Eve, 1871, just two months and fifteen days after the fire, this building, called the North Side Tabernacle, was dedicated.[18]

While in New York, Moody heard about R. K. Remington, from the city of Fall River, who was very generous. He called on Remington and secured a check for a large amount. This new friend took Moody in his carriage to the houses of other rich men in the city. When they parted at the train station, Moody grasped his hand and said: "If you ever come to Chicago, call on me. I will try to return your kindness."[19]

Moody was profoundly grateful for all R. K. Remington had done. He could go home knowing the work of rebuilding could commence in earnest.

But who could rebuild him? He felt shattered and listless. "My heart was not in the work for begging," he said later.[20] At another time, he spoke at greater length of his dilemma. "I got into a cold state. It did not seem as if there was any unction resting upon my ministry. For four long months God seemed to be just showing me myself. I found I was ambitious; I was not preaching for Christ; I was preaching for ambition. I found everything in my heart that ought not to be there. For four months, a wrestling went on within me, and I was a miserable man. But after four months, the anointing came."[21]

If ever a man needed a special touch of the Master's hand, Moody did. That gift came one day while he walked the streets of New York to the house of a friend. "God Almighty seemed to come very near," Moody recalled. "I felt

I must be alone." He hurried to the house of his friend nearby, was shown upstairs, and, on entering quickly asked, half apologizing: "I need to be alone. Have you a room I can use?"

Moody's host graciously showed him to a room without delay. He entered, closed the door, and sat on a sofa—then went to his knees. Almost instantly, he had a deep, unmistakable sense of the presence of God.

Words nearly failed Moody when he tried to tell what happened next.

"Ah, what a day!" he remembered. "I cannot describe it. I seldom refer to it, it is almost too sacred an experience to name—Paul had an experience of which he never spoke for fourteen years—I can only say God revealed Himself to me, and I had such an experience of His love that I had to ask Him to stay His hand. [After this,] I went to preaching again. The sermons were not different. I did not present any new truths. Yet hundreds were converted. I would not now be placed back where I was, before that blessed experience, if you should give me all the world."[22]

As one writer memorably phrased it: Moody had been given a personal Pentecost, an experience literally in an upper room.[23]

"Many a time I have thought of it since," Moody said some years later. "I was wretched no longer . . . If I have not been a different man since, I do not know myself . . . There was a time when I wanted [only] to see my little vineyard blessed, and I could not get out of it. But I could work for the whole world now . . . go round the world, and tell the perishing millions of a Savior's love."[24]

When Moody needed Him most, God came. In mercy, he was given a lasting sense of grace and peace. He felt renewed and strengthened as he never had before.

One sentence captured what he felt: "I was all the time tugging and carrying water. But now I have a river that carries me."[25]

For the rest of his life, this profound sense of God's presence and power shaped Moody's ministry. He did not know it, but what God had given him in this "blessed hour" set the stage for one of the most remarkable missionary tours of the nineteenth century.

9

THE MISSION TO GREAT BRITAIN

*Mr. Moody has been called an uncultivated man.
Well, he has not had an education, thank God, in
the University of Oxford. But, notwithstanding that,
he has a wonderful power of getting at the hearts of
people . . . a great many persons of high station have
been greatly struck with that man's preaching, with
its wonderful simplicity and power.[1]*

—Lord Shaftesbury

That D. L. Moody received such fulsome praise from one of England's greatest reformers, Lord Shaftesbury, was little less than a wonder. Moody was a modestly educated mason's son. Lord Shaftesbury was known the world over as "the poor man's Earl."[2]

Yet it was undeniable: Moody's first gospel mission to Great Britain was a watershed event—indeed, it led to an important article on Moody and his partner in ministry, the composer and soloist Ira Sankey in the prestigious *Oxford Dictionary of National Biography* (ODNB). Alongside *The Oxford English Dictionary*, the ODNB is one of the finest repositories of scholarship in the world.

To be sure, Moody and Sankey were not British. But their influence on Britain was so pervasive and touched so many lives, that their work in Britain may be said to comprise a "multi-biography" all its own. In modern religious history, there has never been anything quite like it. The ODNB's essay on Moody and Sankey is stark in its summary of their impact, stating that they "probably represent the chief cultural influence of the United States on Britain during the nineteenth century."[3]

Moody's mission to Britain lasted just over two years, from June 1873 to July 1875. It is said to have reached its zenith in the final five months, between March 9 and July 21, 1875, when Moody addressed, in total, "over 2½ million people at four venues: the Agricultural Hall, Islington; the Royal Opera House, Haymarket; Camberwell Green; and Bow Common."[4]

This brief summary is impressive. But it is also no less true that Moody's first mission to Britain nearly came to grief before it had started.

In early 1872, Moody had found a place of peace after all the havoc and disruption the great Chicago Fire had brought into his life. The newly built Northside Tabernacle was flourishing, drawing a large and steady attendance. Services there were said to be "meetings fruitful in results."

Aside from this, however, there was little call for Moody to do visitation work on the scale he'd done before the fire. The city was still in ashes "for a large area surrounding the Tabernacle," and relatively few new homes had as yet been built. Little shanties among the ruins were about all there were—and even those were only temporary. So as soon as many people could leave them, they chose to build new, more permanent homes elsewhere. This part of Chicago had once been densely populated. Now, it was something of a ghost town.[5]

Moody's work, such as it had been, was considerably diminished. But what proved a source of sadness on one hand presented an opportunity on another. He had for many years longed to learn more of the Bible from gifted British Christian leaders and educators. That yearning held an added benefit, as a return trip would allow Emma to see members of her family. They decided to travel to England once again and set out in June 1872.

Study and rest were all Moody had in mind to do. He would resume preaching in time, but not for a while.

Or so he thought. One day he attended the Old Bailey prayer meeting. At the close of the service, the Reverend John Lessey, pastor of a church in the north of London, asked him to preach the next Sunday. Mr. Moody agreed.

The morning service proved a challenge, even a source of dismay. The place "seemed very dead and cold," the people "did not appear to be very much interested." As he spoke, Moody felt himself to be "beating against the air." It was as if he preached for "a lost morning."

The next service was scheduled for half-past six that evening. It could not have been more radically different. While Moody was preaching, "it seemed as if the very atmosphere was charged with the Spirit of God." It was as though there was "a hush from heaven upon the people," which Moody found it difficult to fathom. By his own admission, he hadn't been "much in prayer that day." He couldn't understand it.[6]

As was his custom, Moody concluded his sermon by asking any who wished to become Christians to rise, so he could pray for them. Almost all at once, scores of people stood. It seemed like the whole audience had risen.

Moody thought: *They must not have understood me. They didn't know what I meant when I gave an invitation for seekers to stand. Surely, that is what has just happened.*

So, he thought to put his invitation more clearly and repeated it. "All those who want to become Christians," he said, "just step into the inquiry room." At this, most of the sanctuary emptied; virtually everyone present went to the inquiry room. There were so many people that extra chairs had to be brought in. Neither Reverend Lessey nor Moody could believe it. They had never seen God "save by hundreds," rather than "by ones and twos."

Once more, Moody thought he'd been misunderstood. He asked those "that really wanted to become Christians" to rise. Again, the whole audience stood.[7]

Moody truly had no idea what to do, so he again played it safe, and told all those who were "really in earnest to meet the pastor there the next night." It seemed best to let Reverend Lessey and his church leaders sort everything out.

The following day, Moody and Emma set out for Dublin, as they'd planned to do for some time. But just two days later, Moody received an urgent dispatch saying he had to return. Reading the letter, he learned that there had been "more inquirers on Monday than on Sunday."

It was stunning, albeit very welcome news. As soon as they could, the

Moodys returned to John Lessey's church. Meetings were held for ten days. Four hundred people were converted and welcomed into the church. These were pristine days, a beautiful, unexpected time of spiritual renewal.

For Moody, it was a turning point—the like of which he'd never seen.

———◊◊◊———

Not long afterward, Moody heard of inspiring events that had preceded this time of renewal. The Adlard sisters were steadfast parishioners of Reverend Lessey's church; the elder sister participated in the church, but the younger, Marianne, "a mere slip of a girl," was bedridden. Understandably, Marianne found it a hardship at times to be confined to their home. But over time, she discovered there was one thing she could do. True, she couldn't leave home to tell others of the faith she held dear, but she could pray that faith would be given them. Marianne could become their intercessor. All through the day, each day, she kept to this task. Still, she felt disheartened at times. For though she had been praying a long while, no time of renewal had come.

Then, she read a newspaper account of some gospel meetings Moody had held in America. Though she didn't know him, she began to pray that God would send him to her church.[8]

One day Marianne's sister returned home from church to say that "Mr. Moody, from America" had preached in their church. That Sunday, both sisters felt a holy sense of awe and gratitude. It was an astonishing answer to prayer.[9]

As for Moody himself, he always believed that the prayers of these sisters, particularly Marianne, had undoubtedly set the stage for the days of renewal that had come and the incredible time of renewal that would follow one year later.

The news of all that had taken place in John Lessey's church soon spread. Moody soon received invitations from the Reverend William Pennefather, Rector of St. Jude's, Mildmay Park, London, and Cuthbert Bainbridge, a prominent Methodist layman of Newcastle-on-Tyne, to hold meetings. But as Moody had not come prepared for a long stay, he told these friends he had to return soon to America. However, he could leave them with a promise that he hoped to return in 1873. Pennefather and Bainbridge were heartened by this and promised to send him funds to cover the expense of the ocean voyage.

===●/●/●===

Moody, Sankey, and their wives set sail for England on June 7, 1873. They hadn't as yet received the promised funds from Pennefather and Bainbridge, and some months had gone by, but Moody reasoned that could be sorted out on their arrival. They had promised him the funds and to make arrangements for a long series of gospel meetings.

That was good enough for him. He wouldn't hold off leaving just to wait for their letter to arrive. In the meantime, his good friend John Farwell provided them with the money to book passage on a ship called *The City of Paris*. They arrived in Liverpool on June 17, where they were met by Harry Moorhouse.

Sadly, their friend Harry bore dire news: William Pennefather and Cuthbert Bainbridge had died. No sponsorship funds were forthcoming, and no plans for a series of gospel meetings were in place. They'd arrived in England, with nothing more than Harry's somber greeting and a slender supply of pocket money.

On hearing this news, Moody had turned to Sankey and said: "God seems to have closed the door. We will not open any ourselves. If He opens the door, we will go in; otherwise we will return [home] at once."

It was then Moody remembered an unopened letter he'd received just before leaving New York. He took it from his pocket and read it. It was from the secretary of the YMCA in York, England, saying he'd heard of Moody's work among young men in America and hoped if Moody ever came to England, he would come and speak at their association.

Here, hope seemed to flicker, if but a little. Moody said: "This door is only ajar, but we will consider the letter as God's hand leading to York, and we will go there."

After spending one night at Liverpool, Moody, with his wife and children, took the train for London. Ira Sankey and his wife went to Manchester, "to the home of the one man he knew in England"—Harry Moorhouse. Three days later, they all met again at York and began to hold gospel meetings.

The ministers in York were strongly inclined at first "to look upon the newcomers with suspicion and disfavor" and held themselves aloof. Attendance numbers were small to begin with. But gradually, "the meetings grew in interest, the ministers cooperated, and the hymns took hold of the people." These gospel gatherings soon "became the subject of public conversation throughout the community."[10]

"Yes, thank God, I know Mr. Moody," wrote F. B. Meyer, of Christ Church, London. "I have known him ever since a memorable Monday morning in 1873. I can now see him standing up to lead the first noon prayer-meeting in a small ill-lit room in Coney Street, York, little realizing that it was the seed-germ of a mighty harvest, and that a movement was beginning that would culminate in a few months in Free Assembly Hall, Edinburgh, and ultimately in the Agricultural Hall and the Royal Opera-house, London. It was the birth-time of new conceptions of ministry, new methods of work, new inspirations and hopes."[11]

After five weeks of meetings in York, during which several hundred people were converted, Moody and Sankey moved on to the seaport city of Sunderland. Here, "their meetings were still more largely attended." As one writer said, "a better spirit was evident." People in much larger numbers professed conversion. The chapel in which their first meetings were held soon "became too small for the audience, necessitating the use of one of the largest halls in the north of England."

In advance of Moody and Sankey's arrival, posters appeared throughout Sunderland, announcing:

MOODY WILL PREACH THE GOSPEL—SANKEY WILL SING THE GOSPEL

In time, this expression became famous.

Moody and Sankey held gospel meetings for six weeks in Sunderland and its outlying districts, after which, they were invited to Newcastle-on-Tyne. Their work had grown in favor, and "they had now gained the sympathy of nearly all the ministers of all denominations, except those of the Established Church, who, learning that they were both unordained men, refused in any way to countenance them."[12]

After a few weeks of very successful meetings, the editor of *The Newcastle Chronicle*, Joseph Cowan—a member of Parliament for that district—wrote about the gatherings in his paper. He described them as "a wonderful religious phenomenon." On the whole, the *Chronicle* gave "a friendly review and criticism" of Moody and Sankey's work.

Such a prominent public notice proved a watershed event. It was then very unusual "for such a prominent secular paper to discuss religious matters." Cowan's article "created a profound impression throughout England." Invitations to hold services "began to pour in from all sides."[13]

Soon, the fame of the Newcastle revival spread to Edinburgh, Scotland, and ministers and laymen from there came to see it for themselves. The result was an invitation "from a large and representative committee" to hold meetings in that city.

Moody and Sankey accepted, and special advance prayer meetings were soon organized. Everything was done to ensure success. But "there was much prejudice and criticism to overcome." Ira Sankey's singing was said to be "contrary to Scotch ideas." His portable organ was derisively called a "kist full o' whistles" and widely disapproved. Moody's forceful pulpit presence "stood out in peculiar contrast with the staid demeanor and solemn spirit of the ordinary Scotch divine." But persistence ultimately carried the day. Soon Moody's "simple and scriptural style of preaching" began to win critics over.

Aside from the challenges first posed by critics, intense interest had been generated elsewhere. The crowds attending this new round of gospel gatherings were enormous. "No one building," it was said, "could accommodate the people, and three or four overflow meetings were held at the same time. The newspapers gave ample reports of the meetings, and soon the news of the revival was telegraphed all over the country."[14]

In time, this season of spiritual renewal affected all classes of society in Edinburgh. A widely respected clergyman, Dr. Horatius Bonar, declared his belief that "there was scarcely a Christian household in the whole city in which one or more persons had not been converted."[15] People came from miles around to attend the meetings "or to get someone to come to their town or hamlet, and tell of the wonderful work," thus spreading the news throughout Scotland.

—◁◦◦◦▷—

Moody's first meeting with the man who would become one of his greatest friends, Henry Drummond, took place at this time. It was while "organizing services for students" in Edinburgh that they met, as Drummond was then a student himself. Drummond's faith and ability stood out at once, and Moody asked him "to devote the next year or two to work among young men in the cities they visited."

All told, Moody and Sankey spent three months in Edinburgh, and they traveled from there to Dundee. After gatherings in Dundee, they began a four-month campaign in Glasgow that continued until early June 1874. "The career of these men has been like the rolling of a snowball," wrote a minister who'd invited them to Sunderland; "it gathers as it goes; at first a handful, then a hill."[16]

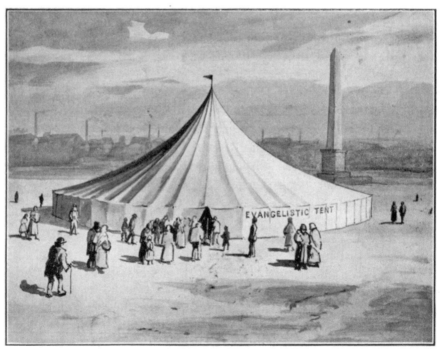

Moody spoke four months in Glasgow, using an "evangelistic tent" for most meetings.

During his final meeting in Scotland, Moody stood on the box of a carriage to address a large crowd at Glasgow's botanical gardens.

The Glasgow meetings took on a life of their own. One of the closing meetings was scheduled for converts only. By ticket, 3,500 people entered the venue. But this number was far exceeded by the crowd on the last Sabbath evening—which was estimated at 50,000.

Given such a huge turnout, Moody chose not to go inside the Kibble Crystal Palace, where the meeting was advertised to be held, but preached to the multitude in the open air, standing on the box of a carriage. For those among the crowd who had chosen to go inside the Palace, Sankey conducted a meeting.

In a word, Scotland was stirred to its depths as never before. Moody and Sankey were taken to heart. Long years later, when Moody died, Lord Overtoun telegraphed: "All Scotland mourns."

———

In September 1874, Moody and Sankey began to hold meetings in Belfast, Ireland. On the first Sunday, it was estimated that four times as many people gathered as could get into the building. They visited other locales in Ireland, and their tour culminated in "immense meetings in the great Exhibition Palace in Dublin." It was said they "had made almost as deep an impression upon Ireland as upon Scotland."[17]

Returning to England, they visited Manchester, Sheffield, Birmingham, Liverpool, and other cities. In each place there were singular "demonstrations of the Spirit and of power." Thousands were converted. Then, on March 9, 1875, Moody and Sankey entered upon their great London campaign, which lasted until July 12.

"Enthusiasm," said one writer, "was intense throughout. Greater crowds than ever attended. The Agricultural Hall in north London was constantly overcrowded, although the capacity was variously estimated from fifteen to twenty thousand."[18]

Meanwhile, it was said that the Royal Opera House, in London's fashionable West End, "with its seating capacity of five thousand, could have been filled three or four times over." Bookstore windows throughout London displayed pictures of Moody and Sankey. Daily newspapers "published extended reports of the meetings. Penny editions of their songbook, *Sacred Songs and*

Solos, were hawked in the streets. Not only was London itself stirred, but the revival became a worldwide wonder."[19]

———⊙⊙⊙———

Lord Shaftesbury later published an account of the great Agricultural Hall meetings of 1875. Referring to the March 31 meeting, Shaftesbury wrote: "[I went] on Good Friday to hear Moody and Sankey; [and was] deeply impressed." Of Moody, Shaftesbury wrote: "The preacher was clad in ordinary dress; his language was colloquial, free, easy, and like common talk." Moody's voice he thought "bad and ill-managed"; yet this was counterbalanced by Shaftesbury's observation that Moody's talk "abounds in illustrations, and most effective ones; in stories, anecdotes, very appropriate, oftentimes bordering on the humorous." More critically, he noted that "there is volubility" in Moody "but no eloquence." Shaftesbury pondered the import of it all: "There is nothing, in short, to win, externally at least . . . And yet the result is striking, effective, touching, and leading to much thought." Finally, Shaftesbury concluded:

> Here come two simple, unlettered men from the other side of the Atlantic. They have had no theological training, and never read the [Church] Fathers; they refuse to belong to any denomination; they are totally without skill in delivery, and have no pretensions to the highest order of rhetoric. They are calm, without an approach to the fanatical, or even the enthusiastic. They seek neither to terrify nor to puff up; eschew controversy, and natter no passions. So it is, nevertheless, thousands of all degrees in station and mental culture bow before them. Are we not right in believing—time will show—that *God has chosen the foolish things of the world to confound the wise?* Moody will do more in an hour than Canon Liddon in a century.[20]

"At this time," one writer noted, "Mr. Moody was only thirty-eight years old. Nobody was more surprised than he at the magnitude of the work initiated in York under such unpromising conditions two years before." Following modest opportunities at the start, Moody "had been led of God to make perhaps the deepest, and most far-reaching religious impression that had as yet been made" upon England, Ireland, and Scotland.

One observer studied Moody closely at this time, "trying to discover the secret of his power." The gentleman, Dr. R. W. Dale, was "one of the leading Nonconformists of England." He sat and watched Moody "for three or four days after he went to Birmingham, at different kinds of meetings." Following this, Dale went to Moody and told him that "the work was most plainly of God," for he "could see no relation between him personally, and the work he was doing."

Moody speaks to a large crowd at the Agricultural Hall
north of London, in 1875.

At this, Moody laughed heartily and said he "would be very sorry if it were otherwise!" But more than this, Dale was deeply impressed with Moody as a servant of the gospel. "He had a right to preach," Dale later said, because "he could never speak of a lost soul without tears of Christly compassion in his eyes."[21]

Many things resulted from this great gospel mission to the British Isles. Thousands were converted, and thousands of nominal Christians were "led into closer communion with God." One writer affirmed that "a spirit of evangelism was awakened, and has never died down." Many inner-city missions and other kindred organizations were established. A spirit of mere Christianity flourished in an atmosphere where "denominational differences were buried to a remarkable degree." Clergymen from all traditions were "drawn into cooperation on a common platform: the salvation of the lost."[22]

Aside from this, a great hunger for a deeper devotional life was awakened.

"Bibles were reopened," said one commentator, "and Bible study received a wonderful impetus." Many marveled that "long-standing [religious] prejudices were swept away." Significantly, no attempt was made by Moody and Sankey to proselytize, and "converts were passed over to existing churches" for instruction in the faith.

Back in America, *The New York Tribune* published a prominent editorial on the mission to England: "There can be but one opinion as to the sincerity of Messrs. Moody and Sankey. They are not money-makers, they are not charlatans ... Earnest and sincere men are rare in these days. Is it not worth our while to give to them a dispassionate, unprejudiced hearing? ... They preach no new doctrine, no dogma of this or that sect; nothing but Christ, and the necessity among us of increased zeal in His service. Which of us will controvert that truth? If the Christian religion is not the one hope for our individual and social life, what is?"[23]

After all had unfolded, Moody and Sankey were in need of a most welcome rest, lasting a few weeks. Following this, Moody preached a farewell sermon in Liverpool on August 3, 1875. Then the two friends and their families sailed for America the next day.

Another important and groundbreaking facet of Moody and Sankey's mission to the British Isles concerned the birth and growth of what came to be called the "Moody and Sankey Hymn-Books."

One writer has said the story connected with these books "is one of the romances of religion and commerce." For, in a very real sense, these books had a mission all their own: a flowering of artistry on the one hand, as hundreds of new songs were written—and on the other, a great increase of devotion among the faithful and newly converted, as basic tenets of the gospel were enshrined in pleasing, often stirring musical settings.

All of this grew out of a discovered sense of need. When Moody and Sankey first reached England, they encountered "a type of hymns in the churches different from what they had been used to, and inappropriate for their purpose." Their solution was an instance of American ingenuity itself: Why not compile a collection of hymns such as they knew from America?

This they did. But they soon hit a setback. Understandably, no British publisher wished to undertake the risk for this kind of publication. And there was a precedent for their reluctance. One publisher had previously tried to publish an American hymnbook. The project sank without a ripple.

Still, Moody was convinced of the need. He undertook the printing of the first hymnbook "at his own risk and expense." He invested all the money he had—about one hundred dollars—in a sixteen-page pamphlet of words and music compiled by Sankey. Copies of this booklet were sold for a sixpence each. Then, a "words only" edition was published, selling for one penny a copy.

Before Moody and Sankey knew it, the supply of both editions was quickly exhausted. Now, a British publisher made a contract offer, which promised "to pay a liberal royalty." Moody consented, thinking the funds that came in "might in part pay expenses for which he had obligated himself personally."

What took place, instead, was a true publishing phenomenon. At the close of the London gospel campaign, and shortly before Moody and Sankey were to return home, the publisher's statement showed that the sum standing to their credit on this royalty account was no less than $35,000, or $750,000 in modern currency.

On receiving this news, Moody and Sankey did something remarkable. They sent word to the London gospel campaign committee, saying "that this amount was at their disposal, to be used for Christian work as they should direct." Moody and Sankey said they "would not take a cent of the money" for themselves.

The committee read this letter and answered with a display of their own character. They "refused to accept the fund," asserting that it belonged to Moody and Sankey personally. It was not their intent, they said, to have Moody and Sankey "pay this large sum for the privilege of preaching."

One writer, commenting on this, said memorably: "Here was a peculiar case—*money going begging for want of a receiver.*"

Eventually, a most fitting solution presented itself. One of the officers of the Chicago Avenue Church in America—the church Moody had founded—happened to be in London at this time. He learned of this scenario and subsequently suggested to the committee that the royalty sum be forwarded to Chicago to complete the rebuilding of that church, which had only partially been rebuilt after the great Chicago Fire. To date, only a first-floor story had been built, then funding from American sources had ceased. For two years, parishioners had gathered in a building covered by "a temporary roof." A better solution was greatly needed.

To the London Committee, and Moody and Sankey, this was wisdom itself, not to mention a solution close to their heart. The funds were transferred, and the Chicago Avenue Church completed. This was the third church Moody began (Illinois Street Church and North Side Tabernacle were the first two), and all are predecessors of today's Moody Church. In the years following, up to 1900, the sale of succeeding hymnbooks generated royalties in excess of one million dollars, or just under 28 million dollars in today's currency.

It is an astonishing tribute to Moody and Sankey's character that "not one cent" of this prodigious sum "ever found its way into their pockets." To oversee the distribution of those funds, an independent board of trustees was established. Under their administration, all of these funds were disbursed among various YMCAs, needy churches, and the schools Moody founded at Northfield.[24]

This munificent act bore a witness all its own.

When Moody died, in late December 1899, the editors of *The Literary World*, a highly regarded British magazine, sent no telegram to solace his family. But they printed a paragraph that was as fine a public tribute as any Moody received in the days following his death. *The Literary World* stated:

> In connection with the death last week of . . . D. L. Moody, the well-known evangelist, it is interesting to recall that that gentleman was the owner of one of the best-paying literary properties in existence. The [Moody-Sankey] hymnbook was offered free to several English publishers in 1873, but one and all fought shy of it. Accordingly, Mr. Moody spent nearly his last penny in getting it printed at his own risk. But lest they should be charged with preaching the gospel for gain, neither of the evangelists would ever accept a penny of the large fortune produced by its million-fold circulation. The royalty was paid directly by the publishers to a committee of well-known businessmen

in London—afterwards associated with a similar committee in New York—who distributed it among various charities.[25]

By example, Moody and Sankey taught their contemporaries a profound and powerful lesson: the gospel never has a better name than when it goes forth in a manner beyond reproach.

GOLDEN DAYS

The revival of 1875 was led by the great apostle of common sense, D. L. Moody. In company with Mr. Sankey, he went to England in 1873 . . . Returning to America, he visited Brooklyn, Philadelphia, New York, and Chicago.[1]

—G. B. Cutten, Ph.D.

D. L. Moody had no shortage of remarkable contemporaries. George Barton Cutten was one of them. Few men have been more obvious exemplars of muscular Christianity.

Born in Nova Scotia in 1874, Cutten held a variety of hardscrabble jobs during his youth: reporter, salesman, even working as a pipe fitter. The story runs that Cutten's uncle, who divined the potential of his restless nephew, locked him in a room, saying, "You can come out when you tell me you're going to go to university." The uncle's tough love worked. Cutten capitulated. At eighteen, he began studies at Acadia University, where he was a standout on the varsity rugby team. He graduated with a BA in 1897. Concurrently, he was ordained a Baptist minister. Five years more and Cutten graduated from Yale with a Ph.D. in psychology and another degree in divinity. He'd also brought his rugby skills with him and took to the gridiron to play American football. Once more, he excelled. A center on the Yale football eleven said, "he played his position so well that he was frequently mentioned for All-America honors."[2]

Away from the playing field, Cutten preached at local churches on Sundays. Soon, yet another career beckoned, that of a highly regarded author. In 1907, he published his groundbreaking dissertation, *The Psychology of Alcoholism*. One year later he published another scholarly book, *The Psychological Phenomena of Christianity*, with the prestigious New York publishing house of Charles Scribner's Sons.

In this book he mentioned D. L. Moody's revival work in America in 1875, noting "a large number of converts [resulting] from Moody's work," and that the "great revival meetings no doubt accomplished much." Cutten spoke also of the hallmark theme in Moody's preaching, "the love of God," and noted how sharply that contrasted with what had been standard sermon fare for so many years: "the wrath of God."[3]

However, Cutten was more than a commentator on Moody's work; he was a participant. "I first heard Moody in 1895," Cutten wrote, "but heard him often afterward."[4] It says a great deal about the character of Moody's gospel mission work that learned men like Cutten found so much that was praiseworthy in it.

※

Twenty years earlier, in October 1875, Moody had just returned to America and was looking to her great cities. "Water runs down hill," he said, "and the highest hills in America are the great cities. If we can stir them, we shall stir the whole country."[5]

America's cities would welcome Moody's revival work, largely due to all that had unfolded during his extraordinary mission work just concluded in Great Britain. Men like Lord Shaftesbury had supported the mission prominently and publicly, and that carried a great deal of credibility. Still others noted the tone of "mere Christianity" that pervaded the mission work throughout the British Isles. Moody's "loyalty to the gospel in all its simplicity" was cited, even as he preached "without championing theological fads." Further, the widespread reporting on the United Kingdom mission fostered a spirit of acceptance and approval. From the largest American cities, religious leaders of all denominations extended cordial invitations for Moody to come preach.[6]

The first "American campaign," as it was called, began in Brooklyn, New York, in October 1875. As in Britain, a spirit of Christian charity and goodwill prevailed. Large venues were selected and programs arranged, all amid a "union of various denominations, in holding meetings for prayer and conference . . . pledging one another to a cordial co-operation."[7]

To accommodate the large crowds that were anticipated, innovative strategies for housing gospel meetings were settled on. Services would alternate between a converted ice rink on Clermont Avenue, and the cavernous Brooklyn Tabernacle on Schermerhorn Street, pastored by DeWitt Talmage.[8]

The Brooklyn Tabernacle was a natural enough venue, but the converted rink was of great interest. Organizers rented the rink for one month, and "chairs for five thousand persons were provided." Attendance at the services grew steadily, and the number of meetings in the rink was increased to allow for greater crowds. A phalanx of "local ministers and prominent laymen assisted Moody and his peerless leader of music, Ira Sankey." Other churches and halls were also brought into use. Soon, "the influence of the mission began to extend beyond Brooklyn."[9]

Prominent media outlets took note. *The New York Tribune* commended this burgeoning movement of spiritual renewal. "There is a common-sense view to be taken of this matter, as of every other," the *Tribune* wrote. "In the first place, why should we sneer because a large part of the multitudes crowding into the Brooklyn Rink are drawn there only by curiosity? So they were when they followed Christ into the streets of Jerusalem or the wilderness, yet they went to the healing of their souls. Or that a still larger part already profess Christianity, and believe all that Moody and Sankey teach? There is not one of them who will not be the better for a little quickening of his faith."[10]

Well aware of humbug and religious hucksterism, the *Tribune* reported that Moody and Sankey could not be tarred with that brush. "With regard to the men themselves," the newspaper stated, "there can, we think, be but one opinion as to their sincerity. They are not money-makers; they are not charlatans. Decorous, conservative England, which reprobated both their work and the manner of it, held them in the full blaze of scrutiny for months, and could not detect in them a single motive which was not pure. Earnest and sincere men are rare in these days. Is it not worth our while to give to them a dispassionate, unprejudiced hearing?"[11]

At the same time, the *Tribune* was mindful that some cultured skeptics had begun to laugh these meetings to scorn. It addressed that quarter of criticism.

"Lastly," its editors commented, "with regard to the method of these men in presenting Christ and His teaching. Men of high culture or exceptional sensitiveness of taste shrink from the familiarity of words and ideas—in which a subject they hold as reverend and sublime beyond expression is set forth to the crowd. They call it vulgarising and debasing the truth."[12]

For the sake of argument, the *Tribune*'s editors were willing to concede this point. In so doing, they posed a pointed question. Granting that this opinion from critics was right, what, from their point of view, was to be done with the crowd?

"They cannot all be men of fine culture, or exceptional sensitiveness," the *Tribune*'s editors countered. Not everyone was "moved to believe, or trust in Jesus through philosophic arguments, or contemplation of nature, or logical conviction, or appeals to their aesthetic senses; by classical music, stained glass, or church architecture . . . [These folk] are plain, busy people, with ordinary minds and tastes. Yet certainly, as Christ died to save them, it is necessary that they should be brought to Him by some means."[13]

Next, the *Tribune*'s editors pointed to the example of Christ Himself. "It was not," they argued, "to the cultured classes that Christ Himself preached, but to the working-people, the publicans, fishermen, tax-gatherers; and He used the words and illustrations which would appeal to them most forcibly. If Messrs. Moody and Sankey, or any other teachers, bring Him directly home to men's convictions, and lead them to amend their lives for His sake, let us thank God for the preacher, and let his tastes and grammar take care of themselves."[14]

Moody spoke four weeks in Brooklyn, from October through mid-November 1875. Great gatherings at the Tabernacle became commonplace. As one commentator, W. A. Candler, observed:

> The morning services were begun at half-past eight, but before six, the people began to gather at the doors. At eight, over five thousand persons were seated in the building, and three thousand, or more, had been turned away for lack of standing room. In the afternoon, twelve thousand sought and could not find room in the building, and meetings were appointed in neighboring churches to accommodate them.

And so for nearly a month . . . multitudes flocked . . . thousands were converted.[15]

=====⚬/⚬/⚬=====

From Brooklyn, Moody, Sankey, and their ministry team went to Philadelphia, where the first gospel meeting was held on November 21 in a freight depot on the corner of Thirteenth and Market streets. This "depot tabernacle" could accommodate seating for 12,000 people, but attendance increased so rapidly that more meetings had to be rescheduled for other venues to meet the demand. "Ministers of all denominations united in the work," wrote W. A. Candler, "and people of all classes attended the services, drawn not only from the limits of the city but from all the region of country accessible to Philadelphia."

Candler also noted that President Ulysses S. Grant was in Philadelphia with government colleagues "to inspect the preparations for the approaching Centennial Exposition," and attended one of the meetings. The president and his party were seated on the platform.[16]

What brought this esteemed visitor? A letter written by the Philadelphia philanthropist and publisher George W. Childs to his friend George H. Stuart. In the letter, Childs had stated: "I hope we can persuade the president and his family, and members of the cabinet, to hear Messrs. Moody and Sankey on Sunday night."[17]

Aside from President Grant, a who's who of notable Americans were also in attendance that memorable December 19 evening. The former Speaker of the House, James G. Blaine, was joined by James A. Garfield, later to become America's twentieth president, along with several other prominent members of Congress.[18]

The New York Daily Tribune sent a reporter. "Three immense meetings were held today by Messrs. Moody and Sankey," the *Tribune* reported. Word had leaked out that President Grant might attend the evening event, and so "every seat was occupied in fifteen minutes after the door was opened." The *Tribune* reporter confirmed that President and Mrs. Grant had attended, along with their son, Col. Fred Grant, and his wife. Moody preached from the text, "I pray thee hear my excuse," a passage of Scripture in which many kinds of people "made excuses for not coming to Christ."

When the service was over, former Speaker Blaine said that Moody was "the most remarkable man he had ever heard." Postmaster-General Jewell, also in attendance, said Moody's remarks "in the latter part of his discourse were wonderful." For his part, President Grant "also expressed pleasure at the services," the *Tribune* reported. And, as a centerpiece for the proceedings, Ira Sankey had performed "several of his most beautiful hymns."[19]

That gathering was the capstone of the Philadelphia meetings, a nine-week campaign that carried on through Christmas and into the new year, closing on January 20, 1876. One visitor spoke for many when he said: "These are golden days for Philadelphia."[20]

⸺◈◈◈⸺

After the Philadelphia mission, Moody returned to Northfield for two weeks of rest. Then, early in February 1876, he rejoined the members of his ministry team in New York City. It was the start of the third and final leg of their gospel campaign, one lasting for nearly three months. It was scheduled to end on April 30.[21]

The advance committee charged with having all in readiness for Moody's arrival had obtained a lease of the Hippodrome, later the site of the [original] Madison Square Garden at Madison Avenue and East 26th Street. To make the best use of the available space, the Hippodrome was "divided into two large halls, each capable of seating about seven thousand persons, and a call was issued by the committee for a private guarantee fund to meet attendant expenses." The planning committee had issued this call for one simple reason. "It must be distinctly understood," they said, "that Messrs. Moody and Sankey refuse to receive any payment for their own services; thus no part of the above fund will be paid to them.'"[22]

Other gatherings had been organized in support of the Hippodrome events. A daily prayer meeting "up town, at Lyric Hall" was largely attended, while "the Fulton Street meeting felt the fresh impulse of revival preparations."[23]

Newspapers published long accounts of the meetings, "in some instances giving verbatim reports of the addresses." One vivid description of an early Sunday morning service came from the pen of essayist William Hoyt Coleman, known later for his prose portrait of Abraham Lincoln.[24] To read what

Coleman wrote of Moody at this time is to be present for meetings unlike any New York City had ever seen.

To the front of the Hippodrome, a high K-shaped platform ran from one gallery to the other along a white partition. "At its center," wrote Coleman, "is a railed projection for the speaker and his assistants, the rails running back to the partition, where there is a doorway with a crimson screen. The right-hand section of the platform holds a melodeon and the choir; the left-hand section the special-ticket holders."[25]

And what of the people who'd waited in the early morning to attend the meeting? As Coleman looked about him, he saw a hall nearly full with "a mixed assemblage of all classes; some very poor, a few not very clean. Many black faces dot the congregation. A large part of those present are evidently Sunday-school teachers. One wonders how so many can come at so early an hour. A man nearby says: 'I built a fire, and got my own breakfast!'"[26]

The fine music that marked every meeting got under way at 7:40 a.m. The choir began to sing, and the congregation joined in. Nearly all had brought "little hymn-books," the Moody/Sankey hymnbooks. And, as the tunes were "simple and spirited," they were sung "in good time."[27]

Promptly at eight o'clock, Moody and Sankey took their places, "one within the rail, the other at the melodeon." As Moody stood, "after a moment of silent prayer," people saw "a short, stout-built, square-shouldered man," with "black eyes that twinkle merrily at times, and a full, but not heavy beard and moustache." As Coleman saw it, Moody's face "expressed fun, good-humour, persistence." His coat was "closely buttoned, with a bit of stand-up collar seen over it." He stood, with his hand resting on the rail, and he seemed to have "a quick, soldierly bearing" that marked every movement.[28]

Moody gave out a hymn—"so rapidly that we scarce catch the words." People's eyes were then drawn to Ira Sankey, "a man of larger build, clear-cut features, and shaven chin." His voice was unmistakable: "clear, melodious, powerful." Coleman thought him "easier and gentler in bearing than Moody," with "enough force and fire in speech and song to hold an audience in perfect quiet." And, when he sang alone, you heard every word and caught "from face and voice the full meaning of the song."[29]

The order of service for the meeting was "hymns and a prayer," with "a solo by Mr. Sankey." Following this, Moody stood to give his message, in this instance a talk on the Old Testament patriarch Jacob.

—◦◦◦—

Coleman gave an insightful study of the evangelist's person and rhetorical gifts. The "message" was unlike anything that might be called a lecture. "Head-long talking would better describe it," Coleman wrote. Moody's voice was "rough, pitched on one key," and he spoke "straight before him, rarely turning to the sides." The power of Moody's address, Coleman thought, lay in his gift for storytelling. "But how real he makes the men!" Coleman wrote. "How visibly the deceiving, scheming Jacob stands before us! And how pointedly he applies the lessons of the patriarch's life."[30]

As he spoke, Moody's gestures were "few but emphatic," his "hand flung forcibly forward with palm open," or "both hands brought down, hammer-like, with closed fists." But such gestures were not frequent, Coleman wrote, for the Bible was "too much in his hands to allow frequent gestures." Continually, Moody referred to his Bible, or read from it, and throughout, he kept it open on the stand beside him. As Coleman sought to describe what he saw, he judged that Moody's talk was "little more than an exposition of a Bible truth," but it was memorable, because it was "a dramatic rendering of a Bible story, with continuous application to his hearers."[31]

Therein lay much of Moody's gift. People who were unchurched, or illiterate, seldom knew the Bible. Moody brought it to life and showed vividly how it related to their lives.

—◦◦◦—

Moody often spoke about "Bible characters," as he called them. Coleman took no notes of Moody's message on the day he visited the Hippodrome, but we can hear something of Moody's thoughts about Jacob, since his talk was one he gave many times over the years. Here and there, he might have added a new touch or two, but the basic message was always much the same. And audiences weren't to know it was a talk he'd given before. On a different night, or in a different city, it would have been a new message to them.

"Jacob," Moody said, "was a man who always had an eye to his own advantage.

He always wanted an agreement, so that he might get the best of it." And here Moody may have paused for effect before saying, "*many of us are like Jacob.*"[32]

Moody had a conversational style of speaking. He knew no other way. When he'd worked among soldiers during the Civil War, he'd talked to them, as a friend would to a friend. He now spoke before audiences that numbered in the thousands, but there was no need to do anything other than he'd always done. People liked being talked with, not being talked to—and there was a world of difference. And if people were helped to understand that Bible characters were people just like themselves, that was a deeply important connection to make. It was a welcome for people to join the family of faith, through a talk that was winsome and compelling.

Jacob the deceiver and schemer stood before the people as Moody spoke. They could see him in their mind's eye. "Jacob," Moody told them, "had gone away with a lie on his lips." He went to his uncle's and began "to make sharp bargains. But Jacob got cheated every time. He worked seven years for his wife, and then he got deceived, and another woman was married to him; and then he had to work seven years longer for the woman he wanted." Here another pause. "You see," Moody said, "Jacob was paid back in his own coin. He lied to his aged father; and now his uncle is lying to him. He deceived his father; and now he is being deceived: and instead of working seven years for Rachel, he worked fourteen—and his wages were changed ten different times. After being there twenty long years, if you will read his life carefully, you will find that he did not make anyone much better."[33]

This was pungent, pointed talk, talk people could relate to. And when Moody came to the place in his remarks where the application came in, people had no trouble seeing the moral woven in his message. Those, Moody said, "who are trying to drive hard bargains with the world, and making the most out of this life—they do not win many people, nor have such a prosperous journey after all. It is a good deal better to be right with God . . . more profitable to have a clear conscience with God."[34]

His close was refreshing and candid. No fire, no brimstone. Just plain dealing, and plain speaking, about matters of the heart. "So let us be careful," Moody said, "and see to it that we are sowing good seed. And if we have told a lie, let us confess it, and ask God to take it away—root it out at once. We cannot afford to be deceitful; we cannot afford to rest in shams, and profess to be what we are not. God wants honesty. God wants truth in the inward parts."[35]

—————◦ʊ⁄ʊ⁄ʊ◦—————

William Hoyt Coleman also recorded what it was like to attend one of Moody's evening meetings at the Hippodrome. If morning meetings tended to be rather more subdued, given their early hour, the evening meetings hummed with activity and anticipation. Gaslights blazed all along the street outside the Hippodrome. Policemen, many with an Irish brogue, walked a special event beat, keeping the throng of people queued up outside in good order.

The evening lecture may have been a different gathering of people, but the crowd was not unlike those listening that morning, though it included many who came after a day's work. The Hippodrome was well illuminated, "the bright light of the many reflectors" falling "full upon the faces of all sorts and conditions of men to say nothing of women and children. A more mixed multitude," Coleman wrote, "would be hard to find."[36]

Surprisingly, the Hippodrome was swept by a quiet stir, but no more crowd noise than this. Then at 7:45, the choirmaster, a Mr. Thatcher, began to lead the choir in singing. He was a skilled conductor, showing "great skill in managing both choir and congregation in combined and separate parts, and in producing tender and powerful effects."[37]

Music was and always would be a hallmark of any gospel meeting where Moody and Sankey were present. And, as Coleman saw it, the reason was not hard to find: they had given the world "capital music." Sankey's melodies were at once captivating, stirring, and easily memorized. His lyrics, or those of his cowriters, were often simple paraphrases of Scripture—but therein lay much of their genius.

The ease of learning melody and lyric lent itself to helping the audience grasp essential truths of faith. Often the words were storylike parables in song, like "The Ninety and Nine."

And Ira Sankey's great gift lay in his ear for melody. It lent his music an unadorned beauty. Further, he could sing the lyrics of a hymn like "Hold the Fort," which roused the spirit with a martial air John Philip Sousa might have envied. In a word, Sankey was versatile and prolific as a hymn writer and performer. As William Coleman saw it, *The Moody and Sankey Hymn-book* was "the best for congregational use ever printed."[38] To hear "Safe in the Arms of Jesus," or "I Hear Thy Welcome Voice," was "to get a new idea of the power of sacred song."[39] Moody and Sankey were fortunate indeed that hymn writers like Fanny Crosby crafted lines like the following, lines that brought heaven near, lines that people left the hall singing—

> *Hark! 'tis the voice of angels*
> *Borne in a song to me,*
> *Over the fields of glory,*
> *Over the jasper sea.*[40]

Distant as we are from Moody and Sankey's day, one hundred years and more, we forget the scores of melodies and lyrics that they and their collaborators gave the world. If the Hippodrome meetings marked an epoch in American pulpit history, the songs that echoed in that vast hall were no less. They were an epoch in modern hymnody. Their power has waned little with the years. The finest songs first published in *The Moody and Sankey Hymn-book* are often recorded today, by artists from a wide array of styles and musical influences. From orchestral music, to the solo piano of scores for films like Ken Burns's *Mark Twain*—from bluegrass to Celtic reimaginings—these songs are not lost to us. They live on.[41]

To return to the Hippodrome at eight o'clock for an evening meeting was to find "Mr. Moody at his post." As William Hoyt Coleman remembered, certain nights required Moody to act like the field general of a gospel campaign. Moody looked down at the large crowd seated before him and could see that many of those in the hall had attended meetings once, perhaps several times before. On one level, he might have been glad to see them. But there was something else to think about: the large crowd outside of people who *weren't able to get in* before the Hippodrome's doors were closed.

So, when it was time to announce another hymn, Moody chose instead to practice some Christian charity toward the outsiders—and urge others to do so. "Now, won't a thousand of you Christians go into the Fourth Avenue Hall and pray for this meeting, and let those outside have your seats?" he asked. This said, some did stand and exit the hall as the hymn began. But many more empty seats were needed. Moody spoke again after the first verse had been sung. "Not half enough have left," he said. "I want a great many more to go out. I see many of you here every night, and if I knew your names, I'd call you out."[42]

Now here was something new under the sun, *a preacher asking people to leave*. Conviction set in, and more people took the not-so-subtle hint. Many of those who had been outside were now shown in by the ushers.

Still, Moody wasn't satisfied. He turned to those seated about him on the platform. "Would some of you be willing to go outside?" he asked. Many did, and soon their places were taken by people who, just a few moments before, thought they wouldn't get in. It was an altogether singular thing.[43]

As Coleman observed, in such meetings ministers of the gospel, no less the unchurched among a Moody audience, were being taught "valuable lessons in their own work: how to make Bible truths and Bible characters more real . . . how to bring the truth into close contact with all sorts of people, and make it stick; how to set old Christians and young converts to work."[44]

Newspapers chronicled all that had been unfolding. One stated: "In the Hippodrome Mr. Moody has gathered day by day the largest audiences ever seen in this city. Lawyers, bankers, merchants—some of whom scarcely ever enter a church, are just as much a part of his congregations as are the second-rate and the third-rate boarding-house people . . . All classes and conditions of men have been represented in these great revival meetings."

Nor would it do, this same paper stated, for Moody to have been anyone other than who he was. That was to his and his audience's advantage. "There is no prospect," the paper opined, "that he will ever conform either himself or his style to the demands of propriety, or to the requirements of grammatical rules. Let us frankly confess, as we bid him good-bye, that we are heartily glad that he is what he is. We would not change him. Make him the best-read preacher in the world and he would instantly lose half his power. He is just right for his work as he is—original, dashing, [with] pell-mell earnestness, downright individuality and uncalculating naturalness."[45]

—◦/◦/◦—

Moody has been called "God's man for the Gilded Age," and indeed he was.[46] That makes his encounter with one of the Gilded Age's most notorious political figures all the more memorable. The story was told by Professor George P. Fisher, of Yale Divinity School, as illustrative of Moody's sincerity and candor.

"I once passed an evening," said Dr. Fisher, "in company with Thurlow Weed . . . long a leader in the politics of New York." The two men had a long conversation during which Weed asked Fisher if he knew D. L. Moody. Weed said that Moody had written him "an excellent letter," which he wanted Fisher to read. The letter had arrived after Weed had sent Moody a very generous contribution. The money was to help defray the expenses of the meetings then held in New York.

Weed later sent Fisher a copy of the letter, which read:[47]

To Mr. Thurlow Weed

My dear Friend:
Yours of the 20th of March, with cheque, came to hand yesterday, and I am at a loss what to do. I am afraid you may put it in with some other good deeds, and they may keep you from coming to Christ as a lost sinner. I wish you knew how anxious I am for you, and how I long to see you out-and-out on the Lord's side. I thank you for the money; but what would you say if I should treat your gift as you have the gift of God, and send it back to you—would you not be offended?

Now as I take your gift, will you not take God's gift, and let us rejoice together? I cannot bear to leave the city, and leave you out of the Ark that God has provided for you, and all the rest of us. Hoping to hear soon of your conversion,

> *I remain your friend*
> *and brother (I hope) in Christ,*
> *D. L. Moody*

In the nineteenth century, Thurlow Weed was one of the most corrupt party bosses ever to come out of New York. For many, he was a troubled enigma. "Tall, slender, awkward and solemn," he walked with a stoop in his shoulders. He was described as a "cunning, unscrupulous" man, notorious for being one of "the horde of plunderers that fattened on our Government" during the Civil War. While "thousands on thousands marched to the front [to give their] lives to the Republic in its time of need," men like Weed "hurried to the rear, to the sound of the enemy's guns, to fatten on the spoils the struggle made available."[48] He was, in short, a war profiteer.

If ever a man needed repentance, or a change of heart, it was Weed. Moody knew that. Many might have treated Weed's letter and check with scorn, and returned it. Many would have accepted it and written a letter to curry favor. Moody did neither of these. Though he accepted the money as to not offend, at the same time he still ran the great risk of deeply upsetting someone who, as a powerful political boss, was not famous for leniency. Weed could have shut down the Hippodrome meetings, or, at the very least, made a great deal of trouble.

Weed had given a magnanimous gift. Moody acknowledged that and seized on that flicker of generosity as a catalyst to something more. It was the act of a friend for Moody to say that God bestows the greatest gift of all—to anyone who will freely accept it. This life, he was telling Weed, is not all that there is. Moody could help Thurlow find the something more that everyone seeks—the something he'd found. Moody's letter was an act of courage, kindness, and a reflection of his character.

———— ✵✵✵ ————

That Moody had a gift for convening gospel gatherings in the best traditions of mere Christianity was acknowledged by one periodical in words that must have been particularly gratifying. While the Hippodrome meetings were in progress, *The Tablet*, a Roman Catholic paper, devoted two columns of one issue to a review of the gospel gatherings. "This work of Mr. Moody," said the writer for *The Tablet*, "is not sin. It cannot be sin to invite men to love and serve Jesus Christ. It is irregular . . . but it may be bringing multitudes to a happier frame of mind, in which the church may find them better prepared to receive her sublime faith."[49]

Nor was the praise of religiously themed periodicals the only such praise that the Hippodrome meetings won. *The New York Times*, not noted for unequivocal commendations of famous preachers, had this to say:

Whatever philosophical skeptics may say, the work accomplished this winter by Mr. Moody in this city for private and public morals will live. The drunken have become sober, the vicious virtuous, the worldly and self-seeking unselfish, the ignoble noble, the impure pure ... The youth have started with more generous aims, the old have been stirred from grossness. A new hope has lifted up hundreds of human beings, a new consolation has come to the sorrowful, and a better principle has entered the sordid life of the day, through the labors of these plain men. Whatever the prejudiced may say against them, the honest-minded and just will not forget their labors of love.[50]

NORTHFIELD

It was touching to see one who had had scarcely any education himself, thus devoting his life to the instruction of others; and the benevolence of [Moody] was shown by the fact that nearly all the [students] of his school were persons who, through the death or misfortunes of their parents, had missed their chance of a good start in life.[1]

—*The Living Age* magazine
(March 1900)

Biographers of D. L. Moody owe his son Will many debts, not the least for his faithful, painstaking research, and his preservation and chronicling of so many aspects of D. L. Moody's life. Many sentences from Will Moody's pen are memorable. But few, perhaps, are more memorable than those published in February 1904 to describe the providential circumstance that led to the founding of the Northfield schools.

Will had the benefit of a fine classical education thanks to his father's generosity and wisdom, and graduated from Yale. His knowledge of Roman legend served him well when he wrote of the Northfield schools: "It is said that the cackling of geese once saved ancient Rome. But it is doubtful if the annoyance caused by poultry was ever known to be the means of locating and developing such a work as is represented by the Northfield Schools. And yet it is true that but for so mean a cause, humanly speaking, these schools would never have been founded."[2]

Therein lies a tale.

In the summer of 1875, after two years' absence on his gospel mission to Great Britain, Moody visited his mother at the family homestead in Northfield. The thought of purchasing a home in his native town hadn't occurred to him. His plan, after a welcome visit with his mother, was to return to Chicago, where he had for so many years previously been active in Christian work.

However, one day his mother's hens got loose and scattered over land belonging to her neighbor. The neighbor was none too pleased and let everyone know about it. When Moody heard of this, his first thought was that his aging mother had no need of such headaches. He knew a way to relieve such a petty annoyance and lost no time in deciding to purchase the few acres of the neighbor's land that lay nearest his mother's boundary line. Such land, he also knew, "was worth less than twenty dollars an acre" and was well worth the comfort it would give his mother.

Within two days, Moody met the neighbor who owned the land and asked him to sell the desired pasture. It was then Moody discovered he had a canny neighbor who scented the opportunity for a windfall. The farmer told Moody he couldn't possibly think of selling that pasture, unless Moody was willing to buy his "entire place of twelve acres, with his house and farm buildings." Moody acted as though nothing was out of the ordinary. He asked the man's price.

"Thirty-five hundred dollars," the farmer replied.

Moody never hesitated. "Done!" he said.

And with that, the paperwork was drawn up, and Moody returned home to tell his mother she needn't worry any longer.[3]

As Will Moody later described it, his father now found himself in a strange position. "He had not so much settled at Northfield, as he had *been settled* by circumstances." There was little else to do, but begin the work of making a few alterations in the old farmhouse, "to meet the requirements of a home in which he could spend a few weeks of rest each year with his family."

The truth was, Moody soon saw this as a very welcome, if unexpected, turn of events. Since the great Chicago fire had taken their home in that city in 1871, he and his wife, Emma, had been without a home. With two children to care for, he had keenly "felt the need of one." However, his only thought at this time about the new home in Northfield was "to keep the place for a few years," or until his family had grown.[4]

—————⌇⌇⌇—————

From such an unlikely beginning came the story of the Northfield Seminary, one of faith bringing hope and opportunity to a place where many had known little of either.

At the outset, hope spread in subtle ways. In August 1875, Moody made his permanent home in Northfield. During his first summers there, he prepared for gospel campaigns held each winter. Early on, he began to hold meetings in his home for Bible study, attended by neighbors. In these, he often had the assistance of visiting friends, pastors, evangelists, and others. It was natural enough that these gatherings fostered a growing sense in Moody of latent opportunities to reach young people nearby—to instill within them a love for Bible study and aspirations for lives of Christian service.[5]

In this, Moody received added encouragement from his younger brother Samuel, who "had long desired the establishment of a high school in his native place, and frequently talked of it."[6]

In 1876, one year after he'd bought his new home, Moody was out driving one day with Samuel to visit a distant pasture. They passed a little cottage on the mountainside, where a mother and three daughters were seated in the doorway braiding hats. Nearby was their father, an invalid paralytic. Stopping for a while, perhaps to water their horses, Moody and Samuel learned that this family, the Sikes family, relied entirely for their support on handicrafts made by Mrs. Sikes and her daughters. Small manufacturers in neighboring towns regularly would send their carts around, supplying straw to families who would perform "cottage work" in their homes. At set times, these carts would return, collecting finished straw hats, and paying modest sums for the work of making them.[7]

Moody and his brother remembered what they saw that day.

Concurrently, Moody took a kind and generous interest in the education of his young cousin Fannie Holton, whom he sent to Wellesley College. Wellesley had been founded as a "school for Christ" by Moody's friend Henry F. Durant. This investment in Fanny's future would later flower in meaningful ways.

—◁ o/o/o ▷—

In the first three months of 1877, Moody held winter gospel gatherings in Boston. It was then he first came in contact with H. N. F. Marshall, a wealthy businessman and philanthropist.

In the spring of 1878, Marshall first visited Northfield and attended a Bible reading in Moody's home. Here, Moody described the hopes he had to start a school for girls. Eventually the visit and discussion would lead to a purchase of land, some sixteen acres in all, almost opposite Mr. Moody's house.

It was a story emblematic of the early history of the Northfield Seminary. When Moody and Marshall stood outside discussing the merits of buying the land, now available for purchase, they soon agreed it should be done. Scarcely had they said as much, when they saw the owner of the property coming toward them, walking up the road.

Moody and Marshall invited the man into Moody's home, whereupon Marshall asked the price of his property. They'd heard it was $2,100, and this price the owner confirmed. Marshall said he would buy the land, wrote out a check, and proposed drawing up a bill of sale on the spot. This was immediately done. "Before the owner recovered from his surprise, the land had passed out of his hands."[8]

Throughout the summer of 1878, the advantages of various places in Northfield were considered—regarding their suitability as a site for Moody's proposed school. In the winter of 1878–79, Moody traveled to Baltimore, where Marshall and he discussed the school for young women in greater detail. The following spring a second lot, of fifteen acres, was bought for $2,500, adjoining the first lot purchased, all with a view toward building Moody's proposed school.

Moody lost no time in finalizing initial plans to open the school. During the summer of 1879, he made alterations to his own home in order to house its first students. The low set, upper story of a long, rear wing was divided into ten rooms on each side of a middle hall, and other improvements were made—at a total cost of about $1,000.

Then, in the autumn of 1879, a third lot, of nearly two hundred acres, was purchased, forming what would become the central location of the Northfield Seminary buildings. This last property, though having a splendid view, was largely "a bare, sandy hillside," thought to be "of small value for farming purposes."

A splendid urgency attended the acquisition of this land, with a dash of cloak-and-dagger secrecy thrown in. It so happened that this large tract of "nearly two hundred acres" was in actuality, and prior to purchase, a collection of several tracts of varying size—all "owned by several different persons." Between "one Friday and the next Monday night," the terms of sale were all concluded in a flurry of activity, several agreements "made separately with each owner for his lot"—no one knowing of any sale, but his own. The total price for all the land acquired was $15,000.

Classes at the Northfield Seminary began in November 1879, with twenty-five students enrolled. The eldest daughter of the Sikes family, Genevieve, was among the students of that first class. Her family must have been deeply proud when they learned she scored the highest entrance examination marks. In time, her academic gifts were shared with others. Genevieve Sikes later became a teacher at the school Moody would later establish for boys, Mount Hermon.[9]

Moreover, Genevieve's sisters, Julia and Mary, also graduated from Northfield—Mary, the youngest, in 1890. From what had been a seemingly commonplace meeting on a mountainside had come a school of blessing for the entire Sikes family. So it would be for generations of others to come.

Of the buildings created for the Northfield Seminary in its early years, East Hall has a special place. This handsome Victorian dormitory was built of brick and granite, with towers on each end, and given a beautiful porch atop "an easy flight of granite stairs."[10] From the hill on which it stands, East Hall commands a superb view. Describing the prospect, as one looks toward the neighboring state of Vermont, the writer T. J. Shanks said, "the range of vision is almost unlimited; the color of the landscape changes gradually from bright green to pale and still paler blue, until at last the actual horizon becomes indistinguishable as mountain peaks melt into hazy sky."[11]

Guests long remembered that Moody would often to point to East Hall and say, "Sankey sang that building up."[12] It was built at a cost of $36,000, with royalty funds collected from sales of *The Moody Sankey Gospel Hymns*.[13]

If Moody was grateful for the place of sacred song in creating East Hall, he knew another profound source of gratitude. At its dedication, he told everyone present: "I want to take this opportunity, while you are all with me, to dedicate this building to the Lord God. When I was four years old, my father died just over there on the hill, and left my mother with nine children. We were poor, and she had to struggle to get even bread for us. It was not in her power to educate us. You know that the Lord laid it upon my heart some time ago to organize a school for young women in the humbler walks of life, who never would get a Christian education, but for a school like this."[14]

H. M. Moore, a friend present for the dedication of East Hall, penned a moving description of Moody's actions after he'd spoken of his father, and the purpose of the Northfield Seminary.

Moody took up his Bible, read Isaiah 27:3, and then prayed.

"The words of that prayer," Moore wrote, "so burned into our souls that many of us remember them to this day. [Mr. Moody] commenced by thanking the Lord that He ever inclined his heart to establish this school. He thanked Him for the kind friends that He had raised up to help in the work, and then continued his prayer by saying:

> O Lord, we pray that no teacher may ever come within its walls, except as they have been taught by the Holy Spirit; that no scholars may ever come here, except as the Spirit of God shall touch their hearts. O God, we are Thine; this building is Thine! We give it over to Thee. Take it, and keep, and bless it, with Thy keeping power.

"I have attended the dedication of many churches," Moore concluded, "some very costly, in which sometimes half a day was spent in dedication. . . . But never in my life did I know of a building so completely given over to God, as this building was in that brief space of time."

There was a touching postscript as well. As Moore recalled: "So impressed were some of the young ladies who came to school that fall with the motto that they went up the mountain, and gathering from the trees some white, clean birch bark they cut out the motto of the school, and placed it upon a black velvet background, and bringing it to some of the trustees soon after the school opened, and showing it to them as the motto of the school, asked them if they would be willing to frame it. The motto was framed, and now hangs in the reception room of East Hall, where many and many persons have visited."[15]

———⌈◦/◦/◦⌉———

What was once only a vision had become reality. When East Hall's cornerstone was laid, *The New York Times* sent a correspondent to cover the August 21, 1879, ceremony.

Henry F. Durant and other honored guests spoke, then Moody himself stood. Holding up before the audience a beautiful silver trowel with some writing on it, he said: "My friends have secured this beautiful trowel with which to lay the stone. It is rather too beautiful for my use on this occasion."

Then he looked over his shoulder toward his birthplace. He paused, then spoke again: "Yesterday I went up to my mother's house, and up into the old garret, where I used to ramble about as a boy, and there I found this trowel." Holding it up, he said: "This is my father's trowel; he used to earn the bread for the family with this; it is a little worn, and a little rusty, but it is quite good enough for me to lay this cornerstone with."[16]

The unnamed reporter for *The New York Times* gave a full account of what followed. The dispatch bore the title "D. L. Moody's Educational Scheme," and its opening sentences read:

Northfield, Mass., Aug. 21. The cornerstone of a new school building which D. L. Moody the revivalist, proposes to erect in the northern part of the Village of Northfield, for furnishing academic instruction to pupils, was laid today. The weather was fine, and there was a large attendance of people from many towns in Franklin County, and from southern New Hampshire and Vermont. The site of the proposed building is . . . near Mr. Moody's Summer residence. The people of the town are much pleased with the prospect of so great an acquisition as a fine academy will be. [Ira] Sankey was present and led the singing . . . Mr. Moody officiated at the laying of the cornerstone, using a trowel [owned] by his father.[17]

Appropriately, the *Times* reporter noted, a copper time capsule was set inside the cornerstone. Among its contents was a recording of Ira Sankey singing the famous hymn *Hold the Fort*, "phonographically preserved on sheet tinfoil." Other items included "a piece of the gravestone of the Reverend Benjamin Doolittle, the first minister in Northfield, who died 130 years ago; a history of Northfield, a photograph of Moody's birth-place, a copy of a volume containing a reading-book, spelling-book, and doctor's book, all in one, owned by Moody's great grandfather; yarn spun by Moody's mother fifty years ago, a copy of *Gospel Hymns*, a Bible contributed by B. W. Jenkins, a Baltimore merchant, and a set of American coins."[18]

Several distinguished guests attended the cornerstone ceremony. Among them were H. N. F. Marshall of Boston, "in whose name the site was bought," and "Edward Kimball, the church-debt raiser."[19]

For Marshall, this day must have brought deep feelings of gratitude. He had given the funds needed to start the seminary. But what of Edward Kimball? He had given Moody a gift beyond price. For he was none other than the same Edward Kimball who'd led Moody to faith in 1855. Were it not for his Christian witness, not a brick of East Hall would ever have been laid, and much else besides.

⟨⟩/⟨⟩/⟨⟩

As the construction of East Hall began in earnest, the Reverend Robert West, editor of *The Chicago Advance*, had "called Moody's attention to the need for teachers in the Indian Territory" of the American West. Accordingly, during the summer after the close of the first school year, a seminary teacher, Miss Harriet W. Tuttle, visited the territory "to learn what Indian girls were to be found prepared to enter the seminary, [and] trained to become teachers among their own people."[20]

Moody's first thought was "to receive into the school a dozen students from the Indian Territory, if so many candidates might be found, free of expense to themselves." But Miss Tuttle found many more "who would have been fitted, and glad to go to Northfield, had the way been open." She selected sixteen, and they "became members of the school with the new year [1880]."[21]

The second year of the Northfield Seminary began "with East Hall full, and a number of day scholars. Besides the two teachers [present for] the first year, two new ones were employed,—Miss Fannie C. Holton, who had completed three years of study at Wellesley, and Miss Alice Rosa Hammond, who had just been graduated at Mount Holyoke."[22]

The third year of the seminary opened in 1881 "with every place full." On September 22 Moody left for Europe, and for the next three years, "excepting the summer of 1883, he was absent in Great Britain or on the Continent," carrying on evangelistic work. During this time, Moody's own home "was given up entirely to the use of the school." For the first two years, teacher Alice Hammond supervised; the next year, it was in the care of Fannie Holton. During this time, about twenty-five girls each term lived there. One observer wrote memorably: "Never was a school more like a home than this."[23]

It was a tragic day in February 1887, when Moody's much loved cousin Fannie Holton died. She was so young and her life far too brief. But that many of the years she lived were years of hope had been due to Moody's faith and generous spirit. He gave as he'd been given.

Two frontispiece epigraphs graced the 1889 edition of *The Handbook of the Northfield Seminary and the Mount Hermon School*. The first was from Frederic Harrison, who'd written: "Man's business here is to know for the sake of living, not to live for the sake of knowing." The second epigraph was taken from the writings of St. Augustine: "The end of learning is to know God, and out of that knowledge to love Him, and to imitate Him as we may, by possessing our souls of true virtue."

To glimpse the early years of life at the Northfield Seminary for young women is to see, figuratively speaking, how the high places of a neglected region were made more beautiful for situation. During Moody's youth, the hills about his home were places where hope too often seemed a stranger. After his return in 1875, grace came to those high places in ways no one, least of all he, could have suspected. Sometimes, the best things come like an outpouring of unlooked-for gifts. The people of Northfield, a place visited by faith, discovered this in myriad ways.

——◆◇◆——

Joy was not least among the gifts that came after the girls' seminary was founded. And D. L. Moody participated in the early days of this new school. One friend, William Covert, penned a Yuletide vignette of Northfield's hallowed hills as the founder and those first "Northfield girls" knew them. "I wish," Covert said,

> every boy and girl could pass through the schools at Mount Hermon and Northfield. Down there Moody would break the rules of the matrons, who were so dignified, and at unseasonable hours of the evening, about nine o'clock, he would sneak a freezer full of ice cream into the girls' dining room, and send up word about it, and they would all come down, knowing that "if Mr. Moody said so," it was alright. And he gathered them together on the hillside in the wintertime to go sliding down in pans, and to go out tobogganing, or to go down on the bobsleds, and he always went along with them.[24]

Moody gave Northfield girls and Mount Hermon boys the education and hope-filled younger years he never had but always wanted. Little wonder that he took unfeigned pleasure in sporting alongside them. The blessing came to him too.

12

MOUNT HERMON

*Great honors may come to this school in future years,
but no honor will ever eclipse the honor it has had in
having had this man of God for its friend and founder.*[1]

—John McDowell

The Mount Hermon School for boys was founded on May 4, 1881, just four miles from Northfield Seminary. Four years later a new boy, age fifteen, arrived at Mount Hermon. He brought an extraordinary story with him.

Born in poverty, John McDowell had been sent at age eight to work in the anthracite coal mines of Pennsylvania as a "wage-earner."[2] About a year later, he became a "breaker boy." He never forgot what it was like.

For ten hours' work a day, he received from fifty to seventy cents. He rose at 5:30 in the morning and put on his work clothes, always soaked with dust, ate his breakfast, and by seven had climbed the dark and dusty stairway to the screen room where he worked. All day, he sat on a hard bench built across a long chute, through which passed a steady stream of broken coal. From the never-ending stream of coal, he had to pick out the pieces of slate or rock.

It was backbreaking work. John had to bend constantly over the passing stream. His hands became cut and scarred by sharp pieces of slate and coal, while his fingernails were "worn to the quick" from contact with the iron chute. The air he breathed was saturated with coal dust. The room he was confined in was "fiercely hot in summer and intensely cold in winter,"[3] John recalled years later.

At age eleven, John became a mule driver. As a "driver-boy" he would descend the mine shaft, clean and harness his waiting mule, bring him to the foot of the shaft, and then hitch the animal to a "trip" of empty cars before seven o'clock. This trip of cars varied from four to seven, according to the number of miners. As the driver, John took the empty cars to the working places and returned with them loaded to the foot of the shaft. They were then hoisted to the surface and conveyed to the breaker where the coal was cracked, sorted, and cleaned and made ready for the market. He was among thousands of young drivers in the anthracite coal mines of the early twentieth century. These boys were in constant danger, not only of falling roof and exploding gas but of being crushed by the cars. Their daily pay varied from $1.10 to $1.25, from which sum they had to supply their own lamps, cotton, and oil.

Then, at the age of fourteen, John's life changed forever. Tragically, he lost his left arm in a mining accident. One cannot imagine how devastating it must have been. But for him, unlike so many others, it proved a severe mercy. Life in the mines was closed to him forever. He might have ended his life as an impoverished, illiterate cripple. But another life beckoned for John McDowell: one made possible by a school D. L. Moody created.

⸻◦◦◦⸻

The Mount Hermon School could trace its origins to three elements: a pioneering vision, a princely gift, and a true instance of poetic justice.[4]

For a start, the Mount Hermon School for boys was a natural second phase to follow the establishment of the Northfield Seminary for girls in 1879. But for almost two years after the founding of that school, plans for a boys' school remained in embryo.[5] Then, in the summer of 1880, Hiram Camp, president of the New Haven Clock Company, paid Moody a visit. A longtime friend, Camp respected Moody's business acumen as much as he did Moody's principled faith. His errand in coming to Moody was straightforward: to seek advice about the drawing up of his will.[6]

Like many businessmen before and since, Moody's advice was concise and direct. "Be your own executor," he counseled, "and have the joy of giving your own money." Camp liked that thought and asked Moody's opinion about a worthy object for his philanthropy. Moody needed little time to frame a reply. Camp's errand seemed heaven-sent, and Moody proceeded to outline what he had in mind with respect to a boys' school.[7]

What appealed most to Camp about Moody's vision was that by design, it would place a fine education within reach of underprivileged boys. He had been a boy like that himself. And Moody's emphasis on work-study, whereby "students were to do a certain amount of work each day," also appealed strongly to Camp, as it reinforced values he thought important.[8]

Now sixty-nine, Camp had worked hard throughout his youth to learn the clock-making trade. At forty-two, he started the New Haven Clock Company. From his own experience, he understood how intellect and creativity are cultivated and shaped through industry and dedication. This union of head, hand, and heart, as Moody described them—that was something he recognized. Stewardship was at its core, a recognition that talents and abilities are a gift from God. Camp could give boys, who were as he once was, a better start than he'd known. Late in life, he'd embraced a faith that taught him to invest in hospitals and libraries—and in that way help make a better world.

Now Moody set the vision of a school before him—a place where all these values could flourish, as boys were given an education rich in opportunity. He said yes to Moody.

Camp's living bequest was a gift of $25,000. Today, that amount is well in excess of half a million dollars. It was a lead gift that could help the school Moody envisioned in the most practical of ways: purchasing a large tract of land.

Next, the reality of poetic justice came into play. At its heart was the redemption of a painful circumstance.

Recall Moody's impoverished childhood. After the death of his father, Edwin, young Dwight watched as Ezra Purple, the mortgage holder, demanded payment from his mother—only four days after she had given birth to twins, and when the family was in great want.

At that time Betsy Moody was grieved and horrified. She quite rightly asked Purple "how he would like to have his daughter turned out of a home" situated as she was, the widowed mother of nine children. At this, Ezra Purple finally felt a pang of conscience and left. But Betsy Moody suffered the further indignity of a visit from Purple's money-grasping son, who came and roughly threatened her.[9]

His uncles Cyrus and George Holton pooled their money and covered the

$400 outstanding on the mortgage. But even that act of grace didn't forestall the cruel conduct of other creditors, who took all they could find, down to livestock that fed the family, even the kindling wood in the shed. All that escaped was a calf hidden in the woods and Edwin Moody's mason's trowel and tools, also safely hidden.[10]

Young D. L. and Betsy Moody's other children came to dread the appearance of Ezra Purple when mortgage payments came due. They would see him coming up the road and say to each other, "There comes the old bear," and scatter. The smallest would hide under the bed until he had gone.

——✦✦✦——

Fast-forward to the fall of 1879, when the 115-acre farm of Ezra Purple was placed for sale at auction. Move forward one more year in time to the summer of 1880, when Hiram Camp gave Moody his gift of $25,000. The farm once belonging to Ezra Purple was still unsold, and it was choice land.[11]

Moody instantly resolved to buy it. On September 20, 1880, Moody took a party of four friends, Hiram Camp, John Collins of New Haven, the Reverend George Pentecost, and George Stebbins, to the old Purple farm, which had been bought only the day before. They explored buildings and tramped the rocks and hills. On their return, they climbed over a fence into a woodland and came upon a large tree shading a clear space of ground covered with moss. It was a good place to rest, so they stopped, whereupon Moody suggested they take time for prayer to "dedicate the Boys' School to God and to His service."[12]

Before they knelt to pray, Moody told them a story only he knew. He told them of "old man Purple," the former owner of the farm, and how he'd once threatened to foreclose a mortgage on his widowed mother's homestead. And he confessed that when he grew older, he'd formed a resolve "that he would someday own the old Purple farm."

But now, in the face of all that had happened, Moody was chastened. "He spoke most reverently," said one of the four friends, "of the way God had ordered events." He could only think that the purchase of this farm for a boys' school was "poetic justice." Most of all, he said he was grateful that, "instead of owning the farm himself, he could lay it at the feet of the Saviour."

John Collins wrote soon after in *The Gospel Union News* of New Haven,

Connecticut: "There may be someday a more formal dedication [of this place] in the presence of a multitude of people, but it will hardly be more solemn than on that morning." Five men knelt to pray, in the deep stillness of a forest, and asked God "to accept and bless the new enterprise."[13]

A onetime cruelty had been redeemed. And Betsy Moody lived to see it.

———◦/◦/◦———

One year later, after the boys' school was well on its way, Moody wrote to Hiram Camp: "Northfield, Mass., July 21st, 1881—let me thank you, my dear brother ... May God bless you in time and in eternity, is my earnest prayer. I am in hopes when you and I are in eternity, the streams you have put in motion will flow on and on, and that we will meet in heaven many who have been brought there through your liberal gift. Yours, as ever, D. L. Moody."

For the rest of his life, Hiram Camp remained a friend to the boys' school. He died in July 1893, well into his eighties. But until that time, he served as president of the board of trustees and "gave liberally to the school each year, especially toward the close of his life." Beyond this, he took "a deep and personal interest in the Christian life and success of scores of boys in the school." Many wrote to him, and notwithstanding the time he had to give to his many business concerns, "he never failed, with his own hand, to reply to their letters." It was said that he "sympathized intensely with poor boys, for he started life as a poor boy himself." Several years after making his first gift, he said: "If I could have that gift back again and see the school reduced to nothing, would I take it? A thousand times no! There is no joy like the joy of giving."[14]

———◦/◦/◦———

But what to call the new school?

Here again, Hiram Camp bestowed a lasting and very fitting gift. "At Mr. Moody's house," he remembered, on "September 20th, 1880, we talked of a name. Some suggested 'Mount Pisgah.' This did not suit. It was then decided to call it 'Mr. Moody's Northfield School for Boys.' But the school was not in Northfield, so it was not liked ... I got to thinking of Hermon. I turned to Psalm 42:6; Psalm 89:12; Psalm 133:3; and Deuteronomy ... After I got home I wrote Mr. Moody asking: how it would be to call it 'Mount Hermon School.'"[15]

So it was agreed. Psalm 133:3 had provided the name—"As the dew of Hermon, and as the dew that descended upon the mountains of Zion: for there the Lord commanded the blessing, even life for evermore."

⎯⎯⎯∘∕∘∕∘∕⎯⎯⎯

John McDowell, the former mule driver who worked deep in a Pennsylvania mine, enrolled at the Mount Hermon School in 1885. Years later he wrote of an unusual encounter. "Just about a week after I entered Mt. Hermon School, Recitation Hall had just been completed, and I was assigned the task of helping to clean the building for my 'work-hour.'" One Saturday afternoon while "cleaning the stairs leading from the first floor . . . a large and energetic man entered the building, and ordered me to go out and hold his horses."

To this, McDowell replied, "I can't. I'm too busy."

The big man repeated the command. McDowell answered:

"I can't go. Mr. Moody and Major Whittle, with some other friends, are coming over here tomorrow to hold a service, and this building must be clean."

It was then the big man's voice boomed the command, "with more force than before."

McDowell stopped what he was doing. He was used to the hard life of work in coal mines. He'd heard worse—from a lot of people. He wasn't going to let this big man push him around. He drew himself up and said:

"There's a hitching post out there—tie the horses yourself! I have to finish my work."

And with that, the big man left.

A little while later, the superintendent of the building came in to see how McDowell was coming along with his task. As they spoke, McDowell asked:

"Who was that big man who ordered me to hold his horses?"

Perhaps the superintendent blanched a little before he spoke. "That," he said, "was D. L. Moody."

If the superintendent hadn't blanched, McDowell did now. "Words can never describe my feelings," he remembered. "I felt I'd missed an opportunity of a lifetime." Worse still, he thought: "I might be expelled from the school."[16]

He wasn't.

The truth was, Moody had been overbearing and later acknowledged it.

The two soon became fast friends, and Moody's appreciation of young Mc-Dowell's grit only grew over time. Despite the loss of his left arm, McDowell "never failed to do his share of work" at Mount Hermon. In fact, his work-study helped put him through school there. More astonishing still, he became the campus tennis champ. He graduated with distinction and later continued his studies at Princeton. By that time, the circumstances of their first meeting had become a standing joke. As McDowell remembered, Moody "told me of the pleasure he found in it." Then the two friends shared a laugh.

In time, Mount Hermon's place in John McDowell's life only grew. He often returned as a featured speaker for many school anniversaries. He later became a trustee and served also as president of the Alumni Association. Ordained as a pastor, he eventually became one of the Presbyterian church's most respected senior clergymen. In 1933, he was "unanimously elected moderator of the General Assembly of the Presbyterian Church of the U.S.A." For some years, his annual Labor Day address "was read from Presbyterian Pulpits throughout the country." He became the author of several fine books. [17] On McDowell's death in 1937, his obituary appeared in *The New York Times*, which reported: "In 1897 Dr. McDowell married Miss Minnie M. Fowler. Theirs was 'a Northfield romance,' the former Miss Fowler having been a student at the Northfield Seminary for Girls while Dr. McDowell was at Mount Hermon. Their only child, a daughter, Mrs. Robert C. Cory, lives at Short Hills, N.J. She has four children."[18]

Sometimes, even the bare recital of life achievements in an obituary carries a powerful story. Had D. L. Moody not been faithful to God's call in founding the schools that became Northfield Mount Hermon, the McDowells, John and Minnie, would never have met, married, or had a daughter: a daughter who in turn had four children.

How many lives, and how many descendants' lives, were forever altered for good because of Moody's vision? That speaks volumes about the ways that faith can be a force for good in the world, not only for one generation but for succeeding generations.

In after years, McDowell and Moody met often. The story of those meetings and their friendship is told in the book *Dwight L. Moody: The Discoverer of Men and the Maker of Movements.* The centerpiece of one of those reunions was a prayer—a very brief, but one prayer McDowell never forgot. As he told the story: "The last prayer . . . which I ever heard from his lips (indeed, the last words I ever heard from him), was offered as I walked home with him from a service he had conducted in Harrisburg. We had reached the house where he was staying and were about to separate, when he put his hand on my shoulder and bowed his head in prayer. It was a short prayer, but it reached the Throne of Grace and my heart: *O God, bless Mac in his life, and work, and use him mightily for Thy glory."*[19]

God answered that prayer.

Another keepsake McDowell treasured was a letter Moody wrote from London just seven years before his death. It stands as a symbol for so many things that Mount Hermon meant to Moody, certainly the great affection he had for "his boys." The letter read:

London, July 8th, 1892

My dear McDowell:
I was glad to get so good a report from Princeton, and am glad the boys are all doing so well, especially Woodhouse. I have written him a letter today. It cheers me to hear that the boys who have gone out from us are doing all they can to hold up Christ. I do not see why Mount Hermon should not become a blessing to all of the colleges in the course of time. Give my warmest love to all the boys, and tell them that I am glad to get so good a report from them. Write me often, and let me know how things go at Northfield this summer.

Yours truly,
D. L. Moody

McDowell penned two tributes to D. L. Moody that were especially telling. Both close this chapter.

"The world at large," McDowell wrote, "has many and good reasons for remembering Mr. Moody as the greatest evangelist of his century. But to us, 'his boys,' he is more than the greatest evangelist of the nineteenth century,—he is our personal friend, our greatest benefactor, the man who gave us a chance 'to make a life,' the man who when urged by supporters of the school to raise the tuition from $100 per year to $200, with the suggestion that those who could not afford to pay the extra $100 should secure some friend to stand for it, said, 'I want to be that friend to every student who enters Mount Hermon.'"[20]

McDowell's second tribute was this: "The greatest privilege of my life was to have known Dwight L. Moody as a preacher, a teacher, and a personal friend. I can truthfully say that I was born in Scotland, but that *I began to live the day I entered Mr. Moody's school . . . at Mount Hermon.*"[21]

13

A SCHOOL AND
PUBLISHER FOR CHICAGO

Let us expect that God is going to use us. Let us have courage,
and go forward, looking to God to do great things.[1]

—D. L. Moody

Some of you may think I oppose theological seminaries.
I want to say I believe we need thoroughly trained men.
I don't think we have enough trained men. At the same
time, we need some men to stand between the laity and the
ministers . . . gap men. We need men to stand in the gap.[2]

—D. L. Moody

Moody's entrepreneurial, innovative spirit served him in many ways. In no instance was this side of his character, burnished by faith, more in evidence than in the circumstances behind the founding of what is now Moody Bible Institute.

MBI was more directly the result of Moody's evangelistic work. As he traveled throughout America, particularly in cities, he saw multitudes not being reached by churches. Over against this glaring need, he also saw many young men and women he thought would be effective lay workers in the cause of Christ, if only they had some special training. How to fit this "supply and demand" was a problem he wished to solve.[3]

Accordingly, on January 22, 1886, Moody went to Chicago and gave a talk on "City Evangelization." He vividly described the needs of "unreached workingmen" and lamented the many churches he saw "closed six days in the week, and often throughout the summer." He told those in the audience of something he'd witnessed firsthand: the success of the Carrubbers Close mission in Edinburgh, Scotland, where "for thirty years, at quarter-past eight every night, someone had stood under a lamp-post, and preached Christ to the working-men, and had drawn them from the streets into the mission."

It was after this moving vignette that Moody said, "I believe we have got to have 'gap-men'—men to stand between the laity and the ministers; men who are trained to do city mission work."[4] With heartfelt eloquence, he described "the great need of more lay Christian workers" and made an urgent appeal for a quarter of a million dollars. "That's not much for Chicago!" he said, and with that amount, his hope was "to open a training school."[5]

Responses to this appeal came quickly. Money was pledged, and preliminary steps were taken. This new enterprise was chartered under the name of "The Chicago Evangelization Society."[6]

For some time, this society pursued its operations in temporary settings such as tents, churches, and the like. But as the scope of its work grew, the need for a permanent home was evident. Further funding was subsequently raised, and on October 1, 1889, its Bible Institute for Home and Foreign Missions, soon known simply as the Chicago Bible Institute, formally opened, with departments for both young men and young women, housed in dedicated campus buildings. At the same time the Chicago Evangelization Society entered new offices within the institute.

The Chicago Bible Institute, the forerunner of the Moody Bible Institute, soon ascribed its founding date as 1886, the year Moody issued his public call for "gap-men" and challenged supporters to raise a quarter million dollars to train them at a Bible institute. Although students first attended classes on September 26, 1889, institute leaders traced their start to Moody's call in 1886 to start the Chicago Evangelization Society and its Bible institute.[7]

―――◦/◦/◦―――

From the start, another person had also been indispensable in the founding of the Chicago Bible Institute. Her name was Emma Dryer, and by any measure she was a remarkable woman.

Like Moody, Emma had suffered a crushing loss as a child: the death of both of her parents. In her time of sorrow, a great mercy unfolded when she was taken in by a caring aunt who provided her with a good home and fine education.

So it was that Emma graduated with highest honors from LeRoy Female Seminary in New York State. Afterward, she would join the faculty of Knoxville Female College in Tennessee, and later, briefly teach elementary school. By 1864 she had become a member of the faculty at Illinois State Normal University, then primarily a training school for teachers.

Clearly, Emma was an educator of stature and accomplishment. And, as those who knew her saw firsthand, the depth of her commitment as an educator flowed from her faith. Indeed for several years, she spent her summers and holidays in Christian settings, undertaking "relief work" but also "teaching, evangelizing, and disciple-making."[8]

But then, in 1870, everything changed. Emma was stricken with typhoid fever and became deathly ill. Her life was feared for. But, as she and her friends believed ever after, God worked a miracle in her life. In her great hour of need, she experienced a complete healing. Following this astonishing recovery, one thing seemed inescapable: God, in His grace and mercy, had spared her life for a special purpose. She vowed to minister to "the needs of the dying world, as never before."[9]

Having resigned her position as head of the women's faculty at Illinois State Normal University, Emma moved to Chicago, not knowing precisely what the future held. She had stepped away from a fine salary and a place of respect and security. What would she find?

The answer wasn't long in coming. For soon after her arrival in Chicago, she met Dwight and Emma Moody.[10]

It is hardly surprising that the Moodys soon took Emma Dryer to heart. For as historian Lyle Dorsett has written, D. L. Moody could not help but admire a woman who had shown so much courage in forsaking all she had known to devote herself fully to relief work. He had wrestled with the same decision in 1860, leaving his business career at the height of his success.[11]

It wasn't long before D. L. Moody and Emma Dryer began to work in concert. At his urging, she took on two new roles: head of the Chicago Women's Aid Society and superintendent of the Women's Auxiliary of the YMCA (a forerunner of the YWCA).

Emma Dryer, once a member of the faculty at Illinois State Normal University, helped Moody to launch the Chicago Bible Institute.

Creative, tireless, and able, she served with distinction in these roles. And in 1873, just before leaving for his first great preaching campaign in Britain, Moody asked Emma to take the leading role in yet another new venture: the foundation of a school to train women (and eventually men as well) in preparation for service in home or foreign missions or evangelistic work. It would be a school that would provide systematic training in the Bible, theology, and practical ministry.[12]

Emma Dryer agreed. She brought her gifts for administration, innovation, curriculum development, and leadership to bear—and worked unstintingly to make this school a reality. And it was a success. Moody's close friend W. H. Daniels unabashedly called this school "Mr. Moody's Theological Seminary."[13]

With the success of this school, Emma Dryer continued to urge Moody at every opportunity to start a genuine training school for young men and women.[14] A visionary in her own right, she could see that from such humble beginnings, the school she started could become much more than it then was.

———◈◈◈———

By early 1883, several Chicago-based friends were meeting weekly with Emma Dryer to pray that D. L. Moody would return to Chicago and help them develop this vision for a new school more fully. Still, their weekly meetings remained just that for another three years. Finally, on January 22, 1886—during a meeting in Chicago to discuss city evangelization—the subject of a training school was taken up in earnest.[15] When Moody rose to address this gathering, his words left little doubt that Emma Dryer's years of consistent encouragement and urging about the Chicago school had given crucial direction to his thoughts. As a friend and counselor, but also as a pioneer in her own right, Emma Dryer's stewardship and gifts had been central to the founding of the Chicago Bible Institute.

Long years later, in July 1924, she looked back on those early days. The work of the first years, she said, "finally gave way to the larger and better work of the Institute. It was directed that way by John V. Farwell and Dr. [Rueben A.] Torrey. I assisted Mrs. [S. B.] Capron in starting the work for women under their direction . . ."[16]

It was characteristic that Emma Dryer's recollections should be heartfelt but brief and marked by humility. Nevertheless, her role in founding the Chicago Bible Institute is secure.

———◈◈◈———

Moody himself had spoken often of his hopes for this new institute. "Many young men," he said, "enter on Christian work far too late in life for them to go through a regular college course. The church ought to take these men in hand,

and give them the chance to do that for which they are fitted." And why, he also asked, "shouldn't devoted Christian women be trained to hold mothers' meetings, and cottage prayer-meetings, and to teach young mothers cooking and dressmaking? That is a practical kind of Christianity."

Churches, as Moody saw it, were vital to the success of this new endeavor. "The churches," he said, "ought also to train helpers to go round among the people and get hold of non-churchgoers, and in that way supplement the regular ministry. The time has come to call out the volunteers."

Next, Moody displayed the kind of intuitive insight for which he was famous. "If a man," he said, "has a desire for a university education, let him have it—by all means. But it is not necessary for everyone to know Latin, Greek, and Hebrew. I regret exceedingly that I never had a college education myself; but I did not get it, and I am doing the best I can without it."[17]

In sum, Moody was saying that this newly founded institute was for people who had a background like his own—too old, perhaps, to attend a college or university—but people who undeniably had gifts that ought to be cultivated, in a setting that could provide some formal training. He believed deeply in the value of college education, and his two sons would both attend Yale. But college, in many instances, wasn't for everyone. The institute that became MBI met a very real need. It still does today.

———

But where to site this new institute? The more Moody thought of his adopted home, Chicago, the more he knew it was the place for a permanent campus. And he knew where in the city to build it. Land and buildings adjoining the Chicago Avenue Church, the church Moody had founded, were accordingly purchased.[18]

Once the Chicago Bible Institute (or CBI) was formally established, D. L. Moody served as president until his death in 1899. Stories of his work and leadership abound, and they underscore the hopes he cherished for this new venture.

Since Northfield was his primary place of residence, and he was so often away on preaching tours, Moody could not stay in Chicago to personally lead the institute. He would visit as often as he could, but could do no more, and there was a true need for a gifted and well-trained administrator who could live in Chicago and shoulder the responsibility for day-to-day supervision at CBI. Moody found such a man in R. A. Torrey, who became the institute's general superintendent and primary teacher of courses in the Bible.

Torrey was highly educated for his day, with a B.A. from Yale, and a bachelor of divinity degree from Yale Divinity School. He had also undertaken postgraduate studies in biblical criticism at two leading German universities, Leipzig and Erlangen. During Moody's lifetime, he and Torrey worked well as a team. Moody worked hard to recruit fine teachers to join the faculty at CBI, while Torrey taught, administered, and implemented Moody's vision for the school.[19]

What was Moody's vision for the Chicago Bible Institute? One of his open letters, distributed nationwide to recruit students for the school, has survived. It was perhaps the last such letter he ever wrote, and was published in the December 31, 1898 issue of the *Outlook* magazine. It gave a marvelous firsthand account of his hopes for the school, while it also provided a unique snapshot of what CBI was like in his lifetime. "The school is open the year round," Moody wrote:

and as the course is in a circle of two years, students may enter any time. Between one and two hundred of those who have passed through the door of the institution are telling the story of the gospel in foreign lands, and more than seven hundred are engaged in home missions and as evangelistic preachers, regular pastoral work, and church visitors, to say nothing about those who have gone forth with the gospel message of song.

The many missions in Chicago give unbounded field for personal work, and the lectures of the morning and the study in the afternoon find practical demonstration in the missions and cottage prayer-meetings of the evenings. Students are not only instructed in preaching the gospel, but in singing it as well. No one doubts the power of song, and many a recruit in the army of the redeemed has received a call in some message of song. . . .

The Institute is undenominational, or, better, interdenominational, and enrolls men and women students. Separate dormitories are provided for both sexes. Representatives from all races have been enrolled as students during the past years, and more than thirty denominations were represented among the students last year. I shall be glad to hear personally from any one who desires to know more of the work of the Institute, at my Chicago address, 80 Institute Place.[20]

Biblical studies, preparation for service in home and foreign missions, with training in pastoral work, music performance, and church visitation—all these were offered in a setting that was coeducational and racially integrated, a place where mere Christianity shaped the faith commitment of students, staff, and faculty alike. And the Chicago Bible Institute was sited in the heart of America's great city of the Midwest.

All in all, the founding of such a school was a remarkable achievement. Moody, Emma Dryer, and R. A. Torrey, with all their colleagues of those first years, had much to be grateful for.

⸻ ❈ ⸻

Moody returned often in the years that followed to be a part of CBI's life as a school. His visits were occasions in themselves, and many revealing stories have survived.

One such story concerns the origin of Founder's Week at the Chicago Bible Institute. Tradition holds that during one February visit to CBI, Moody dashed into one of the classrooms there and shouted: "It's my birthday, let's go for a sleigh ride!"[21]

Such impish, spontaneous, and marvelously disruptive behavior was entirely in keeping with Moody's character. To see these students brought him joy, and though he'd never undertaken studies like theirs, he could spend time with them in a way that they both could celebrate and remember with great fondness.

Starting in 1911, Moody Bible Institute (renamed after Moody's death) would mark the birthday of its founder by suspending classes for a weeklong Bible conference known as Founder's Week,[22] and there was something very fitting about that. But the story of that first "founder's day," so to speak, should have a place all its own. Moody could remember when he'd arrived alone in Chicago, long years before, as a young man of nineteen. The young man he had been would never have believed that he would someday be used of God to play the leading role in establishing a school like the Chicago Bible Institute. It was as Moody later said so memorably: "the God of all grace is able to do great things."[23]

═══◦/◦/◦═══

That Moody cared deeply about CBI and its students was something William Evans knew better than few ever did. The memory of how he came to CBI as a student was etched indelibly on his mind.

Evans was a young immigrant from England and had only been in America nine months in 1890 when he decided to hear the famous evangelist at the Fifth Avenue Presbyterian Church, in New York City. From the start, Evans's arrival in the United States had been noteworthy. He had been converted "the day of his arrival in an Episcopal mission, and thereafter had worked at his trade as type-setter by day, and in the mission at night."

During his talk, Moody "made a strong appeal for men to devote themselves to God's work." Evans sat near the front of the church and listened as Moody spoke.

Then, suddenly, Moody interrupted his talk, pointed his finger directly at Evans, and said:

"Young man, God tells me that this message is for you. Has God ever called you to the ministry? Yield up yourself to the service of Jesus Christ."

Evans sat stunned and breathless and had no idea what to say.

At the close of the meeting, Moody came down to him and said:

"Young man, somehow or other the Spirit tells me that my message today was for you."

Evans then told Moody that he had tried to keep the thought of the ministry out of his mind for nine months and had found no rest in his disobedience to the voice of God.

In reply Moody said, "Pack up your trunk and go to my school in Chicago."

"I have no money with which to go to your school," Evans said with chagrin.

Moody brushed that aside. "Did I say anything to you about money? You pack up your things and go to my school."[24]

And that was that.

Within a few days, Evans was on his way to Chicago, and was soon enrolled as a new student at the Bible institute. Moody interceded personally to make sure Evans's tuition was covered. In time, Evans became a gifted minister, whose life story his alma mater wished its readers nationwide to know more about.

Moody's actions on this occasion were singular in their own right. Many times in the past, he had offered to cover the tuition of a deserving young man or young woman who had been referred to him by a friend.

But in this instance, something profound had taken place. Moody had only a powerful sense of prompting from the Holy Spirit to go by. He was obedient to that prompting. And because he was, the life of a young man he'd never met was forever changed for good.

In time, William Evans became Dr. William Evans. As the first graduate of the Bible institute, he returned to his alma mater to become associate director of the Bible course there in 1901. In the years that followed, he became the director of this course, also teaching Bible doctrine, homiletics, and biblical analysis. Evans was awed that God had opened such doors for him, writing early on to Moody's son-in-law, A. P. Fitt: "I return to instruct in the very school and in the very room where I received the fundamental instruction of my own life . . . to minister to our Lord in the institution from which it was my great honor to carry away its first diploma."[25]

Still other achievements marked Dr. Evans's life at Moody Bible Institute, as it was called by the time he returned to campus. When he died in 1950, *The New York Times* paid tribute to him, saying he was "the man who popularized the Bible for the average reader." And, as an author, Dr. Evans wrote more than forty books, on subjects ranging from sermon preparation to helps for memorizing Scripture. His most popular book, *The Great Doctrines of the Bible*, has remained in print for over one hundred years.[26]

All those who sat in Dr. Evans's classroom, perhaps thousands of students over the years, owed a great debt to D. L. Moody, though perhaps they never knew how deep and far-reaching that debt was.

A decade after the institute was founded, in October 1899, Moody was foremost among those who gratefully reviewed a report of the result and progress the institute had achieved. After his reading, Moody remarked: "I didn't realize we'd done that well!"[27]

Traveling, as he so often did—not just for gospel gatherings but also to raise funds to offset the tuition and operating expenses for the schools he'd established—Moody wasn't always able to track their day-to-day progress as closely as he would have liked. He knew that many gifted men and women had concerted their talents to make this new Chicago institute, in particular, such a success. Reading its report allowed him to have a close view of all that had unfolded over ten years. He might well have called it a ledger of investment for the kingdom.

From its humble beginnings, the Chicago institute had fitted graduates for active service in all parts of the world. Over three thousand men and women, in all, had studied at the institute.[28]

Individual measures of accomplishment told a story all their own. As the twentieth century began, while the institute was still in its infancy, 202 graduates were then in "home and city rescue missions." One hundred eighty were "engaged in evangelistic work as preachers and singers." Three hundred sixty-eight were "pastors, pastors' assistants, and church visitors; many in frontier pastorates." Fifty-eight were "Sunday school missionaries." One hundred eighty-six were "preaching the gospel in foreign lands." Thirty-eight were in "educational and philanthropic work, as Bible and music teachers, superintendents, and matrons of institutions." Sixty-four were "superintendents of city missions and other such institutions in the largest cities of America and Canada."[29]

But this was only to tell part of the Chicago institute's story. Moody knew that for every line of this report, there were other lines unwritten—lines that could have described a changed life on the streets of Chicago—perhaps someone from the very slums where he'd gone as a younger man. That would bring a smile in remembrance.

Close as the school was to the shores of Lake Michigan, history tells us that Moody's vision, and that of his institute colleagues, had a far-reaching ripple effect. Institutions organized on precisely similar lines were founded in other parts of America. What's more, the cities of Toronto, Canada, and Glasgow, Scotland, sent representatives to Chicago to study the Chicago institute. As of 1900, Toronto and Glasgow had created Bible institutes following Moody's model and implemented programs similar to those created by his colleagues in Chicago.

Last of all, Moody lived to see his ideas gain currency among prominent educators. An increase of "the study of the English Bible," and "more systematic instruction of the precise nature that Mr. Moody has given his students" were two reforms taken up by Charles Cuthbert Hall, the president of Union Theological Seminary in New York, and William Rainey Harper, president of the University of Chicago. Still other seminaries introduced kindred reforms.[30]

In 1895, four years before his death, Moody launched an initiative in connection with the Chicago institute that had great influence. This initiative bore a rather cumbersome name, but it did a great deal of good. In concert with his brother-in-law, publisher Fleming Revell, Moody established the Bible Institute Colportage Association (BICA), with offices on the campus of the Chicago Bible Institute. As conceived, it was a mass-market publishing venture that has counterparts today in mass-market paperbacks, audio books, and digital book reading devices. Whether in print, electronic, or audio version, such books are affordable for everyone.

All around him, in train stations and sidewalk stalls, Moody had seen the kind of literature history knows as "dime novels." When he saw these displays, he saw no religiously themed titles among them. Here, he reasoned, was an untapped opportunity. Customers were buying these affordable books in large numbers and their very availability was the key. The books had come to the people—no one had to look hard to find them. They were sold in commonly visited places. If people had ready access to the best titles from religious authors, Moody reasoned, it was yet another way to foster gospel gatherings— one reader at a time.

Once, after preaching in Madison, Wisconsin, Moody visited a store that carried lots of inexpensive fiction books, but not one book on Christian growth. Such books, where available, were costly. "Their price must come down," he argued. He soon learned that publishers had little interest in preparing books that could compete with inexpensive offerings like the fiction titles Moody had seen. So he conferred with Revell and decided to start the BICA.[31]

The goal, Moody explained, was "to supply good literature at a price that is within reach of all." Previously, it had been "almost impossible to buy good reading at a low price." Moody's solution: to issue "some of the most widely known writings of Charles Spurgeon, DeWitt Talmage and others, at fifteen cents a copy," and put them into the hands of people of modest means "through colporters in every locality." These colporters would, in essence, be traveling distributors for this new kind of literature.[32]

Beyond this, Moody had three other goals in view. First, "to carry the gospel, by means of the printed page, into neglected and frontier towns." Second, "to supply pastors and other Christian workers with helpful books (that are not too expensive) to give away to young converts." Third, "to reach non-churchgoers."[33]

And here, Moody cited a telling statistic. "Two-thirds of the population of the United States never attend church," he said. "Experience shows many men and women have been soundly converted by reading good books." As of the time he was writing, September 1895, Moody could report "the experience of the past few months shows us that there is a hunger for such books. Since [our launch] ten months ago, over 160,000 books have been sold, and the output is increasing."[34]

But would it work over the long term? In 1900, when *The Shorter Life of D. L. Moody* was published, the work of the BICA was reviewed to date. The story told in its pages was one of unquestioned, astonishing success. The Colportage Library had clearly hit upon a winning formula. Its titles gained a reputation for a "popular, readable style" from "well-known authors, or books of existing reputation." Moody had also insisted that these books embody the best elements of mere Christianity: possessing an "undenominational character." Last of all, the Colportage Library had to reflect "first-class workmanship," and be sold at a low price.[35]

There were correspondingly large runs for several titles, among them Moody's own book, *The Way to God*, which sold out its first printing of one hundred thousand copies. In all, nearly one hundred titles had been issued by 1900, and backlist titles were in constant demand.[36]

In five years, the BICA and its Colportage Library had become known throughout America and overseas.[37] Prior to Moody's death in 1899, over three and a quarter million copies had been published. In addition to titles in English, translations had also sold well, appearing in Spanish, German, Danish, Norwegian, and Swedish.[38]

The year 1900 marked the one-year anniversary of Moody's passing. His son-in-law, A. P. Fitt, the author of *The Shorter Life of D. L. Moody*, could say: "In a very real sense Mr. Moody is still entering the homes of the people all over this continent, [meeting] their hunger for reading, and telling, by story and sermon, the glorious gospel of the Son of God."[39]

With the Chicago Bible Institute firmly established with its own publishing house, and the Northfield Seminary for Young Women and the Mount Hermon School for Young Men, one might have thought Moody's work as an educator was complete. But one year after students began taking classes at the Chicago Bible Institute, he decided to open a fourth school.

The Northfield Bible Training School was "perhaps one of [D. L. Moody's] most original developments," Henry Drummond wrote in *McClure's Magazine*, and the school had a unique origin.[40]

Touring churches in Chicago, Moody "had learned to appreciate the exceptional value of women in ministering to the poor." He saw, however, that women with proper training "were not always to be found where they were needed most, and in many cases where they were to be found, their work was marred by inexperience and lack of training."[41]

Moody resolved "to start a novel species of training school, which city churches and mission fields could draw upon, not for highly educated missionaries, but for Christian women who had undergone a measure of special instruction, especially in Bible knowledge and *domestic economy*—the latter being the special feature." This was the genesis of the Northfield Bible Training School.[42]

To save money and time in building the school, he looked to a handsome building known throughout the Pioneer Valley. The Northfield Hotel enjoyed the busy summer season yet was shut from October through March. Now Moody proposed the hotel become a school during its off-season. The halls of the Northfield Hotel would be "turned into lecture rooms, its bedrooms into dormitories."[43]

Northfield Hotel, home in the off-season months to the Northfield Training School

And so the first term of the Northfield Bible Training School opened in October 1890. "Six instructors were provided," Henry Drummond wrote, "and fifty-six students took up residence at once." The following year, the numbers in the hotel college almost doubled. "Systematic Bible study [formed] the backbone of the curriculum"; students also learned "those branches of domestic economy which are most likely to be useful in their work among the homes of the poor." This included "cooking, especially the preparation of foods for the sick, and a distinct department devoted to dressmaking."

Its strong, practical component directly benefited Northfield and surrounding communities. "All through the winter," Drummond wrote, "flying columns" of students "may be found scouring the countryside in all directions, visiting the homesteads, and holding services in hamlets, cottages, and schoolhouses."

This school reveals Moody at his innovative best. He perceived a genuine yet unmet need for Christian workers. His creativity was matched in this instance by his sense of stewardship. The Northfield Hotel was never used for better purpose than when it ceased to be a hotel, as it were, to become a very fine school.

By 1900, more than seven hundred women had completed one to four terms at the Northfield Bible Training School.[44] Eventually, in 1908, it was merged with the Northfield Seminary for Young Women. But its nearly twenty-year legacy as a freestanding institution should not be forgotten.

14

THE LANDS OF FAITH

Anything that had a touch of Paul's life in it moved Father deeply. Every place . . . was carefully sought out. The Rev. J. Gordon Gray took Father out to the Appian Way, and when the original pavement was reached, he insisted on alighting from the carriage, and going on foot over the stones which Paul had trodden as he entered Rome.[1]

—W. R. Moody

The founder of Northfield Mount Hermon knew little, if any Latin. D. L. Moody understood the value of Hebrew, Latin, and Greek—indeed, he invoked that trilogy of language in one of his better sermon stories. Yet for fluency, they were an uncharted archipelago. He may have picked up the odd phrase or two in his reading, but little more.[2]

Still, had he been steeped in classical learning, he would have been the first to call the span from 1892 to 1893 a year of wonders (or *annus mirabilis*). That time opened with a sojourn in Europe and the Holy Land. It closed in Chicago, with millions hearing of the faith that shaped the ancient Near East.

Moody's visit to Europe and the Holy Land in 1892 was due almost entirely to friendly solicitude of a cherished family friend, Mrs. Jane MacKinnon. For several years, since January 1887, in fact, she and her husband, Peter, had urged Moody to accompany them on a trip to Palestine. On receipt of that initial winter letter, Moody wrote with great warmth of their kindness and real regret that he could not undertake such a journey. He told Jane MacKinnon:

I could hardly keep back the tears as I thought of going to Calvary, Gethsemane, and the Mount of Olives with you. My heart is with you, and I cannot tell you what a self-denial it is to me not to go. For years I have wanted to do so, and though I have never left my work for pleasure in my life, I think I should have gone this time, if I had not been as I am.

For three years [friends] have been trying to get me to go to Chicago, and I told them that if they would do certain things I would give them three months. They have done what I asked them to do, and so I must stay here now until April or May. I do long to take a trip, and would like to go with you and your husband more than with anyone else; but I must decline . . .

Remember me to all old friends; think of me and pray for me in the Garden, and on Olivet, and at Calvary, and take one good look, when in Bethany, and see if you can see the place where the Master was once seen, and ask Him to come back again.[3]

Five years later, the MacKinnons still kept the hope of a Holy Land tour. In February 1892, they renewed their invitation with friendly importunity. Moody's reply showed his own desire to walk those ancient lands hadn't lessened. Still, he hesitated. He was then on a preaching tour of Scotland and felt it impossible for him to leave his work,"[4]

Paisley, Scotland,
February 10th, 1892

My dear Mrs. MacKinnon:
I would be glad to go to Palestine, but there are some reasons that will keep me.

First, the work. It would be a pity to leave it now, and I am committed until the 1st of April. Second, in April, when it grows warmer, I come down with headache, and suffer a good deal, unless I keep where it is cool. Third, my wife says that Palestine is said to be unhealthy, and no one can go there in the spring. So I think, if ever I see the land of Abraham and his children, I shall have to see it when I go in another body, and it maybe I will see it with Christ Himself.

I cannot tell you how glad I am your husband is better. Tell him I pray for him daily, and trust it will be the will of God to lift him up again. I did not know I loved him so much, until I heard he was so sick.

Mr. Sankey has gone up to London to attend the funeral of Mr. Spurgeon; they wanted me to go, but I could not get away. The churches, halls, etc., were all engaged, and this kept me. I am thankful to tell you the work is good here, and I have much to encourage me, yet I get home-sick at times, and long to see my family. May the blessing of God rest on you and your dear husband is the prayer of

> *Your true friend,*
> *D. L. Moody*

On receiving this letter, the MacKinnons sympathized but would not be dissuaded. They had taken this Holy Land tour to heart and were determined to take Moody with them. They posted another letter, saying they would defer their Holy Land trip until April. Moody capitulated at last and wrote to say he would go with them.

Taking his wife, Emma, and his son Paul, Moody went from Paris to Rome, where he was to join the MacKinnons's party. Along the way, his interest in everything about him was keen. It centered especially on the native people and their ways of life.

Farming on the hillsides captured Moody's attention. To see folk living in little houses "perched like crows in a nest on the edge of the snowline," reclaiming slender patches of land, was a wonder. Once, he said: "Look here! See that hillside farming! That beats all I ever saw. If ever I hear a Northfield man complaining of his farm again, I'll fall on him!" He pointed to his ample girth as he spoke, and everyone collapsed in laughter.[5]

In Rome, the Moodys met up with the MacKinnons. One morning, soon after breakfast, the friends made a tour of the city with a guide. Moody was "unusually silent when going through the beautiful churches," speaking only occasionally.

The Coliseum proved a great attraction. Moody "sat on a huge column that was lying on the ground and surveyed the amphitheatre." He was long lost in thought, knowing how many scenes of cruelty and martyrdom had taken place there.[6]

There were happier moments—many, as it turned out.

Perhaps the best, certainly the most funny, took place when Moody spied an Italian peasant who was stouter in size than he was.

He stopped the man, offered a greeting, and asked Ortini, their Italian guide, to speak on his behalf. "Tell him he's a fine, powerful man," Moody said. Ortini translated.

At this, the peasant smiled at everyone in the party and began to speak rapidly. Ortini listened, then said in English: "He says he was heavier, but he is losing flesh. He is too poor to drink wine. If he had wine, he would look sleek like you!"

Moody laughed and said, "Tell him I'm a teetotaler." Ortini did so. The man stared incredulously and laughed, clearly thinking such a thing impossible.

"Tell him it's true," Moody affirmed.

Still taken with laughter, the peasant produced a loaf from under his coat. He spoke to Ortini, who translated: "You may be a teetotaler in drink, but you are no teetotaler in eating!"[7]

On April 8, the party started for Naples and sailed from there for Port Said, which was reached four days later. Writing from Port Said, Moody observed: "We are now near where the children of Israel passed when they went out of Egypt. The country is sandy and barren, but the canal is a wonder, and it seems strange to be in this land of the Pharaohs, of Moses and Aaron and Joseph."[8]

After coaling their steamer at Port Said, the party sailed on the Suez Canal to Ismailia, the fabled "city of beauty and enchantment," on the west bank of the canal. No one slept. About midnight, they passed the old Syrian Road at Candara, where the ancient Jews and others traveled from Europe and Asia into Egypt. At Ismailia, the party boarded a train to Alexandria that passed through the land of Goshen. Here, Moody's "thirst for information was satisfied," as elsewhere on the tour, by "an early morning ride with a guide, before the rest of the party were up."[9]

Eventually they arrived by train at Alexandria; later they took a boat to Joppa. The Holy Land was sighted on Good Friday. The landing at Joppa was not made until late in the afternoon, and at about four o'clock the start was made for Jerusalem.

Supper was eaten at Ramleh. Mr. Moody finished before the rest and said he would go out for some air. When the party was ready to start, he was nowhere to be seen, and calling failed to reach him. The carriages were entered, and after a while he was overtaken. Impulsively, he had informed the guide that he was going on before. It proved a rash decision, as he soon came upon several local inhabitants who scowled as they passed and spat at him.[10] The carriages had come none too quickly for his liking.

Skirting a potential mishap, the night suddenly turned beautiful. The moon rose brightly over the mountains as the carriages drove on. Quicksilver light touched the peaks. That was worth coming to see.

The party reached Jerusalem at three Saturday morning, and lodgings were taken. After a few hours' rest, a walk was taken about the city, out to the tomb of David, alongside of which was a little house, where, in an upper chamber, it was said that Christ ate the Last Supper.[11]

Many visitors to Jerusalem take in traditional sites uncritically. Moody was not among them. Ever curious and respectful, he nonetheless doubted the true identity of every traditional site save the Temple Mount and Calvary. Most localities were obscure, he felt, "but the hills you cannot change or remove."[12]

That afternoon Moody and his son Paul, just turned thirteen, joined George Mackay and his son Donald on "donkeys and rode to the top of the Mount of Olives." On the way they passed Calvary.[13]

Early the next morning—Easter Sunday—Moody took his Bible and went to the Mount of Olives. Resurrection hope drew near, as it never had before, in that quiet interval.

He preached that afternoon on Calvary "to a large audience" under the auspices of the English Church Missionary Society. It was estimated that "at least three hundred people were present, largely native and visiting Christians."[14]

The impromptu congregation was also joined by some local Muslims and

Jews, curious at the sizeable crowd. Moody was deeply moved at the setting and "preached with an emotion that he had rarely, if ever, equaled in any previous sermon." He began by saying that he "had preached for thirty years, but had never felt the awe of God that he did at that moment."[15]

As Moody spoke, the thoughts and images came in quick profusion. "Mount Moriah and Abraham, the distant hills of Moab and Ruth, Olivet and Christ"—each were taken up and vividly described. Moody's words took on a life of their own. The climax came when he "likened the sacrifice of Isaac to the offering up of Jesus," and spoke of "how Jesus must have felt as He passed this hill in boyhood, knowing that there He should offer up His life." Fervor met faith, and "left an ineffaceable impression on all who heard it."[16]

For so brief a visit as his time in the Holy Land was, Moody found himself returning to favorite places: the Mount of Olives, to which he repeatedly returned, and "the little village of Bethany, over the brow of the hill."[17]

Nor were Christian sites the only places where the party of friends called. George Mackay penned a vivid description of their visit to the Mosque of Omar, just opposite the southern courtyard of the Church of the Holy Sepulcher. "In the mosque," Mackay remembered, "we all wore felt slippers, which they tied on over our shoes. Mr. MacKinnon carried a pair of slippers and put them on. This is necessary, as no heathen foot must touch the sacred floor."[18]

Somehow one of Paul Moody's slippers came off. One of the mosque officers saw it, and near pandemonium ensued. The Arabs nearby became outraged and indignant, shouting and rushing about. Young Paul was terrified. He stood holding his foot up so that he would not further contaminate the floor. Emma Moody was no less fearful. Pale with worry, she was trying to help her son, "and looking as if she would give anything to get out alive."

After what seemed a chaotic eternity, a wise attendant retrieved a new pair of slippers. Paul quickly donned both, and the tempers that had flared so quickly slowly subsided. Violence could well have resulted but mercifully did not. A hasty departure followed.[19]

A happier incident by far followed soon after. One morning at five o'clock, in company with George Mackay, Moody went to the Mount of Olives. It rained, and as they ascended, "a beautiful rainbow spanned the city, its base resting on the Temple court at one end, and just beyond the Gate of Herod at the other." The sight stopped them in their tracks. It seemed "a rainbow of promise of the glory to come at Jerusalem."[20]

When they reached the crest of the mountain, they discovered "a glorious view of the hills of Judaea, the Dead Sea, and the Jordan Valley." Stopping "on the Bethany spur of the mountain," the two friends read the story of Lazarus and of the ascension of Christ. A time of reverent prayer followed. Moody asked the Lord to come again quickly, and to sanctify their visit to that spot by their growth in grace. He was deeply moved. Both friends were loath to leave the mountain. It was fully eleven o'clock when they returned. They had been gone for nearly five hours.[21]

On his second Sunday in Jerusalem, Moody rose at 4 a.m. to catch the sunrise on the Mount of Olives. He wanted "to see the sun come up beyond the hills of Moab." Rejoining his party at breakfast, he couldn't hide his happiness. He said that he had seen the sunrise, and that as he "looked over this land of promise," he saw Moses's face in his imagination, "surrounded by the sun as a halo."

He marveled at it all. "The beautiful eastern view from the Mount of Olives" seemed to transmute distance. He knew the Valley of the Jordan, the Dead Sea, and the hills of Moab were more than twenty miles away, yet they seemed far closer—less than five. Clearly, the land held an enchantment all its own.

That same day, in the afternoon, Moody "preached beneath Calvary on the west." The heart has its reasons, Pascal once said. Moody could number each memory that his sojourn brought with it. Time would only hallow them.[22]

The following day, Moody, Emma, and Paul went one last time to the Mount of Olives. One wonders what they said to each other. What is certain was the gift of time they shared in this storied place. Too soon, they had to leave. At noon, they started for Joppa.

George Mackay always remembered their parting. "Thus ended my three weeks with Mr. Moody," he wrote. "It had been a blessed experience for me." The company of friends was furthered diminished when the MacKinnons left as well and returned to Egypt.[23]

For a time the Moodys returned to Egypt themselves. Several days were spent in Cairo, "visiting the Pyramids and other points of interest." Then, in the first week of May, they started for Italy. That month was spent in Naples and Florence, traveling to the Italian lakes and Switzerland. By the end of May, Moody was again in England, having been absent for two months. All in all, it was the longest vacation he'd taken since he entered business as a boy of seventeen.

This visit to the Holy Land remained a vivid, living memory. Moody constantly referred to it afterward in private conversations and sermons. Most of all, he looked forward with deepened appreciation and joy to the restoration of Israel, "when the feet of the Messiah shall once more stand on Olivet."[24]

31 JAN 2024

	TIME
SE	10:00
	11:00
CK	1:15
	2:30

15

DELIVERANCE AT SEA

*The North German Lloyd steamship Spree has been towed
into Queenstown Harbor with her shaft broken, and the
compartment under her second cabin full of water.*[1]

—*The New York Times*

D. L. Moody, with seven hundred other souls, nearly lost his life at sea
in late November 1892. The near disaster became headline news in *The
New York Times*. For many, this incredible escape from peril became the stuff
of legend. For Moody, and others among his fellow passengers, it was the stuff
of miracles.

On Wednesday, November 23, The S.S. *Spree* set sail from Southampton,
England, bound for New York City. D. L. Moody and his eldest son, Will, had
boarded on a picture-perfect day, as Moody himself recalled: "My last day in London was a pleasant one; a day of promise it might have been called, for the sun
shone out brightly after some of those dark, foggy days so common in London."[2]

Moody was glad to be returning to America, where the hills of Northfield
beckoned, as they so often did. He longed to get back.

Three days out from port, in the early morning, there came "a terrible crash
and shock," as if the *Spree* "had been driven on a rock." Will Moody jumped
from his berth and ran on deck. A few moments later he returned, telling his
father, "The propeller shaft has broken, and the ship is sinking."[3]

At first, Moody did not think it could be as bad as that. He dressed quickly
and went out on deck. Soon he discovered that what Will said was true. Initially,
the *Spree*'s captain told frightened passengers there wasn't any danger. But
when some of the second-cabin passengers tried to return to their berths, they

were met by fast-rising water. They rushed back on deck, their belongings left behind.

Captain Willerode and his crew were doing all they could to save the ship. But despite their gallant attempts, the water pumps seemed useless. Water was pouring into the ship too rapidly to be controlled. "We were utterly, absolutely helpless," Moody recalled. "We could only stand still on the poor, drifting, sinking ship, and look into our watery graves."[4]

Preparations were under way for the last resort. Lifeboats were made ready, provisions set out, and life preservers distributed. Ship's officers were armed with revolvers to enforce their orders. All that remained was a final decision to launch the boats at once, or wait.

Captain Willerode faced a terrible choice. The seas were so heavy it seemed the lifeboats could hardly stay afloat. Meanwhile, as Moody himself learned, two passengers "had loaded revolvers—ready to blow out their brains if the vessel should go down, preferring death by bullet to death by drowning."[5]

The waiting game subsisted throughout the day. Then everyone aboard passed a harrowing night. Passengers looked at one another, "with blanched faces and trembling hearts," as though "trying to read what no one dared to speak." Distress rockets "flamed into the sky, but there was no answer." The *Spree* was drifting out of the sailing lanes commonly used by other vessels.[6]

———

At noon the following day, Willerode told everyone the flow of water was under control, and there were hopes of drifting toward some passing vessel. All the same, many were alarmed because the ship's bow was now high in the air. Her stern seemed to settle into the water more and more.

As for the weather, seas remained very rough. The *Spree* rolled from side to side with fearful lurches. It seemed that if she pitched violently but once, the safety bulkheads would have burst. The captain did what he could to keep up hope by telling passengers they should probably drift in the path of a ship by three o'clock that afternoon. But as night closed in, there had been no sign of a smokestack or sail.[7]

Understandably, to this point, no mention of a special religious service had been made. It was thought such a suggestion would produce panic. But as the second night after the accident came on, Moody asked his friend and fellow passenger, the Civil War hero General Oliver Otis Howard, to request Captain Willerode's permission to hold a service in the ship's saloon.

To this, Captain Willerode readily agreed, saying, "Most certainly, I am that kind too," by which he meant he was a person of faith. This done, notice was quickly given of the service. Nearly every passenger attended. "I think everybody prayed," Moody said.[8]

D. L. Moody leads passengers in prayer on the S.S. *Spree* after a huge rock damaged the propeller shaft and the ship took on water.

During the hastily called service, Moody stood with one arm grasping a pillar to steady himself on the reeling vessel. He read from the Ninety-first Psalm. Then everyone prayed God would still the sea and bring them safely to port.

As he was reading Psalm 91, Moody experienced something extraordinary. The words of the Bible passage took on a meaning they'd never held for him before. "It was a new psalm to me from that hour," he recalled. "The eleventh verse touched me very deeply. It was like a voice of divine assurance, and it seemed a very real thing as I read: 'He shall give his angels charge over thee, to keep thee in all thy ways.'"[9]

Thinking that more Scripture might offer comfort, Moody began to read aloud from Psalm 107. As he did, a German passenger translated each verse for the benefit of his countrymen.

⎯⎯◦◦◦⎯⎯

Yet even as he read, Moody was himself being transformed. "I was passing through a new experience," he would later say. "I had thought myself superior to the fear of death. I had often preached on the subject, and urged Christians to realize this victory of faith."[10]

Moody later recalled that during the Civil War he had "been under fire" without fear. "I was in Chicago during the great cholera epidemic," he also remembered, "and went around with the doctors, visiting the sick and dying . . . I remember a case of smallpox where the flesh had literally dropped away from the backbone, yet I went to the bedside of that poor sufferer again and again, with Bible and prayer, for Jesus' sake. In all this I had no fear of death."[11]

But on this sinking ship, it was different. To be certain, as he said, "there was no cloud between my soul and my Savior. I knew that if I died there, it would be only to wake up in heaven. That was all settled long ago."

No, it was something else that filled him with dread. "My thoughts," he said, "went out to my loved ones at home—my wife and children, my friends on both sides of the sea—the schools, and all the interests so dear to me." When his mind turned to these things, and as he realized "that perhaps the next hour would separate me forever from all these, so far as this world was concerned, I confess it almost broke me down. It was the darkest hour of my life!"[12]

As Moody remembered: "I could not endure it. I had to have relief." Finally, as he and the other passengers prayed, relief came. "God heard my cry, and enabled me to say, from the depth of my soul: 'Thy will be done!' Sweet peace came to my heart. Let it be 'Northfield or Heaven,' it made no difference now."[13]

Soon after the service had concluded, night came. Moody returned to his room, went to bed, and "almost immediately fell asleep." He had never, he would later say, "slept more soundly in all my life."

About three o'clock the next morning, Moody was aroused from a sound sleep by the voice of his son. "Come on deck, Father!" Will said.

Moody got out of bed and quickly went out onto the deck. Once there, Will pointed to a far-off light, rising and sinking on the sea. It proved to be a light from the steamer *Lake Huron*, whose lookout had seen their distress rockets, and thought they'd come upon a vessel in flames. "Oh, the joy of that moment," Moody recalled. "Seven hundred despairing passengers stood on deck, and beheld the approaching ship! Who can ever forget it?"[14]

General Howard gave a detailed account of all that took place in his autobiography. As Howard wrote:

> After midnight Friday, we were about eleven hundred miles on our way, when the main shaft of the propeller broke, sending two large fragments through the bottom of the steamer. The bulkheads had not been closed, and for a time about half the compartments speedily filled with water.
>
> Of course, the compartments were instantly shut off from each other by the bulkhead doors, and the water was pumped out from every compartment, except the last two near the stern. These two could not be secured without straining the ship, and producing a great leakage.[15]

Howard described how the *Lake Huron* rescued the stricken steamship. By nine o'clock Monday morning, the *Lake Huron* "was towing the *Spree* by two strong cables, and we were quietly dragged for eight days on a smooth sea back to Queenstown, Ireland. As soon as we touched land, most of the passengers ran to the nearest church. It was of the Methodist persuasion, and when the house was well filled, Moody mounted the pulpit and preached a sermon from the text, 'God is Love.' We all gave thanks."

Moody took a ship for his return voyage sooner than General Howard and his family did. Howard "returned by the *Harvel*, a sister ship of the *Spree*. When he arrived in New York City, he learned "newspapers were filled with opposition to Moody's theory [of deliverance], which he expressed in the brief phrase, 'Prayer saved the ship.'"

As soon as Howard had disembarked, correspondents clustered about him. They "asked me for the facts," Howard remembered. He told them: "Mr. Moody's prayer had been, 'Please send us a ship, and smooth the waves so that we shall not be drowned.' The *Lake Huron* did come in time to our rescue, and we had a smooth sea for eight days back to Queenstown, Ireland. What we asked for came. Whatever our belief, surely we were made to feel, as Moody said, that 'God is Love.'"[16]

MOODY AT THE WORLD'S FAIR

Let anyone visit Northfield, with its noble piles of institutions, or study the history of the work conceived, directed, financed, and carried out on such a colossal scale by Mr. Moody during the time of the World's Fair at Chicago, and he will discover for himself the size, the mere intellectual quality, creative power, and organizing skill of the brain behind them.[1]

—The Literary Digest
December 22, 1894

Moody never ceased to marvel over the miracle of his deliverance at sea. For the rest of his life, he spoke of it, reverently, in his sermons. At least one reason for his deliverance soon became clear. For had he perished in November 1892, he would never have led the great six-month mission at the Chicago World's Fair of 1893.

When plans for this great conclave of commerce and industry were announced, Moody immediately recognized the possibilities connected with it. Millions of people, from all over the world, would be coming to Chicago. They were coming, literally, to his doorstep. He was uniquely positioned to make the most of this event, with a long established base of operations there. And, since 1889, Chicago had been home to the Bible institute he'd founded. He had a host of friends and coworkers who could be mobilized.

In 1892, when plans for the World's Fair were far advanced and its exposition buildings nearly complete, Moody was overseas conducting gospel gatherings in Great Britain. But he wasted no time in telling coworkers and colleagues that the World's Fair was, in his phrase, "the opportunity of a century."[2]

Then, too, when death had come so close aboard the *Spree*, Moody made a vow connected directly with the hopes he cherished for a mission at the World's Fair. As he recalled:

> when the announcement was made that the steamer was sinking, and we were there in a helpless condition in mid-ocean, no one on earth knows what I passed through as I thought that my work was finished, and that I should never again have the privilege of preaching the gospel of the Son of God. And on that dark night, the first night of the accident, I made a vow that if God would spare my life, and bring me back to America, I would come to Chicago, and at the World's Fair preach the gospel with all the power that He would give me.[3]

But not everyone saw the World's Fair as "the opportunity of a century" or had such a clear sense of calling about it. More than a few Christian leaders and groups were outraged over news that the World's Fair would be kept open on Sundays. There were some who wanted to launch a boycott of the fair; still others wished to file a lawsuit.

Moody saw things in a completely different light. He couldn't fathom why so many had such a wrongheaded, separatist mentality.

Moody's resolve called forth a tribute from one of his great friends in New England, A. J. Gordon of Boston, who later said: "Now I like the spirit in which [Moody] undertook this work. Some said, 'Let us boycott the fair;' others said, 'let us appeal to the law, and put in money enough to prosecute its managers, and compel them to shut it up.'"

Moody's plan, according to Gordon, was "to present so many attractions, that the people from all parts of the world will come and hear the gospel." And that, Gordon said, "is actually what has happened . . . It is a remarkable movement."[4]

Here, Moody was at his unconventional best. Where others saw obstacles and were bent on contention, he saw opportunities and sought to extend a welcome—with a message of hope, to those visiting the World's Fair.

The fair, or as it was also known, the World's Columbian Exposition, officially opened on May 1, 1893 and closed on October 30, just shy of a full six-months.

Moody's gospel campaign at the fair would showcase his administrative skills. His plan was both simple and inspired. As Chicago was then naturally divided into three sections by "the forking river that flowed through it"—the North Side, the West Side, and the South Side—a church center for each section was selected. On the North Side, the church Moody founded, the Chicago Avenue Church, was chosen, while the First Congregational Church was chosen for the West, and the Immanuel Baptist Church for the South. Still later, other churches were offered and occupied, but these were the first three.

Thankfully, gifted coworkers helped Moody shoulder the burden of this enormous outreach initiative. Many prominent Christian workers, "from all parts of America and Europe," traveled to take part and lend their talents.

There was a need for them. "Buildings and tents sufficient to hold large audiences" had to be secured. Rosters of speakers and singers had to be scheduled. A carefully targeted advertising campaign was designed and implemented.

Fund-raising was chief among the tasks Moody took on. Daily expenses would be $800–$20,000 per day in today's money. This covered daily expenditures for the rental of halls, as well as the cost of advertising, salaries, and lodging for speakers, clerks, and others. To maximize his effectiveness, Moody enlisted a large volunteer force of secretaries, who "wrote appeals under his direction." He also secured "the co-operation of the religious press in giving full notice to the work," and this "aided greatly in securing the generous support of the Christian public."[5]

The gospel campaign began on the Fair's first Sunday, May 7. Moody preached in the Chicago Avenue Church on the morning, afternoon, and evening of that day. His introductory sermon was on "The Elder Brother," as described in the parable of the prodigal son. "There are quite a number," Moody said, "right here in this city today . . . [people] very religious in outward observance, but they do not know how to sympathize with a prodigal, nor help those who try to lift him up."

Moody went on to say that "there is not one of the Beatitudes the elder brother had not violated." Outwardly righteous, "internally he was all wrong," Moody said, "and yet he resembles many Christians today—nearer than they suppose." His father longed for both his sons to be with him, "and that is just what God the Father wants; He has room for us all." But many people, Moody said, "want the benefit of religion themselves, while they grudge it to their neighbors."[6]

Moody's desire, in taking up this text, was "to disarm and expose the prejudices which often excite opposition to the work of saving the lost."[7] He'd been deeply concerned that so many professed Christians saw the World's Fair as something to be opposed, and thought nothing of the myriad opportunities this great gathering held for offering a welcome to Chicago's visitors, and sharing the gift of faith with them. Moody knew millions would be coming—eventually some 27 million people did come, averaging 150,000 people a day.[8]

Could contentious believers not spare a thought for them? His choice of sermon had a central point: to commend the gospel outreach mission he had so close to heart. Chicago had once welcomed him as a young man seeking his way in life. What's more, didn't the idea of a gospel mission get to the heart of faith—of sharing faith, as a grateful return for the matchless gifts faith had bestowed? Moody wanted his audience to understand that the answer to that question must always be yes.

Having set the stage for why such mission should be undertaken, Moody thought it right to show that the commencement of the fair, and the coming of so many, was rightly a cause for celebration. If Christianity was "the blessed hope," what could be better than to schedule a week of "praise services" to be held each night at the Chicago Avenue Church? Apart from the grand spectacle of many gifted voices lifted in song—a series of free concerts for World's Fair visitors, as it were—Moody wished to embark on this great venture of faith by inspiriting those who had to work with him. For some, the prospect of starting a work like this was daunting, even "forbidding and discouraging."[9] It was as though a message was being conveyed through this gift of music: "the joy of the Lord is my strength."[10]

Certainly, it was an uplifting beginning to things, and indeed, this approach had its intended result. The work of the gospel mission soon began to expand weekly, and "it was presently necessary to call other churches into use."[11]

Here, however, another challenge presented itself. Such churches as might have been used "were not always suitably located to reach the masses of people," so Moody hit upon an innovation born of necessity: he decided "to hire theaters." Seemingly an excellent solution, for a time "desirable halls and theaters could not be secured at any price, on account of previous engagements."

Moody, not wishing to curtail any momentum that had been growing for the gospel campaign, thought to offer great sums to secure much needed facilities. He "offered $18,500 for the use of the Auditorium Theater alone on Sundays, but was refused." This was a princely sum, equal to $475,000 in modern currency.

After much effort, "a footing was obtained in the Haymarket Theater." From this time forward, until the end of the campaign, Moody preached there every Sunday morning, save for a few Sundays, when he was called away from Chicago.[12]

⸺◦/◦/◦⸺

The gospel mission grew apace, and other theaters and halls were rented. Ultimately, ten such venues were secured by Moody—some used on Sundays only, others throughout the week.

But these were stationary places. Moody and his colleagues saw the wisdom in having mobile ways of conveying the gospel. To that end, five large tents were brought into constant use, "being pitched in strategic points in the midst of non-churchgoing communities." Aside from this, two "gospel wagons" were custom-designed and outfitted, for use in holding open-air meetings, and distributing tracts. In theory, this brought the entire city of Chicago, even outlying communities, within reach. Lastly, a store "in the heart of the city [was] rented and fitted up as a mission hall."[13]

Another particular challenge was presented by the neighborhood that had grown up, seemingly overnight, around the fairgrounds. As one writer put it: "here, on the open prairie, hotels and other buildings had grown up like gourds, without any effort to keep corresponding pace in providing church accommodations." This Moody addressed by securing "the use of half a dozen tents, and tabernacles, and hotel parlors."[14]

———✺✺✺———

Amid these rapid-response initiatives, some of "the most notable meetings of the campaign" now began to take place, to judge from the crowds that came. Among the largest, most popular settings were Tattersall's Hall and Forepaugh's Circus tents.

Tattersall's Hall could seat up to fifteen thousand guests and was near Chicago stockyards. This huge arena had many times been the venue for major political conventions and Wild West shows. With an infectious flair, Moody sought to turn Tattersall's unique setting to good advantage. When he announced the start of meetings there, he said: "We've got something better than Buffalo Bill, and we must get a bigger audience than he does!"[15]

Forepaugh's Circus tent, set on Chicago's lakefront, represented an even more novel and larger venue. While the great circus tent was being prepared for a meeting, "a circus man chaffingly asked if Mr. Moody expected to get three thousand hearers."[16] However, it proved an inspired choice. For "crowds surged in until no more could gain admittance." Fifteen thousand people came for one morning service.[17] The circus manager's jaw dropped, but he was nothing if not quick on his feet. He soon took to advertising the Sunday slate of programs as follows:

HA! HA! HA!
THREE BIG SHOWS!
MOODY IN THE MORNING!
FOREPAUGH IN THE AFTERNOON AND EVENING!

One observer recorded what it was like to attend a service at Forepaugh's Circus. "The surroundings were the usual circus furniture—ropes, trapezes, gaudy decorations, etc., while in an adjoining canvas building was a large menagerie, including eleven elephants. Clowns, grooms, circus-riders, men, women, and children—eighteen thousand of them, and on a Sunday morning, too! Whether the gospel was ever before preached under such circumstances I know not, but it was wonderful to ear and eye alike."[18]

One Sunday in the circus tent, Moody preached from the text: "The Son of man is come to seek and to save that which was lost" (Luke 19:10). A writer present at the meeting wrote, "The Spirit of God was present. The hush of heaven was over the meeting. Tears rolled unheeded down the faces of those whose hearts were touched."

However, toward the close of Moody's sermon, "there was a slight disturbance, and a lost child was passed up to the platform." Moody held her up so that her parents could see her. A few moments more and her anxious father came to the platform.

Moody placed the child in his arms, then waited a moment before telling the crowd: "That is what Jesus Christ came to do: to seek and to save the lost, and restore them to their heavenly Father's embrace."[19] The immediate illustration "came home to many with great force."

Forepaugh's Circus represented just one type of meeting, among many others that were held throughout the 179 days of the World's Fair. In other venues, scattered in and around Chicago, specific groups were gathering—men's meetings, women's meetings, children's meetings; temperance meetings, soldiers' meetings, jail meetings; open-air and cottage meetings. Nor were these meetings confined to English-speaking people. There were "meetings for Germans, Poles, Bohemians, French, Jews, and Arabs in the Fair grounds," with preachers from overseas speaking in their native tongues.[20] Christians assembled in meetings for praise and prayer, some lasting all night.

Moody and his coworkers placed special emphasis on outreach to visitors who knew no English. If the world had suddenly become their parish, they felt they must serve their new parishioners. Consequently, many prominent European ministers and evangelists rallied to Moody's banner in Chicago. Dr. J. W. Pindor, of the Silesia province, came to preach to the Poles; Joseph Rabinowitz, of Russia, to the Jews; Theodore Monod, of Paris, to the French; and Dr. Adolf Stoecker, of Berlin, to the Germans.

In addition to these, other preachers, teachers, singers, and lay leaders came to Chicago, including John Paton of the New Hebrides, and Thomas Spurgeon and Henry Varley, both of Australia. Cordial cooperation from other prominent World's Fair visitors, like Count Bernstorff, from Berlin, and Lord Kinnaird, of London, was also secured during their stay in Chicago.[21]

—⟨◦/◦/◦⟩—

During the final weeks of the World's Fair, organizers rented the Central Music Hall for a daily, two-hour (from 11 a.m. to 1 p.m.) midday service. This fostered a palpable sense that the gospel mission was reaching a point of climax.

Moody urged Christians everywhere to pray and labor with unremitting diligence. "Friends, help fill up the churches," he said. "Let us see whether we can't wake up this whole city. There is now before us the grandest opportunity for extending the Kingdom of God that this country has ever seen. Hundreds of thousands of people will come in during these last weeks of the World's Fair. It is possible to reach them with the gospel message."[22]

Moody now sought to rent all the theatres he could get. The total daily expense of the gospel mission had run to $800; Moody now estimated he could spend $8,000 a day (or $200,000 a day in today's currency) if only sufficient funds could be obtained.[23]

In light of this need for increased funds, Moody sent out renewed requests through the many secretaries who ably assisted him. At the same time, Moody placed a renewed emphasis on "concerts of prayer," asking God to provide for the many new initiatives about to get under way.

At one point, the need for added funds was a cause of great concern. Receipts had been falling off, and one evening, the faculty of the Chicago Bible Institute were gathered with Moody at dinner. During the meal, the growing financial need was discussed, and the business manager was asked the amount that the gospel campaign was in arrears. "Seven thousand dollars," was the reply.

It was a somber admission, and no one knew where the necessary funds might come from. The after-dinner meeting continued, but it was soon interrupted by the arrival of a boy bearing a telegram. It was handed to Moody, who read it intently. A few moments later, "he cried with emotion: 'Deliverance has come!'" The telegram read: "Northfield conference sends greeting. Six thousand dollars in cash. More to follow."[24]

On this extraordinary news, the meeting was halted to offer "earnest prayers of thanksgiving." The time came for Moody to pray, but no one heard his voice. After a few moments, "the silence grew heavy." Then, all gathered there heard him begin to pray in a broken voice, "choked with sobs." Moody's future son-in-law, A. P. Fitt, was present. He later wrote of this watershed moment, saying: "none who heard it will ever forget it."[25]

This instance of timely provision became a powerful symbol of the prayerfulness that undergirded the entire World's Fair gospel campaign. As Fitt recalled: "During the entire campaign unusual stress was laid on prayer as an indispensable condition of success. Indeed, it was a campaign of prayer, as much as a campaign of preaching and song. Not only did the leaders in the campaign pray without ceasing, but they labored to bring the people into the same spirit. Prayer was a prominent exercise in the meetings. Special seasons of prayer were also observed."[26]

Moody knew how central prayer had been to everything. He spoke of it at the closing meeting of the gospel campaign. Even as he thanked all those who had worked so tirelessly with him—such a welcome task—he thought it deeply important, in a larger sense, to give credit where credit was truly due. "God has outdone all our expectation. He has gone away beyond our faith."[27]

According to statistics kept by the Chicago Bible Institute, 1,933,240 people attended events set in motion by Moody and his coworkers for the World's Fair Campaign.[28] Nearly two million people had heard the gospel.

One Chicago pastor, Dr. Frederick Campbell, spoke for many when he said that Moody had "once more proved himself to be a most remarkable instrument in the hands of Providence . . . If ordinary preachers had a little more of his audacity, with the faith and works which should accompany it, they would achieve greater things."[29]

In an interview, Moody himself expressed profound gratitude. "The principal result of our six months' work," he said, "is that millions have heard the simple gospel preached by some of the most gifted preachers in the world;

thousands have apparently been genuinely converted to Christ, and Christians all over this land have been brought to a deeper spiritual life."[30] Moody had kept the vow he made on board the *Spree,* and his prayer was one of renewed thanks that God had spared him. He had redeemed the time he'd been given—and would continue to do so during his remaining years.

THE PLACE OF CHARACTER

Shall we not meet as heretofore,
some summer morning?[1]

—Charles Lamb

The Reverend Charles Inglis, of London, knew Moody well. The two men shared thirty-two years of friendship.[2] Once, as he was concluding a visit with Moody and leaving the room, Moody asked a rather considerable favor.

Inglis agreed to help, then stopped and said: "How is it that I do things for you that I would not do for anybody else on earth?"

Moody flashed a smile, and said: "If you haven't found out, Inglis, I'm not going to tell you!"[3]

Inglis was also present when Moody met Prime Minister William Gladstone in London. "The place was so crowded," Inglis recalled, "that Mr. Gladstone had to sit on the stairs of the platform." Afterwards he came up to Mr. Moody.

"Mr. Moody," he said, "I wish I had your voice."

Moody was ready, and said: "*I wish I had your brains.* We would get on splendidly together."[4]

Inglis recalled those stories and others in 1918 while speaking to students at the Moody Bible Institute. He spoke of Moody's humility. "He was a very teachable man willing to learn lessons from anyone capable of teaching him." As proof, Inglis began to describe the debt Moody owed to Harry Moorhouse—"a man who was very small, and not very good-looking," Inglis said, "but one of the most marvelous men I ever knew in giving Bible readings."

Moorhouse could, Inglis said, speak inexhaustibly on a text like John 3:16, yet what had been his background? He had been "one the most expert pick-pockets of Manchester," Inglis said. "For months after he was saved, he never went out without wearing thick gloves—for he said it was a part of his nature to pick pockets."

Inglis marveled that someone who'd overcome such challenges in life could have helped Moody understand how to study the Bible. But grace put no one beyond the hope of redemption and rebuilding a life. Moorhouse was proof of that. He had "little education," Inglis concluded, and "never graduated from any seminary—yet it was he who, under the blessing of God, was made such a blessing to D. L. Moody."[5]

<hr />

During his mission tours of England, the last of which took place in the 1890s, Moody met some who were famous, and many times, people who were part of the British aristocracy.

Once, in London, some 23,000 people were present for a gospel gathering in the cavernous Agricultural Hall. At one point during the evening, Ira Sankey brought an English nobleman forward and introduced him to Moody.

As Inglis recalled the conversation, Sankey said, "Allow me to introduce you to Lord Camberdon" (here, for propriety's sake, Inglis had used a fictitious name for this British lord).

"Glad to see you, Lord Camberdon," Moody replied. "You couldn't have come at a better time. I've been watching two old ladies down there. They've been trying to get a seat, and haven't been able to. Here are two chairs. Will you carry them down for them?" The noble lord did as he was asked.[6]

On another occasion, Ira Sankey himself received a bit of ribbing from Moody. "We were having a campaign at Sheffield," Inglis remembered, "in York-shire, England." At the close of one afternoon's meeting, Inglis, Moody, Sankey, and other friends went back to their hotel for supper.

Everyone ordered what they wished, and Inglis recalled that "Sankey had a great weakness for beef steak and fried onions." Sankey placed his order, and in due course, the waiter brought back a rather fragrant dish. Inglis long remembered what happened next.

"Mr. Sankey had got some onions on a fork and was just putting them into his mouth, when Mr. Moody said:

'Sankey, do you expect to speak with inquiring souls tonight?'

'Why, yes,' Sankey replied.

'Then put down those onions!'"[7]

Moody was just as willing to indulge a joke at his own expense. The evangelist was anything but sanctimonious.

The gospel meetings were drawing tremendous crowds during one London campaign. "Think of a man preaching to sixty thousand people in one day!" Inglis exclaimed. "The crowds were so dense that the people would sit from the afternoon's meeting right through until the evening meeting, so as to secure a seat."

One great London meeting was held on November 4, which Inglis explained was "the day before Bonfire day"—England's day for firecrackers and celebrations.

Moody was unaware of this, and it soon got him into trouble. Aware that people were sitting through two meetings, without supper, he urged them:

"Now, then, if you want a seat tomorrow, bring along some crackers with you."

"Of course," Charles Inglis recalled, "Mr. Moody meant what we call biscuits."

But his audience didn't know that. They began to roar with laughter.

Moody was flummoxed and said, "What are they all laughing for?"

Inglis told him.

"Why, you've said to bring crackers tomorrow, and it's Fireworks Night. They'll blow the place up!"

Moody stepped quickly to the edge of platform and shouted as loudly as he could:

"Biscuits, biscuits! Not crackers, but biscuits!"[8]

But perhaps the finest story Inglis shared with his audience that day at the Bible institute spoke powerfully of Moody's humility.

One night, after a meeting toward the close of the Chicago World's Fair, all the preachers had left except Moody, Inglis, and one other man. The three decided to return to Moody's hotel room and talk. Their discussion centered on various meetings that had been held in different places that evening.

Moody asked the unnamed gentleman: "What kind of a meeting did you have, brother?"

"Oh," was the reply, "not a great service. I didn't feel I should trouble the people with concatenation remarks."

Concatenation—a word as incomprehensible now as it was then. Moody looked slightly confused.

At that point Inglis listened to one of the worst displays of rudeness he ever heard. The unnamed gentleman, seeing Moody's questioning look, said:

"Oh, I don't suppose *you* know the meaning of that word, do you?"

Inglis wanted to knock the man to the ground. Moody did something different.

"No," he said quietly, "I don't know the meaning of the word."

"Would you like me to tell you?" the man asked, compounding the offense.

"Yes," said Moody, again very quietly, "I am willing to learn from anybody."

The man defined the term as Moody listened. Meanwhile, Inglis marveled at Moody. "When told the meaning of the word, Dwight L. Moody was the greatest man in my vision. I have seen him preach to five and twenty thousand people and hold them spellbound. I have seen hundreds of people converted in a single meeting. But, D. L. Moody was never a greater man in my estimation than that night in that room."[9]

Those who came to know Moody well, as Inglis did, saw many instances of Moody's humility. True enough, he was often decisive and direct, sometimes off-putting when he was—but he also strove to listen and learn throughout his life—and he had a profound awareness of his shortcomings. With refreshing honesty, he freely admitted he was a work in progress, saying things like: "It's easier for me to have faith in the Bible than to have faith in D. L. Moody: for Moody has fooled me lots of times!"[10] On another occasion, he said: "Character is what a man is in the dark."[11] In short, Moody strove to cultivate character—to be consistent when people were watching and when they were not.

When *The Congregationalist and Christian World* magazine published a lengthy tribute to Moody fifteen years after his death, its editors called Moody "one of our greatest Americans."[12] They devoted fifty-six pages of the issue to Moody but deemed the tribute not sufficient "to contain all our special Moody material in both pictures and articles." So they planned to publish the overflow throughout several issues, starting from mid-November and closing on December 22, the date of Moody's passing.

Those fifty-six pages were filled with closely set type. *The Congregationalist* had published, in essence, a small book. A tribute of this size measured his influence, even as it showed that influence hadn't waned. Elements of Moody in his prime were scattered throughout.

The Congregationalist's editors aimed "to help the present generation" realize his "spiritual stature and the world-wide influence."[13] They wished "to reconstruct that vivid personality, to project it in bold, strong outlines," before readers "of today and tomorrow," while those who knew Moody well were still alive to share their recollections.

The editors stated that Moody's list of achievements was "a long and shining one." They summarized the founding of his schools in Northfield, Massachusetts, and the Bible institute in Chicago, as well as his successful gospel hymnbooks in partnership with Ira Sankey, and the founding of a publishing house, the Bible Institute Colportage Association.

"Something of a dynamic character," *The Congregationalist's* editors concluded, "came at a critical moment for this indifferent schoolboy . . . It transformed him, not all at once, but slowly and irresistibly. It made him the greatest lay worker in the Kingdom of God in the nineteenth century."[14]

Among Moody's greatest character traits were a passion for the gospel on the one hand, and a willingness to innovate and accept change on the other. In this respect, Moody's example was a welcome reproach to Christians who rested in comfortable conformity, according to *The Congregationalist*. "Mr. Moody's life showed in the clearest fashion that sense of mission." Moody's faith was the more compelling because it exhibited the "impression and enthusiasm of one who is sent."[15]

Moody's contemporary C. F. Goss once said that Moody "tormented the navigators in easy sailing."[16] There was something to this, and the editors for *The Congregationalist* detected it as well. "There was nothing conventional . . . about Mr. Moody or his work." Today, we have a phrase that captures what they meant: "thinking outside the box." "His mind was alive and alert to all passing opportunities, and quick to learn—even from those with whom he disagreed," *The Congregationalist* editors concluded. The result was "creative work in education and evangelization," and something else all too rare: "a genius for inspiring others."

"The real significance of Mr. Moody's life and character" the magazine's editors argued, was that they might prod "the church and the individual to rise to a sense of mission." Then came three pointed questions:

> "Have *we* any message for the world?" they said. "What are *we* doing with the machinery and the prestige of Christ's Church, and with the money raised by His people?" Last of all, they asked: "If *we* have a message, why are we not more in earnest in pressing it upon the attention of a needy world with something of the same tact and affection and sturdy faith in Christ?"[17]

⚬⚬⚬

No one knew about Moody's commitment better than son-in-law, A. P. Fitt, the Irish-born husband of his daughter, Emma. Fitt drew attention to Moody's deep sense of consecration, writing of "his devotion to God, in the simple, full, evangelical sense. . . . He had one supreme aim in life—to please God, more especially in the salvation of others through faith in Lord Jesus. All his plans in educational and other lines were tributary to that aim. All the elements of his character were conditioned by this devotion."[18]

Nor had Moody's profound sense of gratitude over his conversion ever lessened. As Fitt expressed it, Moody "never lost his first love. I was in Boston with him in 1897, and he showed me where he had been led to accept Christ as his Savior over forty years before. That vital experience continued as a fresh, animating force in his life to the end."

Fitt saw Moody's frailties but also his sincerity. Many sons-in-law have had occasion to see flaws in their father-in-law's character. Moody could sometimes be brusque, short-tempered, or peremptory. Many men charged with great responsibility are, when pressures mount. But when Moody was, he was also quick to seek forgiveness. These were all-too-human frailties.

But beyond such things, Fitt could say he found it a blessing that he could not recall "one shady act or word during those years that I served and knew Mr. Moody intimately." Fitt had left his homeland and crossed an ocean to join the Moody family. When he looked back on that choice, he knew it had been well made. His father-in-law was a man of tried integrity.

Ultimately, it was in the home, and in his family relationships, that Fitt judged "Mr. Moody was best and greatest." For though few beyond the hills of Northfield knew it, "family joys and sorrows were mingled" during Moody's last years. As Fitt wrote: "four grandchildren were born, of whom two died. Mr. Moody's aged mother also died. The public does not know the tenderness and simplicity of that great heart, but this is the side of him that remains undimmed with me."[19]

Moody also was a lifelong learner. Indeed, his few years of formal education seemed only to feed his appetite for knowledge.

"Mr. Moody was not popularly known during his lifetime as an educator, nor as an educated man. He really was both," wrote Henry Franklin Cutler. Dr. Cutler, the principal of the Mount Hermon School, held a degree from Amherst College. "The great schools which [Moody] founded entitled him to a place among educators, and his skill in the selection of courses and of teachers proved his right there."

In his essay, "Mr. Moody's Appreciation of Education," Dr. Cutler wrote that Moody's wisdom and learning were hard won. "Soon after his conversion," Cutler stated, "he came more and more into the companionship of educated men, and this seemed always to spur him on to get information for himself."

So he set himself a task. "In those years," Cutler wrote, "he formed the habit of rising early in the morning to read and study, and this custom he kept up to the very end of his life." In addition to this, Cutler stated that for many years, Moody engaged "several persons to read for him. These readers made outlines of books and marked passages which he ought to see and read. In this way Mr. Moody became a widely read man."[20]

Moody also sought the acquaintance of learned friends and mined their collective wisdom. "His contact," Cutler said, "with students and professors in the universities of Great Britain and in the colleges of this country made him alert to acquaint himself" with their learning and challenges. Moody's great desire was "to get at facts" in terms of essentials. As a case in point, when Cutler assumed his duties at Mount Hermon, Moody often stressed how important it was "to teach the Hermon boys to spell and write. Sham and slipshod work he despised, and could tolerate neither in himself nor in others."

In Cutler's view, all these things combined to make Moody "in the best sense of the word, the educated man that he was. He was never at a loss in the discussion of any topic theological or philosophical, and he was well informed along scientific lines."

For Cutler, Moody's sterling commitment to higher education was "shown by the number of boys and girls he sent to college, and by his desire to emphasize the courses in his own schools leading to university work. For him, an educated man meant a great new added power in the world, and if to this greatness he could add goodness, his ideal man was complete. He used to say, 'There are great men in the world; there are good men in the world; but there are few who are both great and good.'"

Last of all, though Moody was often incredibly busy, he did all he could to get to know the young men and women who attended Northfield and Mount Hermon. Cutler wrote: "In those earlier years, while he was with us, he seemed to know everyone. He was interested in their homes, in themselves and in their futures. He wanted to help everyone who came here, and he wanted everyone to go out from here to help others."[21]

If Henry Cutler described Moody's attainments as a self-educated man and an educational pioneer in his own right, Sir J. Kynaston Studd, president of the Polytechnic Institute in London, England (the forerunner school of the University of Westminster), knew about Moody's influence in two of England's finest universities, Oxford and Cambridge.

Studd, who was later Lord Mayor of London, said of Moody, "There has been no man in my life whose friendship I have more valued, or whose influence has helped me more."[22]

Studd met Moody at Cambridge in 1883. "It was at the early morning meeting in the Corn Exchange," he remembered. "This meeting was open to all the town, but Mr. Moody's visit was to the undergraduates of the university, of whom I was one. My heart sank when I heard him, for his way of speech was not our way of speech, his accent was not our accent, and I feared what undergraduates, full of spirits and ready to make fun of anything, would do."

One Sunday night, over one thousand undergraduates were present to hear Moody. A majority were there to listen—but "a considerable minority to make fun. They applauded Mr. Sankey's most solemn solos, they made fun of Mr. Moody's words." In such circumstances, the meeting, said Studd, "could not be regarded as a success."[23]

The following Monday and Tuesday nights, "some 200 turned up and remained quiet but unmoved—no impression seemed possible." On Wednesday, Moody called the mothers of the town together "to pray for the boys." That evening some 300 undergraduates were present. At the close of Moody's address, an invitation was given "to any who were interested to go into the gallery," which was to be the "Inquiry-Room."

There was no response till the third or fourth appeal. Then one man went slowly up the stairs in the sight of everyone. He was soon followed by fifteen or twenty more. The tide had turned.

On Sunday night, Moody discovered that some 1,700 undergraduates had come to hear him. After the meeting, fully 400 undergraduates went into the inquiry room. "The result of the mission was remarkable," Studd remembered. "Men who were then converted are now occupying foremost positions in Christian work."

At Oxford, however, the opposition to Moody's meetings took a different form. "The first evening," Studd recalled, "some undergraduates holding prominent places in the university occupied the front seats and made fun of all that was said."

At the close of the service, Moody went to them directly and said: "Gentlemen, I think you owe me an apology. This was a free meeting, you came in of your own accord, and the least that you could have done would have been to keep quiet or leave."

Remarkably, the young men were chastened. As Studd described it, "The men saw the fairness of Mr. Moody's remarks, and apologized." Moody then said it was not sufficient to apologize, because "they had done wrong publicly." They ought, in consequence, to come again another night, occupy the same position, and "show by their good behavior that they were sorry." Further chastened, the young men consented. In fact, such plain dealing completely turned the tables and won them over. Perhaps guilt was the reason, but on the spot, they invited Moody to have lunch with them.

Studd's purpose in telling these stories was "to show Mr. Moody's great power. He not only overcame a very real prejudice, but inspired an equally deep respect and admiration." With only a modest education himself, Moody respected learning in others. He had engaged the collegians with respect but also with logic.

As for Studd's respect personally for Moody, he much admired Moody's "ability to make God and religion natural to everyday life and circumstances —to strip everything of cant and conventional terms." Studd saw Moody as a man of "practical common sense," a trait "counterbalanced by a very warm heart and deep sympathy," that often gained him the victory when argument failed.[24]

One day at Stratford he was invited to tea by the acknowledged head of the atheists. The conversation turned to a future life, the host repudiating any belief in or desire for a future life. His wife and children were having tea together with them. Mr. Moody asked, "Supposing one of these children were to die, would you not wish to meet them again?" The host, true to his opinions rather than his heart, replied, "No"; and Mr. Moody answered, "I don't think I should like to sit here as one of these little ones, and to think that it would not matter if I died, and that I should be forgotten." The argument was ended.

Moody had a large heart, Studd concluded, and few, if any, who ever really knew him, failed to love and admire him.

⸺◦/◦/◦⸺

Nobel Laureate John R. Mott owed a great debt to Moody, but before exploring the nature of that debt, it should be said that Mott owed a great debt to Sir J. Kynaston Studd as well. As Mott's biography for Nobelprize.org states, when a student at Cornell, Mott thought his life's work was "a choice between law and his father's lumber business, but he changed his mind upon hearing a lecture by Studd. Three sentences in Studd's speech, he said, prompted his lifelong service of presenting Christ to students: 'Seekest thou great things for thyself? Seek them not. Seek ye first the Kingdom of God.'"[25]

As for his debt to Moody, Mott's article "Moody's Power with College Men" did much to repay it. "My knowledge of Moody," Mott began, "was confined largely to observing at first hand his work among the college men of North America and to studying the results of his activities among the students of Great Britain." Based on his studies, rooted in "the testimony of undergraduates and graduates," Mott determined that Moody "exerted a greater influence upon them than did any other Christian worker of his day—with the single exception of that exercised by Henry Drummond among students in Edinburgh."[26]

What accounted for this? Mott had given the matter much thought and concluded that much of Moody's appeal lay in Moody being "a truly great preacher." For those inclined to be skeptical, Mott pointed to a stubborn fact: "If we may judge by results," he stated, there was "no greater preacher in the closing decades of the nineteenth century." Mott went further, insisting: "the combined judgment of . . . students of both sides of the Atlantic for a generation may be trusted to place a preacher of righteousness where he belongs."

Mott thought next of elite universities of Britain and America, writing, "It is a significant fact that the men of Oxford and Cambridge, of Yale and Princeton and of that 'college of colleges'—the Northfield Student Conference—assigned Moody a central position among the preachers of their day." And Mott had vivid memories of the sermons that seemed to resonate most powerfully among the students he'd observed. "The sermons," he wrote, "which most mightily moved students were the one on 'Sowing and Reaping,' the one on Daniel (he always pronounced the word Dan'l) and the one in which he described how he came to devote his life to Christian service." Mott had felt their power himself, saying: "I have heard him deliver each of these sermons possibly ten times or more, and invariably a profound impression was made."[27]

Here Mott paused to offer a classic Moodyism. Mr. Moody, he remembered, used to say that "a sermon did not amount to much that would not stand repeating fifty times."

This *bon mot* aside, Mott hastened to say that "the note of reality in Moody's preaching appealed strongly to college men." They were impressed by his "downright honesty and transparent sincerity." He was "absolutely devoid of sham and affectation." He never played to the house, as many speakers did. Mott judged him to be "tremendously frank and direct. He was wholly unconventional, and never flattered, or paid compliments. He was bold as a lion in exposing hypocrisy, and in attacking individual and social sins. The students saw that he practiced what he preached, and accepted him."[28]

For a host of college men, Mott said, Moody "brought religion out of the clouds, and made it a present-day and every-day personal and practical relationship and experience." No collegian "who ever heard his incisive comments on the Ten Commandments, and his pointed applications to modern life, will ever forget them. They cut like a mighty plowshare through the sins of college life and of society."

Mott then described what he called Moody's "wonderful heart power," something that "went far to explain the wide range of his influence." What was this power? As Mott understood it, Moody "won men by his kindness, as well as persuaded them by the truth."

Mott spotted two character qualities that influenced the college listeners. In addition to the evangelist's kindness, there was again his humility. "His enormous influence with college men," Mott said, "cannot be explained apart from his unaffected humility. The great teacher must ever remain a disciple. Nothing was more impressive at the student conferences than to see Moody, after introducing a speaker, go down from the platform and take a seat at his feet," jotting down notes of what was being said.[29]

As Mott saw it, Moody's "openness to new ideas, and responsiveness to new plans" did much "to give him such a strong hold on growing, studying, ambitious young men." But there was something else too: a "willingness to receive criticism and to confess faults." That revealed "genuine greatness of soul."

Mott understood that this side of Moody's Christian character was something wrought arduously in the school of surrender. Moody, as he and anyone who knew him well understood, "was one of the most masterful of men, and one of the strongest personalities of his generation," yet he was nonetheless "modest and self-effacing to a marked degree." The last sentence of Mott's long article was in many ways the best. "Wherever," he said, "Moody spoke or worked or lived—Christ loomed large."[30]

Harvard philosopher William James, like so many observers in this chapter, found Moody's story one worth knowing—so much so that he purchased a set of the two-volume *Shorter Life of D. L. Moody*.[31] And Moody's name appears in the pages of James's classic text, *The Varieties of Religious Experience*, published in 1902.

Though James's writing was learned and often profound, it could at times be something of a tangled skein. The words James wrote about Moody were intended as a compliment—still, they need a bit of unraveling:

> If an Emerson were forced to be a Wesley or a Moody forced to be a Whitman, the total human consciousness of the divine would suffer. The divine can mean no single quality, it must mean a group of qualities, by being champions of which in alternation, different men may all find worthy missions.[32]

James was arguing here for the importance of individual people as they seek to make meaning of life. History, he was saying, should be grateful for Emerson because he was Emerson and not wish to him to be as John Wesley was.

By the same token, Moody, as an individual, was an ornament to his faith and beliefs. We do wrong to wish he was another Walt Whitman or to wish Whitman was another Moody. Each of these four men, James believed, had a unique mission—disparate missions, for which posterity can be grateful.

That James placed Moody among this foursome underscores Moody's stature as a faith-leader of the late 1800s. In one sense, two sentences in a long book like *The Varieties of Religious Experience* may not seem like much. But it would be wrong to think this. What James wrote about Moody, in tandem with his contemporaries, says a great deal.

18

THE BANNER OF HEAVEN

In an age of great preachers, Moody was perhaps the
tallest and most mighty among them . . . He toured the
U.S. and England, giving his solution to the gigantic
crossword puzzle of the universe.[1]

—*Time* magazine (1928)

If Moody had far-reaching influence and fine family relations, he also had an eloquence uniquely his own. As one might suspect, his sermons were the setting where that eloquence was most often on display.

Commonly recurring traits made Moody's sermons distinctive. The first lay in his gift for casting an arresting phrase—often just a line, not much longer—of great pith, imagery, or insight. To read the best of them is to see that Moody's remarkable program of self-education, described one chapter earlier by Dr. Henry Cutler, had borne fruit.

For example: many a philosopher would be proud to own these lines from Moody: "Truth never grows old; truth is as young today as it has ever been. Talk of the old truths wearing out! Don't you enjoy the rays of the same sun which has been shining these thousands of years?"[2]

In a similar vein, Moody sounded much like C. S. Lewis when he stated: "A usurper has got this world now; but Christ will have it soon. The time of your redemption draweth nigh, when He returns to set up his kingdom, and reign upon the earth. He will rend the heavens, and his voice will be heard again. He shall descend from heaven with a shout. He will sway his scepter from the river to the ends of the earth. The thorn and the brier shall be swept away, and the wilderness shall rejoice. Let us rejoice; we shall see better days."[3]

Victorians who cherished mere Christianity had a friend in Moody when he said: "Catholics have the same Savior as the Protestants—one Shepherd, one Christ."[4] Moody had felt this way for many years, saying on another occasion that Christianity "is not belief in a creed only. A man may have a creed, and no Christ." He continued:

> A creed is all right in its place, but if you live on creeds, you will never get a living Christ. Suppose a friend should ask me to dine with him. To reach his house, I must go in the street leading to his home; but if I do not go into his house, I do not get my dinner. Now a creed is the road or street; very good as far as it goes, but if it does not take us to Christ, it is worthless. God does not ask you to believe a creed, but a person, and that person is Jesus Christ.[5]

It says much that over the course of his ministry, Moody sought and won the friendship and respect of many Catholics. This was the more noteworthy, in that the nineteenth century was a time when the divide between Protestants and Catholics was often a yawning chasm.

Moody was always a bridge-builder, as the writers of the *Catholic World* noted in a moving posthumous tribute to Moody, published in July 1900. "Many Catholics," they wrote, "who knew and loved Mr. Moody may perhaps have wondered why so religious a man was never attracted to the Catholic faith. The answer is doubtless to be discovered in many of his published sermons, where he avowed such strong repugnance to all bonds of faith made by creed or dogma. He believed that a simple promise to be loyal to Christ was all-sufficient."[6]

At the same time, those who cherished mere Christianity knew Moody was a kindred spirit when he famously quoted these lines from Abbé Mullois, chaplain to Napoleon the Third: "The end of preaching is to reclaim the hearts of men to God. Nothing but love can find out the mysterious avenues which lead to the heart. . . . If then, you do not feel a fervent love and profound pity for humanity, be assured that the gift of Christian eloquence has been denied you."[7]

Moody's own gift of Christian eloquence was displayed when he said:

Perhaps nothing but the shortness of our range of sight keeps us from seeing the celestial gates all open to us, and nothing but the deafness of our ears prevents our hearing the joyful ringing of the bells of heaven. There are constant sounds around us that we cannot hear, and the sky is studded with bright worlds that our eyes have never seen. Little as we know about this bright and radiant land, there are glimpses of its beauty that come to us now and then.[8]

Over time, the breadth of Moody's reading shaped his sermon craft. He beautifully invoked St. Augustine when he spoke of humility. "Someone," he said, "asked Augustine what was the first of the religious graces, and he said, 'Humility.' They asked him what was the second, and he replied, 'Humility.' They asked him the third, and he said, 'Humility.' I think that if we are humble, we have all the graces."

"The showers fall upon the mountain peaks," Moody continued, "and very often leave them barren because they rush down into the meadows and valleys, and make the lowly places fertile. If a man is proud and lifted up, rivers of grace may flow over him, and yet leave him barren and unfruitful, while they bring blessing to the man who has been brought low by the grace of God."[9]

Has anyone, since Moody's time, offered a more graceful definition of the word *revival*? As he phrased it, this word "simply means a recalling from obscurity—a finding some hidden treasure, and bringing it back to the light."[10] And Moody once movingly challenged false notions of obscurity when he said: "Small numbers make no difference to God. There is nothing small that God is in."[11]

Seldom has the hope of heaven found a more telling expression than in these lines from Moody: "The world is in darkness, and the gospel offers light. Because man will not believe, the world is dark today. But the moment a man believes, the light from Calvary crosses his path, and he walks in an unclouded sun."[12]

And what of our obligations to foster a better world through helping the less fortunate? "If we are going to help the poor widow and those fatherless children, we must do it now," Moody said. "God has sent us to make the world brighter and better, and to help those that carry burdens."[13] These words might well have been the credo for the Northfield and Mount Hermon schools. Moody had been poor, and he had been fatherless. Many of the first students given a place in his schools were no different. His schools were a sterling affirmation that he never forgot where he came from. They were one of the best things about his Christian witness.

———⟨ᴏ/ᴏ/ᴏ⟩———

Aside from this, Moody's disdain for sham and hypocrisy was often voiced, as when he said: "Where one man reads the Bible, a hundred read you and me. That is what Paul meant when he said we were to be living epistles of Christ, known and read of all men.[14] I would not give much for all that can be done by sermons, if we do not preach Christ by our lives."[15] On another occasion, Moody insisted: "There are too many religious meetings which are sadder than a funeral. They are hindrance to the cause. They breed people with faces bearing an expression as chilling as an east blast from the lake."[16]

Caustic saints also set Moody's teeth on edge. The thought of them prompted lines like: "The man that hasn't any love in his religion, I don't want it. The man that hasn't any love in his creed may let it go to the winds; I don't want it. 'By this shall all men know that ye are my disciples, that you have love one toward another.' That is the fruit of the Spirit."[17] This passage had a counterpart when Moody said: "Don't go to church just to criticize. Anyone can do that. If you feel inclined to criticize, just stop and ask yourself whether you could do it any better. Some make only one mistake: that of finding imperfections in everybody and every thing."[18]

Nor did Moody have much patience with what one of his more learned friends would have called the *odium theologicum.* "I make a point," Moody said, "of not discussing disputed passages of Scripture. An old divine has said that 'some people, if they want to eat fish, commence by picking the bones.'"[19]

Moody was often one to look to wisdom from faith traditions beyond his own. When he found a pearl of wisdom, he was the first to share it, as when he said: "I want to give you a motto that has been a great help to me. It was a Quaker's motto: 'I expect to pass through this world but once. If, therefore, there be any kindness I can show, or any good thing I can do to any fellow human being, let me do it now; let me not defer nor neglect it, for I will not pass this way again.'"[20]

And the best of Moody's preaching showed how deeply he had taken Harry Moorhouse's sermons on the love of God to heart. "Love," Moody said, "is the greatest of God's gifts, and of all the Christian virtues. I don't think we shall require faith when we get to heaven. Before the throne of God, we shall walk by sight, and not by faith. Nor shall we need hope there, as we shall have attained to the full measure of possession. Faith and hope will be past, but love will still reign."[21]

Aside from his gift for framing an arresting phrase, or lines that were, by turns, moving or insightful, Moody's sermons showed him to be a master of what could be called "the pocket parable."

To foster a sense of fellowship and shared purpose, for example, Moody told a story from the days of America's pioneer past. "Away out in the prairie regions," he once said,

> when meetings are held at night in the log schoolhouses, the announcement of the meeting is given out in this way:
>
> "A meeting will be held by early candle-light."
>
> The first man who comes brings a tallow-dip with him. It is perhaps all he has; but he brings it, and sets it on the desk. It does not light the building much; but it is better than nothing at all. The next man brings his candle; and the next family bring theirs. By the time the house is full, there is plenty of light. So if we all shine a little, there will be a good deal of light. That is what God wants us to do. If we cannot all be lighthouses, any one of us can at any rate be a tallow candle.[22]

Another pocket parable appeared in the pages of a book published just after Moody's death. Its title was his one-sentence summary of the gospel: *The*

Way Home. In its pages, Moody offered a concise, memorable rendering of the parable of the Good Samaritan.

"At last," Moody said, "a Samaritan came down that way, and he looked down on a man beaten by thieves, and had compassion. He got off his donkey, and took oil and poured it into the man's wounds, and bound them up. He took him out of the ditch, helpless as he was, placed him on his donkey, and brought him to an inn, and took care of him.

"That good Samaritan," Moody concluded, "represents your Christ and mine. He came into the world to seek and to save that which was lost."[23]

Still another pocket parable may have been one Moody thought of often in connection with the Northfield and Mount Hermon schools. He'd heard the story from his friend Dr. John Hall and told it often. "My friend," Moody said,

> once told of a boy who'd been sent by his mother off to school. When the time came to graduate, he wrote home saying he wanted his widowed mother to be there on graduation day. She wrote that she couldn't come. She hadn't a new dress, and had turned the skirt of her old one once, and couldn't turn it again. The boy said he could not graduate without her; she had to come. He persuaded her to come.
>
> She wasn't dressed very well.
>
> When the people assembled, it was discovered that the best seat in the hall was reserved for somebody. Soon that young man came proudly down the aisle with his mother leaning on his arm. He escorted her to that seat. She didn't know that he'd carried everything before him, and he was Valedictorian of his class. When he won the prize and the medal set around his neck, he walked down and put it on his mother. He kissed her, and said: *"I should never have had it, but for you."*[24]

Moody knew what it was to owe his mother a debt beyond price. He captured that once, in one sentence. "There was nothing," he said, "in President Garfield's life that touched me so much as when, the moment after his inauguration, he turned and kissed his aged mother."[25]

One favorite pocket parable centers on "the glorious hope" Moody looked to in heaven. He likened it to a city, saying: "There is one city in the universe of God without a cemetery; one city without a hearse; one city where there is no night, no sorrow, no weeping; one city where Death never enters, where there is no separation, where there are no gray hairs and bending forms. There perpetual youth is stamped upon every brow; there they live on and on forever, a life as pure as God's life, and as lasting as God's life. It is in the reach of everyone."[26]

⸻ ⚬⚬⚬ ⸻

Last of all, one of Moody's pocket parables was in reality a true story, and it captured the imagination of a Pulitzer Prize winning poet. In 1938, Robert P. Tristram Coffin wrote a review of *My Father: An Intimate Portrait of Dwight Moody*, a memoir published by Paul Moody in 1938. Coffin was a former Rhodes Scholar at Oxford, and at this time, professor of literature at Bowdoin College.

Moody's name, Coffin wrote, "was on a book that spelt holiness and rest and music to me," a reference to Moody and Sankey's bestselling songbook, *The Gospel Hymns*. For Coffin, Moody was "the preacher who cracked open the skies for thousands and let the unearthly light come through."[27] A highlight of this new book about Moody was a story that showed Moody's flair for the unconventional. "Dwight Moody's fondness for speed," Coffin wrote,

> showed in his prayers. He made them short. He won his greatest convert by stopping a long-winded prayer. It was in London. "While our brother is finishing his prayer," he rose and said, "let us sing hymn number so and so."
>
> So an indifferent young Englishman turned his face west, found him an icy empire to heal bodies and minds in, won a knighthood the best possible way, and wrote his name forever on Labrador. It was Sir Wilfred Grenfell [the great medical missionary and benefactor].[28]

Humor was an arrow in Moody's quiver. When the occasion called for it, as in this instance, he quickly notched it to his bow. Sir Wilfred Grenfell, and thousands throughout Canada, could be grateful he did.

⋰◦/◦/◦⋱

What fostered Moody's sermon eloquence? Apart from his oft-demon-strated ability to turn a memorable phrase, or his gifts as a storyteller, he constantly furnished his mind with fine thoughts. Things of eternal moment kindled within him, and he sought them wherever he could find them. This facet of his character shone in the pages of *The Shorter Life of D. L. Moody*, written by his second son, Paul Moody, and his son-in-law, A. P. Fitt. As they remembered, Moody

> used to say "it would be worth going a thousand miles, to get a good thought." With what keenness he listened to other preachers for good thoughts and illustrations, and how his face lit up with a smile as he took out the notebook he kept in his hip pocket for nuggets! He urged this habit of making notes of all the good things one read and heard . . .
>
> He was an untiring Bible student. He usually arose about day-break in summer, in order to have two or three hours alone with his Bible and his God, while his mind was fresh, and before the activities of the day divided his attention. The walls of his library [were filled] from floor to ceiling with bookshelves.[29]

A story from Moody's friend William Daniels put the capstone to this side of his character. "If," said Daniels, "Moody met anyone from whom it seemed probable he might obtain an idea for use in his pulpit, he would salute him with: 'Give me something out of your heart. Tell me something about Christ.' At table in [Chicago's] Farwell Hall restaurant, where he and his *confrères* dined together, he would ask one and another around the table, 'What has been your best thought today?'"[30]

⋰◦/◦/◦⋱

Books were Moody's university. C. H. Spurgeon, one of the finest preachers of the nineteenth century, once presented Moody with a set of his collected works. He read them all, cover to cover.[31]

Marshall Hazard, a prominent banker, had known Moody during his youth in Chicago. As he vividly remembered, "The contrast between Mr. Moody as he now is—and Mr. Moody as I first knew him is simply amazing. Those who have known him from his earliest beginnings, find it next to impossible to realize the change that has taken place in him. Those whose acquaintance with him is but recent can hardly conceive of the difficulties . . . through which he has struggled up to the present."[32]

Given Moody's constant reading, it's worth asking the question: What writers had a place in his library? The answer is close at hand. Turn the pages of his book *One Thousand and One Thoughts from My Library*, published in 1898, and many fine selections from the authors he read are there, set in a gallery of learning. Lines from the poem "The Mission of a Good Book" set the tone by way of a preface. What are the hallmarks of a good book? In this poem we learn—

> *It will go anywhere, sea or land,*
> *Gets into cabin or palace,*
> *Reaches those otherwise unreachable,*
> *Waits its time to be heard,*
> *Is never tired of speaking.*[33]

Moody cited 225 authors in *One Thousand and One Thoughts*, covering nearly all the centuries from the advent of Christianity to 1898.

Of ancient writers, Moody owned books that held the wisdom of Anselm, Augustine, Seneca, and Tertullian. Christian mystics were represented in the writings of Madame Guyon, Madame Swetchine, and Thomas à Kempis.

Catholic writers were also on his shelves. Apart from those already cited, Moody's book held selections from Francis de Sales and Nicolas Caussin. The Anglican/Episcopalian tradition was well represented in passages from Richard Baxter, Phillips Brooks, Richard Cecil, John Newton, Jeremy Taylor, and H. W. Webb-Peploe, prebendary of St Paul's Cathedral, London. Puritan writers had a place as well, among them Thomas Brooks and John Flavel.

One Thousand and One Thoughts often cited women writers. Two have already been mentioned, Madame Guyon and Madame Swetchine, but selections also included Geraldine Guinness, Frances Ridley Havergal, Leila Mott, Elizabeth Prentiss, and Hannah Whitall Smith. Many dissenters as well, from across the denominational landscape, were in Moody's book, including John Bunyan, Thomas Chalmers, Timothy Dwight, A. J. Gordon, Matthew Henry, Blaise Pascal, and Charles Spurgeon.

One key theme sets *One Thousand and One Thoughts* apart. Although it's a fine anthology in its own right, it also stands testament to the emphasis on mere Christianity that pervaded Moody's life and career. To remember this is to remember one of the best things about Moody during the heyday of his life and ministry.

19

YALE AND THE COMING OF SUMMER

Let never day nor night unhallow'd pass
But still remember what the Lord hath done.[1]

—*Henry VI*, William Shakespeare

As 1898 began, Moody turned sixty-one. It was said that he "rode the crest of the wave in campaigns, institutions [and] home."[2] Just days after his February 5 birthday, a series of meetings began that would confirm his place among the great preachers of the nineteenth century.

The capstone, reported *The New York Times* on Valentine's Day, February 14, was a "monster meeting in the Hyperion Theatre" of New Haven, Connecticut, "where 2,000 people were turned away for lack of room."[3] It was one of several visits Moody made in the 1890s to speak before large gatherings of students from Yale.

That monster meeting occurred on Sunday evening, February 13, and there had been a morning meeting as well. "In all the services," the *Times* reported, "unprecedented interest was taken by the students." The Young Men's Christian Association had sponsored the evening gathering, which "was so largely attended that the students not only crowded the big hall to suffocation almost, but filled the stairways as well," reported the *Times*, "and at the close, a delegation from each class requested . . . Mr. Moody to remain several days, or if that [was] impossible, to return to Yale again in the near future."[4]

After the evening meeting, Moody granted an interview. In it, he offered a stalwart defense of Yale, based in large part on the very positive experiences that both his sons, first Will, then Paul, had known there. "I have been pretty well acquainted with Yale for twenty years," he said, "and I have never seen the university in as good condition, religiously, as now. My oldest son graduated here, and if my other son, who is now in the freshman class, gets as much good out of Yale as his brother did, I shall have reason to thank God through time and eternity."[5]

Clearly this visit, above others he'd known, meant a great deal. "I can honestly say," he told the *Times* reporter, "I have never spent so good a day at Yale as today has been, and I never saw so earnest and inquiring a crowd of young men as that which attended service this evening."[6]

At Senior Glen in Northfield Moody met with senior students at 6 a.m. on most mornings. During the summer Northfield conferences, he also met with college students informally in this glen.

The meetings Moody held at Yale, and the reception they received, were part of his special relationship to that university—a relationship stamped with mutual respect.

In 1901, the distinguished New York publishing house G. P. Putnam's Sons published a collection of essays called *Two Centuries of Christian Activity at Yale*. One entire chapter was devoted to "Yale and the Northfield Student

Conferences," and Moody's lasting influence was several times cited elsewhere. "Within the last decade and a half," wrote H. B. Wright, "the desire of Yale men to see and know more of what is going on in the religious world . . . has found expression in an annual pilgrimage of sometimes as many as a hundred or more Yale students for a ten days' conference with students of other colleges, at Northfield, Massachusetts."[7]

Northfield was a hallowed place for Wright, class of Yale, 1898. He had a keen eye for detail, and his memories of the summer conferences were fresh for their having taken place just a few years before he put pen to paper. For him, they were living memories.

"As we near the ground," he wrote, "every spot has some bit of interest to the newcomer, or awakens fond memories in the veteran of past conferences. Round Top and Senior Glen recall those informal hours in the early morning, or on a Sunday afternoon, when [Mr. Moody], seated in his big armchair beneath the trees, answered informally the numberless questions of life and practice raised by the eager inquirers who sat at his feet."[8]

To hear Wright tell it, Moody was like Samuel Johnson in more than his ample girth. Yale students, and many others, were like James Boswell in Moody's presence: grateful to catch gems of wisdom and counsel.

The gatherings with Moody were not solely reverent spiritual moments. Often a story was spun with pith and humor, for they knew Moody to be a gifted raconteur—one part Mark Twain, the other C. H. Spurgeon.

That Moody and Spurgeon were kindred spirits was no mere conjecture. Charles Inglis, one of Moody's British friends, had firsthand knowledge of the close friendship Moody and Spurgeon shared. Both had an irrepressible sense of humor, as Inglis fondly recalled. "Now on a Saturday," Inglis wrote, "no man on earth would have gone in to see Charles H. Spurgeon. I know a man who attempted to get in. He said to the secretary, 'Don't tell him my name. Tell him I am the king's son. I would like to see him.' And Spurgeon sent this message back: 'Tell him I am waiting on the King [that is, preparing a Sunday sermon] and I cannot see anybody.'"[9]

Charles H. Spurgeon, a great friend and early role model for D. L. Moody

D. L. Moody (circa 1890)

D. L. Moody (circa 1895)

But Moody was proof against such an interdict. Inglis understood why. "There was no man in London that loved Dwight L. Moody more than Charles Haddon Spurgeon," Inglis said. "On one occasion Moody was leaving London, and he had not seen Mr. Spurgeon. He wrote to him and said, 'I know that you never see any one on Saturday; it is your day for preparation. It is the only day I have to visit. A friend and myself would like to see you, but I presume you cannot break your rule.' He got back a postal the next day with these words on it: 'Come, sinners, come. C. H. Spurgeon.'"[10]

—————

The Northfield conferences featured well-known speakers, typically recruited by Moody himself.

H. B. Wright had come to know Stone Hall well—"made memorable," he wrote—"by the first of the great addresses of Henry Drummond upon *The Greatest Thing in the World*, which awoke the college world of America in 1887." That handsome venue stood "near the centre of the ground, while behind [it] rise those quiet Northfield hills with their undisturbed retreats, in which many a man has wrestled out alone his life problems."[11]

Seen in this light, Northfield was both a place of retreat, of solitary reflection, and a place for fellowship. Both were part of forming Christian character, and Wright learned of them firsthand during the times he walked those hills of the Pioneer Valley.

What was it like to glimpse Northfield from a coach or carriage as it drew near? Wright's memories of that were vivid. "As we enter the seminary grounds, just after supper, the buildings rise all about, bright with college flags and college colors, while far above and crowning all, from the top of the great auditorium, floats the Stars and Stripes."[12]

—————

Recreation was a centerpiece of the Northfield conferences, and the steps of East Hall were a gathering place. There one might find "a group of Yale men are instructing their Harvard and Princeton friends in the intricacies of the fascinating game of 'peel.'"

Those caught up in the game might occasionally catch a sound other than cheers from competing sides. "From Marquand down in the valley," Wright remembered, "a college song is borne up faintly on the evening breeze, and when it dies away, a sharp and stirring college cheer from another direction answers the arrival of some belated delegate to the conference." Friendly rivalry, horseplay, and welcome reunions from past summers—all were part of the benison Northfield gave.[13]

—✦✦✦—

The summons to Round Top was something all collegians present for the Northfield conferences came to cherish. Wright was no exception. It took but a moment to remember what it was like to walk there, just before dusk, to hear an evening meditation, or sermon.

"After a while," he wrote, "a convent bell of unusual sweetness begins to toll slowly from the tower of East Hall . . . the crowds about the buildings disperse, and little groups of men, with their coats on their arms, pass over through a field of standing grain to Round Top, a small knoll directly back of Mr. Moody's house. Here in the calm of the gathering twilight . . . the sun goes down in red and gold behind the hills, leaving the still waters of the Connecticut all aflame in the valley below."[14]

To read these words is to know why the Northfield grounds are treasured still by generations of visitors. For many, their forefathers knew Round Top gatherings just as H. B. Wright described.

—✦✦✦—

Some of the finest speakers from America and Britain brought their best words to Round Top, men like A. J. Gordon from Boston, or H. W. Webb-Peploe, the prebendary from St. Paul's Cathedral, London. Seated on the grassy crest of that hill, the Yale men and other conferees would hear "talks frankly and fairly on the choice of a life work."

At the close of the evening meeting, as Wright remembered, "the convent bell breaks the stillness again, the twilight has deepened into dusk . . . hills are dotted here and there with lights, which peer from out the farmhouse windows, and a long straight row of gleaming specks, moving in and out on a horizontal line half way up the opposite hills, betokens the arrival of the evening express at South Vernon."[15]

As for the deep connection between Yale and the Northfield conferences, Wright wanted his readers to know that his alma mater had been there from the start. As he wrote in 1901, "For fifteen years college students have gathered from all over the land, and, indeed, in recent years, from all lands, to discuss methods and to receive an inspiration for efficient Christian work. Yale has been vitally connected with the movement from the start."[16]

Wright detected Yale's presence in the very inspiration for the Northfield conferences and took pride in that. "It is probable," he said, "that Mr. Moody was greatly influenced in his decision to start these conferences by the cordial reception he met with at the hands of Yale and Princeton men when on an evangelistic mission to these colleges in the early eighties. Of the two hundred and fifty students who gathered at Mt. Hermon, across the river, in 1886, at his invitation, seven were Yale men."[17]

And Yale collegians had always been numbered among the largest groups to attend the Northfield conferences each summer. "In the size of its delegation, Yale has from the beginning generally led the institutions of learning represented, which now number one hundred or more. [In] 1900 the total of Yale men on the grounds was one hundred and twenty-seven, nearly a fifth of the whole conference."[18]

What was the reason Northfield proved such a magnet for collegians? Wright thought he knew the answer. "The secret of the attractiveness of these conferences and the ready response which they have met with from college men everywhere are not far to seek. Northfield stands for a healthy, hearty, common-sense Christianity."[19]

Muscular Christianity was also a hallmark of the Northfield conferences—athletics of all kinds were highly prized there. Wright witnessed everything the gatherings had to offer. Over the ten days of the conference, there were "tennis tournaments and track meets," and Yale, Wright was quick to say, "has been more than ordinarily successful on account of the large size of her delegation." There was also a baseball series, "generally ending in a final struggle between Yale and Princeton, unless perchance some smaller college triumphantly produces its varsity battery." And Northfield could boast some of America's finest athletes among its delegates, among them football great Amos Alonzo Stagg.[20]

Athletics, formal and informal, reinforced the great sense of camaraderie that marked the Northfield conferences. Wright spoke fondly of the "opportunity to meet students from other colleges and from other lands, both formally in the many receptions, and informally at the daily swim in the Connecticut." High jinks, if not officially on the program, were very much a part of it all. There were "clandestine raids on the pantry and on each others' quarters, in the rivalry for the possession of the big bell and in the flaunting of the college colors from the highest point on the grounds."[21]

As the Fourth of July always fell within the ten days of each Northfield conference, the afternoon and evening of that day were "given over to a patriotic and intercollegiate celebration unparalleled elsewhere." The order of the day called for "field day games . . . held with the regulation track and field events which call for skill—plus just enough of those of the more amusing and less exacting type such as the sack and potato races and the obstacle race, through the deceptive waters of the duck-pond, to leave the final result to luck rather than to skill." Later, in the evening, the great auditorium became "one mass of college emblems and colors, each section being occupied by the delegates of a certain college, which, at the time appointed, sings its college song and gives its college cheer."[22]

———

H. B. Wright understood the essence of the Northfield conferences. He described their overarching message as "the Ten Commandments preached in the spirit of the 13th of First Corinthians." Mere Christianity was much in evidence too. "The emphasis," Wright said, was "laid on the Bible as the guide of life, the presentation of the claims of the ministry and missions, the appeal for consecrated laymen in every profession, [and] the utter absence of all denominationalism, or, better, the union of all denominations." All these things, Wright said, "combine to give the college man a better and a truer view of life, and to lead him to think seriously upon his own place of work in the world."[23]

Many fine colleges, Ivy League and otherwise, sent delegates to Northfield. But for Wright, "Yale owes to the Northfield conferences a peculiar debt of gratitude . . . The Northfield delegation, bringing together as it did, each year, men of all classes and departments, of varied circumstances, with concentration of interests and singleness of purpose, did much to conserve the force and to adjust it to the newly developed university. At Northfield, even with a delegation of over a hundred, all class lines are broken down, and in a few days, men come to know one another as they meet in the common dining-room and at the delegation meetings as would be well-nigh impossible at New Haven."[24]

All these things made the Northfield conferences special, but there was one other aspect that Wright placed high in his estimation—and, since Moody had only been dead for about a year when he wrote this brief memoir—there was a poignancy to what he wrote next.

"Until last year," Wright said, "the Yale men always enjoyed the peculiar privilege of meeting and knowing Mr. Moody personally, in the little receptions which he invariably gave, sometimes by classes, at other times to the whole delegation, at his home. The quick flash of his humor, and his kindly interest in each man, won for him the unbounded love and admiration of all the Yale men who came to Northfield."[25]

And those years Yale gave back to Northfield—in many ways.

Wright remembered them all. "It is pleasant," he wrote, "to think that Yale has been able to render something to the conferences in return for what she has received. The evening delegation meetings, which were started by the Yale delegation of 1887, have since been adopted by all the colleges of the conference. The fact that the Yale delegation has generally led in point of numbers has made it an example and guide for many others."[26]

What was the tally of good that Yale collegians found in Northfield? In his closing thoughts, Wright counted the blessings. "*Down from these Massachusetts hilltops,*" he said, "*after days of precious privileges, eight hundred Yale men have come since 1886 . . .* All have felt a new force in their lives. The enthusiasm and consecration which they have brought with them have been contagious and have been a mighty leavening force for good in the YMCA, the church—and through them—in Yale."[27]

20

NO PLACE LIKE HOME

*He was beloved in general society; but if he
sparkled there, he shone at home.*[1]

—Samuel Wilberforce

As 1898 passed into 1899, D. L. Moody kept to a taxing schedule of gospel meetings. He would soon turn sixty-two, but to all appearances, he was like the prophet of old, "his eye was not dim, nor his natural force abated."[2]

And so he traveled to a half-dozen cities in Colorado, speaking at evangelistic services during the months of November and December. For three weeks, he stayed in Denver, then it was off to other western hubs: Pueblo, Canon City, Leadville, Florence, and Greeley. His expectation was that he would "spend Christmas at Colorado City."

Each service was "well attended and . . . heartily supported by the local pastors and secular press." In January 1899, he devoted a month in Arizona, beginning in Phoenix. After services in Tucson, and several other Arizona locales, it was on to California for meetings in San Diego and afterward, Los Angeles. After that, it was a return east, where he was "due to preach at Yale University on April 16."[3]

———

The tour out west yielded one vignette that spoke to Moody's depth of character and humility. D. B. Towner, the featured singer and member of the music faculty at the Chicago institute, recalled, "After Mr. Moody's meetings in Oakland, Cal., in the spring of 1899 . . . we took the train for Santa Cruz.

We were hardly seated, when in came a party of young men, one of whom was considerably under the influence of liquor and very badly bruised, with one eye completely closed, and terribly discoloured."

Despite his badly swollen eye, the drunken young man somehow recognized Moody. He "began to sing hymns and talk very loudly." Moody, who was probably very tired from travel, did not wish to be put upon. He caught up his bag and said, "Towner, let's get out of this."

It was then Towner reminded him that the other passenger car was full. Moody took it with ill grace, protesting that "the company should not allow a drunken man to insult the whole car in such a manner."

Presently the conductor came. Moody called his attention to the drunk in the rear of the car. Whereupon the conductor did his duty, going to the young man and saying a few words in a low voice to get him to settle down. Whatever was said, the young man got up and followed the conductor into the baggage car. There he bathed the young man's bruised eye, and bound it with his handkerchief. Within minutes, the young man fell asleep.

Moody saw it all and was chastened into silence. After a while, he turned to his friend Towner and said, "That is an awful rebuke to me. I preached against hypocrisy last night to a crowd, and exhorted them to imitate The Good Samaritan. Now, this morning, God has given me an opportunity to practise what I preached, and I find I have both feet in the shoes of a hypocrite." As Towner remembered, Moody "was reticent all the way to Santa Cruz, but he told the incident that night to the audience, confessing his humiliation."[4]

Moody need never have said anything publicly. That he did was a self-imposed cautionary tale—a practice in humility. The temptation to lose himself in the waves of adulation he constantly met with must have been very strong. Many a person could have become hopelessly conceited in such circumstances. He didn't.

That, in itself, says something. As the distinguished biographer Lyle Dorsett has written, Moody "traveled incessantly, lived in hotels, suffered loneliness, and experienced the headiness of being idolized and sought out by millions; yet he stayed faithful to his wife and managed to help her raise three children who became admirable adults."[5] Moody wasn't a perfect man—he knew that only too well. But he was a good man. That he kept trying, despite his lapses and failings, was part of that goodness.

What was Moody's preaching like at this point of his life? Clearly he was the born storyteller, shown in a visit to Texas about this time. Some artists work in oils; he painted word pictures that were at once vivid and instantly relatable.

"I was down in Texas," he said, "and I happened to pick up a newspaper . . . They called me 'Old Moody.'" That stung a bit, and he said so.

"Honestly," he said, "I never got such a shock. I had never been called *old* before. I went to my hotel, and looked in the mirror."

Here, he grew thoughtful for a moment. Then, with a dash of humor, he drew on the experience he'd just described for a conclusion that was winsome in its application to Scripture. At the same time, he summoned a poet's skill. Here, his story about mortality became something more. It beckoned to the hope of heaven.

"Friends," he said, "I never felt so young in my life as I do tonight; I cannot conceive of getting old. I believe that I have a life that is never going to end. Death may change my position, but not my condition, not my standing with Jesus Christ. Death is not going to separate us. That is the teaching of the 8th chapter of Romans.

"Old! I wish you all felt as young as I do here tonight. Why, I am only sixty-two years old! If you meet me ten million years hence, *then* I will be young."[6]

The month of May 1899 brought with it glimpses of forthcoming events. There came the announcement of the "Twentieth Anniversary of Northfield Seminary," scheduled from Saturday, June 10 to Friday, June 16. Reunion Day was set for Wednesday, June 14.[7]

It was a time remembered ever after as fine and wonderful.

When the seminary had opened on November 3, 1879, there were no dedicated buildings for classes. Instead students and teachers met in the dining room of Moody's home. Twenty-five young women had comprised that first group of students, among them two of the girls he had seen in their mountain home with no hope of an education. Their plight had inspired the formation of the school. They were now among the finest alumnae of the seminary.[8]

Now, twenty years later, words of love and gratitude were a recurring phrase. Current students, faculty, staff, and alumnae could look out at five hundred acres of land and see nine dormitories, a gymnasium, a library, a recitation hall, an auditorium, and farm buildings. There were now nearly four hundred students, "with a staff of teachers and matrons numbering thirty-nine."

One common testimony stood out. Many who came thinking "to obtain enough education merely to get along better in life" had instead discovered what it was to have "their whole course and purpose changed." They'd learned to love God with their minds and their hearts—many themselves becoming teachers and missionaries—all finding ways to give for what they had been given.[9]

Northfield shone among America's schools for its sterling, innovative philanthropy. Hundreds of students had been "either orphans or half orphans"—fatherless children, as Moody had been, or without a mother's guidance. Still others had been "poor, [without] means to attend other schools." Betterment, on a generational scale, was Northfield's continuing bequest. Faith brought that blessing near.[10]

⸺⚬⚬⚬⸺

Just two weeks after the seminary's twentieth anniversary celebrations, Northfield hosted "The World's Student Conference," scheduled from Friday, June 30 to Sunday, July 9.

It boasted an impressive roster of speakers, including the future Nobel Prize Laureate John R. Mott; Robert Speer, prominent as a leader of the Student Volunteer Movement; and Reverend W. H. P. Faunce, the newly elected president of Brown University. Moody himself rounded out the list.[11]

Several days after the World's Student Conference closed, Moody attended the YWCA conference. Robert Speer and Moody reprised their roles as featured speakers.

Moody's final summer event was the seventeenth annual General Conference for Christian Workers, held from August 2 to August 20. Apart from

Moody and longtime friends like H. C. Mabie, international speakers were also in residence: G. Campbell Morgan and Sydney Selwyn, both from England.[12]

Moody's summons for conferees to gather, dated June 1, was a call for renewal: "I am glad to send out this invitation to my fellow-workers," he wrote, "because I believe that such a gathering was never more needed than this year. Many thoughtful men have come to feel strongly that the hope of the Church today is in a deep and widespread revival."[13]

"In response to this invitation," Moody's son Will wrote, "the largest gathering ever held at Northfield met during the first three weeks of August. The [entire] Presbytery of New York engaged Weston Hall, and sixty of its pastors and members were entertained there, several accompanied by their wives. Three or four of the leading pastors of the city were among the speakers at the Auditorium and on Round Top."

For his part, G. Campbell Morgan imparted many a blessing to those who heard him at this time, but he always remembered what Moody and Northfield had given him. His recollections of Moody bring these days to life. "My personal acquaintance," he said of Moody, "was not of long duration, according to the measure of the calendar." If, however, he said, we could count time as the heart measures it, "then I might claim to have known him; for it has been one of the greatest privileges of my life to have come very near him in the ripest years of his life."[14]

Morgan had first heard Moody in England, "in 1883, during his second visit to Birmingham. Bingley Hall was being crowded by day with eager crowds, who had come by train from the whole surrounding district."

Thirteen years later, Morgan made his first visit to America. "Among other work, I had promised Mr. Moody to speak at the Chicago Institute to his students. The Northfield Conference was in session, and I managed to get a few hours there."

Morgan had arrived late at night, found his quarters, and gone to bed. The next day, however, he was off and running. "It was a field day for me," he wrote, "and a revelation. I attended meetings from morning till night. Everywhere Mr. Moody was the moving spirit . . . He seemed to make everything go before him.

In the intervals of the meetings, he gave me a drive round the campus in his buggy. Every point of interest was pointed out, and in a few brief words, [he told] the story of how the different buildings were [built]."

"Passing one house, Moody quipped: 'People sometimes ask me how I found Northfield. I tell them, *it found me*. I was born here!'"

Then, Moody drew the reins to stop his road wagon, and speak to a group of children. "Have you had any apples today?" he asked.

"No, Mr. Moody," they replied.

"Then go down to my house," Moody said, "and tell them to give you all you want." Away they went, remembered Morgan, and so did Moody, both happier.

Then, it was "down a narrow lane, and through a gate," to where a man was hard at work in a field.

"Biglow," said Moody, "it's too hot for you to work much. Half a day's work for a day's pay, you know, while this heat lasts."

Morgan had been given a near view of life in Northfield, with Moody for a guide. "I sat by his side and watched," Morgan said, "and began to understand the greatness of the man whose life was so broad, that it touched sympathetically all other phases of life."

That night, after the evening meeting, Morgan was invited to gather with other Northfield conference speakers in Moody's home. "Then," Morgan recalled, "for the first time, I saw him in a new role, that of the host. He sat in his chair, at the head of the table, and helped the ice-cream, directed the conversation, and listened . . . to every word that others spoke."

The talk "turned on the most serious subjects," among them elements of inner spiritual life. The evening wore on, and too soon it was time for Morgan to bid Moody goodbye, as he was "to depart by an early train on the morrow."

"Oh," said Moody, as though it were the most natural thing in the world, "I shall see you in the morning. You are to preach at ten o'clock!"

That stopped Morgan in his tracks. It was the first he'd heard of it. "What did I do?" he remembered—"I preached."

As he looked back on it, Morgan said, "I did as he told me—as others, and better men—have ever been glad to do. That was his way. He printed no programme of the Northfield Conferences. He gathered around him a band of teachers and speakers, and then as the days moved on," he directed them "according to the necessities of the case." After speaking the next morning, Morgan did have to hurry away, but in that brief stay, he said, "Moody had become much to me. Strong, tender, considerate—from that day, I more than reverenced him, I loved him." [15]

⚬⚬⚬

To see Moody in and around Northfield or Mount Hermon in the 1890s, was to see him wearing his ubiquitous straw hat, driving his road wagon, or phaeton, off-road at a speed passengers found exhilarating by turns, or slightly alarming.

Moody escorts Ira Sankey on tour of the Northfield campus in his horse-drawn buggy.

His British friend F. B. Meyer once called him "the most fearless of whips." Meyer smiled at the thought. "Where have I *not* been in that buggy?" he recalled. It was "the most natural thing in the world" for Moody to leave the road, "climb over a ditch and hedge, and make straight for the top of a grassy slope because he wanted to show you a view." Or, if that was not the case, he would take a steep descent through "a plowed field into a glen, to explain his method of [bringing] water from the spring to Mount Hermon School."[16]

Others among Moody's friends long remembered those wagon or carriage rides. J. Wilbur Chapman was one of them. "To take a morning ride with D. L. Moody," he said, "was to see God in all nature." That "love of nature," he said, "was manifest in every turn of the road." At such times Moody would say: "Look at that!" pointing to "a beautiful picture of a running stream, and bending boughs of trees, through which the morning sun was breaking." Or, he would exclaim: "Listen!" as "the whole of the forest on either side of the road seemed vocal with the song of birds."

At such times, Moody often grew suddenly reverent. "Isn't it beautiful?" he would ask. Lost in the thought of it all, he would say the same phrase over and over. Chapman marveled at how often he too could see something more of God's presence—in nature, or a reverent heart—because Moody helped him to.[17]

Scholar Henry Drummond, a Fellow of Edinburgh's Royal Society, left a vivid picture of Moody as he was at Northfield in the 1890s. Drummond's lengthy and informative essay was first published nationwide in *McClure's* magazine, with specially commissioned illustrations and inset photos—still later, it appeared in book form.[18]

As the *Harvard Crimson* reported, Drummond was a favorite speaker at Harvard, Williams, Princeton, and Yale.[19] He was grateful for what those visits to great centers of learning afforded, but Northfield was the only place that prompted a long tribute in prose.

"To gain just the right impression of Mr. Moody," Drummond had written, "you must make a pilgrimage to Northfield." So stated, that's precisely what Drummond offered his readers. If they couldn't come to Northfield, he would bring Northfield to them.

"Take the train to the wayside depot in Northfield," Drummond said, "or, better still, to South Vernon, where the fast trains stop. Northfield, Moody's birthplace and his home, is distant about a couple of miles, but at certain seasons of the year you will find awaiting trains a two-horse buggy, not conspicuous for varnish, but famous for pace, driven by a stout, farmer-like person in a slouch hat."

Once seated, the driver and buggy made straight for "a spacious hotel," called "The Northfield," whilst the driver "answered your questions about the place in a brusque, business-like way," indulging, very likely, "in a few laconic witticisms." He might touch on "the political situation," or offer a shrewd observation about "the last labor strike."

Presently, Drummond wrote, "on the other side of the river," the eye was drawn to "one of those luscious, grassy slopes, framed in with forest and bounded with the blue receding hills, which give the Connecticut Valley its dreamlike beauty—the great halls of the new Northfield, which Mr. Moody has built, begin to appear."

It was, Drummond said, quite a sight. "Your astonishment is great," he wrote, "not so much to find a New England hamlet possessing a dozen of the finest educational buildings in America—for the neighboring townships of Amherst and Northampton are already famous for their collegiate institutions—but to discover that these owe their existence to a man whose name is, perhaps, associated in the minds of three-fourths of his countrymen, not with education, but with the [lack] of it."

But once "deposited at the door of the hotel," Drummond said, "a more astounding discovery greets you. For when you ask the clerk whether the great man—Moody himself—is at home, and where you can see him, *he will point to your coachman, now disappearing like lightning down the drive,* and—too much accustomed to Mr. Moody's humor to smile at his latest jest—whisper, '*That's him!*'"

Nothing "could more fittingly introduce you to the man," Drummond wrote, "or make you realize the naturalness, the simplicity, the genuine and unaffected humanity of this great unspoilt and unspoilable personality."

Drummond then offered a postscript to his vignette. "At the beginning of each of the terms," he observed, at Northfield or Mount Hermon, "hundreds of students, many of them strangers, arrive . . . At such times [Moody] literally haunts the depots, to meet them the moment they most need a friend, and gives them that personal welcome which is more to many of them than half their education."[20] Moody would help them stow their luggage, get everyone seated, and conduct them personally to start a new chapter in their life.

One wonders why he set such store by doing this. But perhaps the reason isn't hard to find. Long years before, when he arrived at seventeen without a penny in Boston, there had been no one to collect him at the train station. He could be the friend to offer a welcome he never received.

———⊙/⊙/⊙———

Rides in Moody's phaeton were as much a part of some people's store of Northfield memories as any of the fine buildings that Drummond described. James McConaughy, writing for the *Youth's Companion*—a magazine made famous in Laura Ingalls Wilder's Little House books—captured distinctive qualities that Moody never lost. If anything, students felt renewed vigor when he returned to Northfield each year after the close of a preaching tour.

"Much of Mr. Moody's influence with the students," McConaughy said, "was undoubtedly due to his interest in their amusements, and his love of honest fun. He never outgrew the boy in his own nature."

Moody, McConaughy continued, "did everything in his power to encourage open air amusements." He took part in the sports "on both sides of the river," but "took special delight in giving a holiday of his own now and then." In the fall this was "Mountain Day," and "for many a girl the happiest memories of seminary life cluster around those glorious autumn days on Strobridge Mountain, just back of the seminary."[21]

Moody, McConaughy knew, "dearly loved a harmless joke." Once in the early days at Mount Hermon, while he was acting as "anchor" for one side in a tug of war, he planted himself in front of a large tree, round the trunk of which, without being seen, "he slyly got a turn or two of the rope." Then he sat there "and shook with laughter while the other side, headed by one of the teachers, tugged away in vain."

One spring, some seminary girls were taken in by one of Moody's shenanigans—only this one had a catch. It was the close of afternoon of field day sports. Moody drove up with his market wagon and invited a number of the girls to take a ride. The wagon quickly filled, and the party drove off in high spirits.

It wasn't long, however, before "Mr. Moody turned off from the main road toward Round Top, slyly remarking, 'You girls must pay for this ride; there's a job of work to be done.'" Then he lowered the boom: "some burdocks had appeared in the fresh grass" on the crest of Round Top. Moody pointed to them and said, "Weed those, and you'll have paid the fare for your ride!"

Sure enough, there was a set of the necessary tools. Moody set the girls to work, laughing all the while. As it happened, there weren't all that many weeds in the event, and the work was soon done. But, as McConaughy wrote, "they accomplished the task so well that Moody told them he should 'speak a good word for them to all the young farmer-lads of the neighborhood!'"[22]

In 1898, "one of the most characteristic photographs of Mr. Moody ever taken was caught one day . . . when he had given a clambake to the whole school, and was sharing a game of 'duck on the rock' with his boys."

Moody was just as happy to have the tables turned on him. McConaughy described an instance when one of the Mount Hermon boys challenged him to run a race. Moody accepted at once, "but stipulated that the boy should carry a handicap equal to the difference between his own weight and Mr. Moody's." McConaughy dryly observed: "As this would have been something like one hundred and fifty pounds, the race was never run."[23]

Moody was a welcome presence too over Christmas vacations. At times he would visit and "play crokinole [a board-game version of shuffleboard] and halma [an American form of Chinese checkers] with those of the seminary girls who, having no homes to go to, were spending their holidays as best they could." Always competitive, it was take no prisoners. He played these games, McConaughy wrote, "as he did everything else, with spirit and enthusiasm, and was seldom beaten."[24]

If Don Quixote had his Rocinante, Moody had a favorite horse of his own: a gray mare named Nellie Gray, given to him by a good friend, Julius J. Estey, a businessman from a dozen miles away in Brattleboro, Vermont.[25]

For years, Moody and Nellie Gray were fixtures for a radius of more than twenty miles in and around the greater Northfield area.[26] Once the two were sighted at Mount Hermon, the boys "would rush down the hill and shout to see him coming." As one of them recalled: "Any one of us would run across a ten-acre plowed field to unbar a gate for him, if his gray mare started that way."[27]

D. L. Moody with college students, baby granddaughter Emma, and Lion, one of two family mastiffs

Nor was Nellie Gray the only four-footed friend wont to travel with Moody. His wealthy friend John Wanamaker had given him a pair of English mastiffs.[28] One of them, called "Lion," was never far from Moody's side. Journalist Edwin McAlpin wrote of the bond that existed between this faithful dog and his master.

"One summer's afternoon," McAlpin said, "I had the rare privilege of visiting Dwight L. Moody in his garden at Northfield. While we were chatting together his big mastiff persisted in pushing himself against his master. Time and time again Mr. Moody absent-mindedly shoved him away. At last the dog's affection intruded on his thought. With an unmistakable but affectionate push, Mr. Moody exclaimed: 'If I was only as faithful to my Master as Lion is to his, I would have nothing to complain about.'" A very human moment had brought home a facet of faith.[29]

Whenever Moody set out in his phaeton, Lion trotted along behind. Sepia-colored pictures still exist of them both. Local folk knew that to see Moody coming was to know that Lion wasn't far behind. And sure enough, in time to come, puppies with mastifflike features began to crop up—in many places. Leash laws were a thing of far distant future, and inasmuch as Moody wanted to have more dogs like Lion at his side, he never had the dog neutered. One wonders if neighbors with Lion-like litters of puppies were so grateful.

Moody's phaeton was a vehicle for transport and conversations with friends and even faculty in Northfield.[30] But many residents remembered him as the grandfather in his carriage. In 1895, he'd become a grandfather for the first time. Will and May Moody had a little girl, Irene Moody, on August 20, 1895. In December, A. P. and Emma Fitt had a little girl, whom they called Emma.

Four Generations: D. L. Moody, his son Will, and his mother, Betsy, who is holding great-grand-daughter Irene

"Do you know I have a granddaughter? I am taking a present over to her," he shouted from his buggy to a summer visitor one August morning, pointing to a basket of doughnuts. He was happy as a schoolboy on a holiday and told the news to everyone he met.

Later that day, he made a second trip to Mount Hermon to see baby Irene, this time bringing over an immense cauliflower, the best his garden had produced."[31] It's not quite clear how the cauliflower was to be helpful for a newborn, but Moody took any excuse, however dubious, to make another visit.

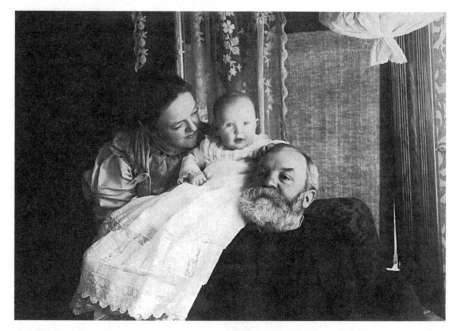

Moody with granddaughter Emma and daughter, Emma

On December 10, 1896, just before little Emma Fitt's first birthday, he wrote her a touching letter. "In six days you will be one year old," he said—

> and your grandmother will make you a cake, and have it all frosted over with white sugar, and they will put one tiny little candle in it.
>
> It will be one year ago, next Tuesday night, [that] I was sitting up for your grandmother, and when it got past midnight, I thought I would go up and see why she did not come home, and I heard you cry for the first time. The tears of joy came to my eyes, and I have thought a great deal of you ever since. Soon after, my mother died, and you seemed to come to take her place, and you have been a dear, good little girl. . . .
>
> I am going to steal up to your home next summer and take you out riding before your parents get up. Only think, of some fine June morning, we can go up Lovers' Retreat. The birds will sing you a beautiful song. What times we will have together! I get real homesick thinking about it. [32]

Emma's father, A. P. Fitt, wrote: "And so [Mr. Moody's] loving heart went out to his grandchildren, and they in return, loved none better than him. In the summer months, he would usually be seen with one or more of them seated beside him as he drove around town." [33]

One friend remembered that Moody had "learned to perfection the art of being a grandfather. I saw him one morning driving with his little four-year-old granddaughter into the yard of his house. The child had gone to sleep in the buggy, leaning against him. Rather than disturb her, he had the horse gently unharnessed, and taken away, while they sat on. Presently he, too, was overcome with sleep." [34]

So many of the things that endeared him to friends, family, and associates were themselves associated in some way with those rides and rambles. It's easy to see why those rides were such a tonic for him. Traveling incessantly, as he did for long stretches of time—across the Atlantic, or far from home somewhere in America—he was deeply grateful to get into comfortable old clothes, hitch up the wagon, and take a trip through the countryside.

As few men ever have, he loved telling "the old, old story" of faith. But he loved coming home too. The sight of Moody in his carriage was a metaphor of his family happiness, his life in Northfield, and its people.

One letter captured it all. "I am thinking next Wednesday morning I will look out on dear old Northfield, and will take a walk about and see things. I am just longing to see you all, and to sniff the fresh morning air. It is a great joy to think that in so short a time I am to be free once again."

At such times, the mind and spirit can find rest just in not being harried by appointments (even very welcome ones like gospel meetings), and in not being the center of attention, or in not having to give of yourself. Moody's bursts of humor and affection were natural enough. They were part of his character.

But they were also part of a grateful return for coming home. It was where he was happiest in his later years. If his childhood in Northfield had been marked by poverty and hardship, his later years there were the reverse.

Faith hallowed Northfield, bringing blessings his younger self could never have imagined. That he lived to see it all, and revel in it, was just one gem among the many bright treasures of grace he knew.

THE LAST CAMPAIGN

In garments glorious he will come,
To open wide the door;
And I shall enter my heavenly home.
To dwell forevermore.[1]

—Harry Barraclough

On November 8, 1899, D. L. Moody set out for a series of gospel gatherings in the American West. The centerpiece: he would conduct a week of meetings in Kansas City, Missouri.

On the way, he stopped in Philadelphia, where preparations for future meetings were well under way. He turned west, with a brief stop in Chicago to address some administrative items at the Bible institute. Still, he'd left time to speak to the young people there. It was said the two talks he gave to the students "were marked by unusual power."[2]

Soon after, Moody boarded a train for Kansas City. However, he arrived there a sick man, with a recurrence of the heart trouble he'd been warned of in late 1892, on the eve of his return to America to undertake the great campaign at the Chicago World's Fair of 1893.

On his arrival in Kansas City, Moody felt a great weariness, but he did not think to consult a physician. A bit of rest was what he needed, he thought. Then he would be all right.

As he settled in on Sunday, November 12, he wrote a letter to his friends Jane and Peter MacKinnon in Scotland. Bringing them near, if only in the mind's eye, was a comfort. The letter was poignant and introspective—with thoughts of mortality. To read it is to sense Moody knew all was not as right with him healthwise as it should have been. The letter read:

> *My dear Mrs. MacKinnon:*
>
> *I am off here all alone, thinking of the past, and you and your good hus-band have come into my mind, and I just long to see you both once more. It would do my eyes good to see you all, and ride down that western coast [of Scotland] once more. I wonder if I should like your new house as well as your old one.*
>
> *I cannot tell you how much I miss dear [Henry] Drummond. It does not seem possible I shall not see him again on earth. What a good time we shall all have when we get to heaven!*
>
> *Only think, what a lot have gone home since 1873, when we first met. I get homesick for them sometimes, and yet I would not be off, until the work that the Lord has given me to do is finished. The work is sweeter now than ever, and I think I have some streams started, that will flow on forever. What a joy to be in the harvest field, and have a hand in God's work!*
>
> *Will you give my warmest love to all old friends, and take much for yourself?*
>
> *Your loving friend,*
> *D. L. Moody*[3]

The first services in Kansas City were memorable, despite Moody's not feeling well. He rose to the occasion. Trademark wit seasoned his sermons on the hope of heaven—the more quick to win their way, for the sharing of laughter at intervals over the course of the evenings.[4]

A chorus of five hundred voices had been gathered to open and close the gatherings, under the capable baton of a good friend, Professor C. C. Case. But, as the choir was comprised largely of Methodists and Presbyterians, Moody couldn't resist a bit of ribbing. Arminians and Calvinists singing in close harmony. Ne'er shall the twain meet—it was too good an opportunity to pass up.

"There's good material in that choir," Moody told Case. "They sing famously well. At first, I'm told, there was some difference between the Methodists and Presbyterians in the manner of their singing. The Methodists sang fast, and the

Presbyterians sang slow. *The result was peculiar*—but we have taught them to pull together pretty well now."

If Case's choir was innovative for sheer numbers, the other group to perform during the Kansas City meetings dealt in more typical fare. It was billed as an "Old Men's Quartette, and gave balance to the program. Five hundred voices could raise awe-inspiring song; a quartet fostered a more subdued, more subtly reverent tone.

Still, there are always some bugs to iron out for any great gathering of people, and this first meeting was no exception. The hymns had been printed for the audience, but afterward the rustling in handling them threatened to drown out Moody as he prepared to preach. So, just before he began his sermon, Moody said: "All who have sheet hymns, please hold them up high."

All at once, 5,000 hands were lifted, holding sheets of paper. "The effect," one observer noted, "was that of a Chautauqua salute." Moody looked on.

"Now shake them," he said. All at once, a noise several times louder than what had been heard filled the hall. People smiled and some laughed. What was to come next? This wasn't what a gospel meeting was supposed to be like, was it?

That's what the roguishly subversive Moody had been counting on. He began to laugh himself, then said in his stentorian voice: "Now sit on those sheets! I only wanted you to see what a noise they'd make, if you kept handling them."

People laughed still more and took the point. The sheets were safely stowed away, and the vast auditorium became "a region of silence." Moody could now be heard to best advantage. [5]

That first service was to begin at three o'clock in the afternoon, but well before that time, the great auditorium was filled. It was necessary to close and lock the doors. Several thousand people were turned away.

At night, an overflow meeting crowded the Second Presbyterian Church nearby, and great crowds of people went home, unable to get into either meeting. There had been notable gatherings in the great Kansas City Convention Hall on former occasions, but even its dedication services, with the featured attraction of John Philip Sousa's world-renowned band, had failed to bring together such a throng as that assembled to hear Moody preach. "It was," said one writer, "the greatest meeting in point of attendance in the history of the Mississippi Valley."

The second day, Moody's evening sermon was followed by an after-meeting in the Second Presbyterian Church, just across the street from the convention hall. The church was filled. Many, unable to find a seat, stood wherever they could.

Moody took his place, and the old hymn "Just as I Am" was sung. Afterward, he gave a message "in a simple, conversational way." It was, said one observer, "just as though he were sitting by the side of each one before him."

Moody set out the timeless truth of the gospel and closed with a story from his time of relief work with the Christian Commission during the Civil War. Many men, he said, on both sides of that conflict, had trusted Christ— some only just before they died of their wounds. It was a powerful story.

Here Moody paused a moment. "The church was still," said one who was there. "The ticking of the clock could be distinctly heard." Then Moody spoke:

Great Hall in Kansas City, where Moody held his final evangelistic campaign

"Will anyone say he will trust Christ?" From far back in the church, there came a low, but firm, response, "I will." At this, Moody stepped to the edge of the platform and "with his eyes questioned those before him." The responses increased, then began to come faster. In a few minutes fifty people had said "I will."

On the third day, Tuesday, the after-sermon meeting was once more the setting for a moving scene. One of the most prominent businessmen of the city was converted. His decision, voiced unreservedly and with conviction, had a marked effect. Many who had been hesitant took courage from his example. "The result," one observer wrote, "was a decision on the part of many."[6]

On Wednesday came the first indications that Moody's health was breaking down. Speaking twice a day, without amplification, in so large a building as the Kansas City Convention Hall would have placed a physical strain on healthy men. Moody was neither healthy nor as young as he once was. After the evening meeting, he told the local ministers who'd organized the event that he "was almost exhausted" and "must have some rest." It pained him to say so, but it would be impossible for him to lead the inquirers' meeting that typically followed in the church. And with that, he "went at once to his room at The Coate's House," that he might "rest and be ready" for the great meetings to follow on the morrow.

On Thursday afternoon, Moody showed further signs of exhaustion, "though," as one friend said, "anything like a total physical collapse was not apprehended." One of the city ministers asked him how he felt. His answer was subdued. "*Not big*," he said.

By nightfall, his appearance had changed. His face was flushed, and he was sweating profusely. Several times, he was "hardly able to support himself, and it seemed as though he would fall from weakness." The pauses between the points of his sermon lengthened.

Somehow, Moody got through his message. But one wonders why those who saw him struggling didn't discreetly step to his side and ask if he was able to continue. Meanwhile, the 15,000 people in attendance that night were unaware, but they were hearing the last sermon D. L. Moody would ever preach.

His sermon title was "Why Not Be a Christian?" His text was taken from

Luke14:18. Lines from that talk, as with the best of Moody's sermons, still speak across the years. He'd always retained the gift for speaking effectively to people with little or no church experience. He drew word pictures that his audience readily understood.

"Let any man," Moody said, "get an invitation from President McKinley to go down to the White House to some banquet. There is not a man here but would consider it a great honor to receive such an invitation. But only think of the invitation that I bring tonight! It comes from the King of kings!"

That set the table for his message. He then expanded on his theme. "The invitation," he said, "is 'whosoever will, let him come to this feast.' Tonight, my friends, let me say that you are invited, every one of you."

It was a message as old as Christendom itself, this invitation to place one's faith in Christ. It lay at the very heart of Christianity. As Moody explained, it was the greatest gift ever offered to humanity.

"You know what it is to take a gift," he said, "you know what it is to put trust and confidence" in someone. Who, he asked, was more deserving of our trust and confidence than God Himself. "Cast yourself unreservedly upon the Lord Jesus Christ," he said. "If you do, you will be saved." God calls to each one of us. "Why not accept His invitation?"

Having set this invitation before his audience, Moody must have surprised a good many when he suddenly became self-deprecating.

It may be, he said, some of you are thinking: "I would like to become a Christian; but I have a prejudice against revival meetings, and against a layman too. 'If it was a regular minister,' some might say, 'if it was our regular minister, I would accept the invitation.'"

Moody took himself out of the equation. "If that's your difficulty," he said, "I can help you. You can just get up, and go out of the hall, and run right over to your minister, and have a talk with him. Your minister would be glad to see and talk and pray with you. And if you say you do not want to be converted in a special meeting, like this one, there are regular meetings in all the churches throughout Kansas City."[7]

Moody's desire here was to remove any hindrance to faith. If people weren't quite sure what to make of him, if they were more inclined to trust a pastor or clergyman they knew, that was just fine. And if a revival meeting like this was something they'd come to see out of curiosity, but an event where they felt uncomfortable making a declaration of faith, that was all right too. What mattered most was saying yes to Christ. Whether in this convention hall, or in a nearby church—it mattered little to him *where* people said yes to faith, so long as they said yes.

—◦/◦/◦—

Moody then moved to a description of what a welcome in heaven would be like. It was the "blessed hope" he'd held out to so many, for so long.

"Lift your eyes heavenward tonight," he said.

Mothers; you have loved children that have gone on before you. They will be at the marriage supper of the Lamb. They will sit down with Abraham, Isaac, and Jacob, in the kingdom of God. Will you be missing?

Young man, you have a sainted mother there—a loved father there. They are beckoning you heavenward tonight. They have been gathering from the time the holy Abel went up . . . gathering out of the four corners of the earth. The purest and best of earth are here. They are in heaven. God wants you and me to be there.[8]

Following this vivid passage, Moody made a refreshingly honest admission. Candor had always been a hallmark of his preaching and was so now.

"Many of you," he said, "will get up and go out of this hall, making light of the preacher, laughing at everything you have heard, paying no attention to the invitation. I beg of you, do not make light of this invitation. It is a loving God that invites you."[9]

He painted one last word picture. What would it be like, he wondered aloud, if everyone there that night were to accept heaven's invitation. What words could they say? Perhaps, their reply would run something like this: "To the King of Heaven: While sitting in the Convention Hall on November 16th, 1899, I received a pressing invitation from one of Your servants to be present at the marriage supper of Your only begotten Son. I hasten to reply. By the grace of God, *I will be present.*"

He left the thousands who sat before him that night with two final questions. "Who will sign that?" he asked. "Who will set to their seal tonight to saying that God is true? Make up your mind now. Don't go away till the question of eternity is settled."

Afterward, Moody returned to his hotel room, completely spent. He told those with him he'd "never felt so feeble before." Worse still, he said he "hadn't been able to lie in bed for three nights" but had taken all his rest in a chair, sleeping only a few minutes at a time.

Still, it was difficult for him to realize the full extent of his weakened condition. So it was that on Friday morning, November 17, a little before noon, he asked to be taken for a drive. Doubtless, he thought that getting some air might help.

Sadly, it didn't. He came back thoroughly exhausted. Only then did he "relinquish the hope of preaching that day." He sent for one of the ministers of the committee, the Rev. Dr. M. S. Hughes, of the Independence Avenue Methodist Episcopal Church, to preach that afternoon. In making his request, he let off a flash of his old spirit. "You Methodists are *always* prepared to preach," he gently teased.

Upon consultation with a physician named Dr. Schauffler, it was decided that Moody should return to Northfield at once. As this decision was made, he was sitting in his armchair, breathing heavily, his face puffy and bloated. He complained of a swelling in his limbs and said he "had a feeling of oppression about his heart."

Even then, he let go of finishing the Kansas City meetings reluctantly. "I'm afraid I shall have to give up the meetings," he said. "It's too bad." Then, he grew silent, lost in thought, before speaking again: "It's the first time in forty years of preaching," he said, "that I've had to give up my meetings." He was silent again, then spoke quietly of how painful it was to leave.

Every effort was made to get Moody a special railroad car, but none could be secured. In the event, a car belonging to the American Baptist Publication Society was secured. The car even had a name, "The Messenger of Peace." The Rev. S. G. Neil placed it at Moody's disposal. So he began the homeward journey, accompanied by his physician and a few friends.

One of them was Charles M. Vining, who long remembered the journey.

"When the train pulled into Detroit," he wrote, "it was over an hour late. Unless at least half of this time could be made up, the eastern connection for the through Boston train could not be made."

As the train stood in at the Detroit station, the engineer came back along the train until he reached "The Messenger of Peace."

"Whose car is this?" he asked.

One of Moody's friends, then standing outside, said: "It's a special car, taking Mr. Moody, the evangelist, home. He was holding meetings in Kansas City, but was taken ill. We're about an hour late, and if we don't make up the time, we won't make the proper connections for Boston."

At this, the engineer responded: "Look here, fifteen years ago I was converted by Moody, and I have lived a better and happier life ever since. I didn't know Moody's car was on tonight, but if you want me to make up the time for you, I'll do it. Just tell Mr. Moody that one of his friends is on the engine. Then hold your breath!"

The engineer proved as good as his word. As soon as the train got clear of Detroit, he pulled the throttle open. It was later said that he made the fastest time ever over this part of the journey. When Moody and his party awoke the next morning, they were on the Boston train. Charles Vining stayed with Moody all the way, right until the train pulled into East Northfield. Just as it was about to depart for the return trip to Kansas City, Moody said to him: "*Tell them they have caged the old lion at last.*"[10]

TO THE WESTERING SUN

*D. L. Moody, whose illness obliged him to cancel a number of
appointments in November and December, is steadily improving.
With complete rest and relaxation . . . it is thought that Mr.
Moody will be entirely restored to his usual strength and vigor.*[1]

—The Record of Christian Work

This notice in *The Record of Christian Work* was published before the close
of December 1899. Its editor was sanguine in saying D. L. Moody would,
with rest, recover.

Readers might well have thought the same. The magazine's recurring feature, "Thoughts for the Quiet Hour," appeared with the byline, "conducted by
D. L. Moody," just as it had done so many times.

"We hoped," said Moody's eldest son, Will, "that a complete rest would
[bring] restored strength and health; and in many ways, there was cause for
encouragement. The doctors gave us assurances that, barring accidents or com-
plications, there was every reason to hope for the best."[2] Still, the doctors spoke
of the possibility Moody might not recover. It was real enough.

In the waning days of November, the best medical treatment was secured.
At the same time, Moody followed the scriptural admonition to call in the elders of his local church and be anointed with oil—along with a prayer for the
restoration of his health (James 5:14). He was now bedridden.

―――⟨ଡ/ଡ⟩―――

For five weeks, Moody remained in this state. We know something of what
it was like because of a writer for *The New York World* named Lavinia Hart.[3]

She was allowed to spend a day in East Northfield in mid-December. Her account is the more valuable for the rare glimpse it gives of this time.

As Hart's carriage arrived, she was drawn to the beauty of Moody's hometown. "The view from Mr. Moody's place," she wrote, "is wonderfully good, and restful to eyes grown used to narrow streets and pavements and chimney pots. A wide valley slopes from his house to the Connecticut River, and beyond are the Winchester hills, with the Green Mountains rising loftily behind them."[4]

As for the Moody homestead—the farmhouse Moody had once bought on little more than a whim—it had been transformed into a living space that was another name for welcome.

Lavinia Hart took note of that too. "The Moody home," she wrote, "is a big white structure with green blinds, almost hidden by massive elms. There are dainty white chintz curtains at the windows, with fluted ruffles falling over boxes of bright flowers, and within there is something about the old-fashioned rockers and cushions, round tables and books, and the cozy glow from open fires, that makes one feel it is really a home."[5]

For all this warmth of detail, other lines from Hart's account were by turns poignant, even unsettling. Her article itself bore the title: "Pen Picture of the Life of Dwight L. Moody, Now Closing." Underneath were several descriptive taglines. One of them read: "While Life Ebbs Away, He Worries About the School He Has Helped to Sustain."

※ ※ ※

Hart was granted a brief interview with Emma Moody. What she shared of her husband's plight and concerns was deeply moving. "He has no thought," Emma said,

> but to recover; there is so much to be done, and things press so hard upon his mind. I devote all of my time to diverting his thoughts from his work. He is very cheerful. When he is not in pain, he is trying to make us laugh. We show him none of his mail, nor speak of anything from the outside world.
>
> Yet we cannot keep him from thinking. The schools are a source of worriment to him. You see, the students pay only half the cost of

tutorage, and the other half has been secured through Mr. Moody's efforts. If those efforts were to cease, it would mean the downfall of the schools, and they have been the dearest hope of his life.

And what of Emma herself? "During the five weeks of Mr. Moody's illness," Hart told her readers, "Mrs. Moody has scarcely left his side." Emma's bravery and devotion were mirrored in her words. She said: "I do not have time to weep, nor have I the inclination. I am confident he will recover, for he cannot yet be spared; there is so much work for him to do." All this, Lavinia Hart reported, "was said softly, for no one speaks above a whisper in the Moody home." Nothing, Moody's doctors had said, must be permitted to disturb his rest.

Emma spoke too of little things—things only a wife would know. Part of what endeared her husband to her lay "sometimes in what he did not say, when most of us would have spoken—or the pressure of his hand, or an act of kindness which no one but the one who needed it would ever know." She admired her husband's courage, kindness, and faith. None knew them better than she did.

Lavinia Hart, surrounded as she was by all the fine buildings of the Northfield Seminary, took note of what they said about Moody's legacy. "His power to win souls," she wrote, "has been no greater than his power to win from those who could help the necessary funds to carry on the work." Then followed a quote from Moody himself, one Emma might have obtained for her.

"Giving," Moody said, "is as essential a part of true religion as believing. No one knows how much blessing is to be derived from giving, until he has tried it. It works both ways."[6]

═══◦◦◦═══

Miss Hart was also able to glean samples of Moody's table talk from family members and friends who'd gathered to help during his sickness.

First of all, she learned Moody was fond of calling Northfield "the West Point of Christian Work." In that vein, she wrote with appreciation of how Northfield and Mount Hermon were "schools designed to give to young men and women, who could not otherwise afford it, a good preparatory college education."

One could not be in Northfield, or in close proximity to Moody, without hearing one of his stories. He was the Mark Twain of the Pioneer Valley, and good stories were never far from him. Perhaps as a way of spending the time, or lightening the mood of her visit, Lavinia Hart was treated to a telling of one of Moody's favorites—though her account is silent as to who, among his family and friends, might have shared it.

It ran as follows. There once was a converted miser to whom a neighbor in distress appealed for help. The miser decided to prove the genuineness of his conversion by giving the neighbor a ham. On his way to get it, the devil appeared, whispering, "*Give him the smallest one you have.*" A struggle followed. Finally, the miser took down the biggest ham he had.

"You are a fool!" the devil said.

At this, the farmer replied, "If you don't keep still, I'll give him every ham in the smokehouse!"

This led, in turn, to a reflection from Miss Hart and a closing tribute. She began by writing: "Mr. Moody believes in the efficacy of stories." His family and friends told her why. "Men will listen to a story," Moody so often said, "when they won't listen to Scripture . . . The moral of a story remains with them a long time, and often sets them thinking along lines they refuse to consider in sermon form."

Then came Lavinia Hart's tribute. "Mr. Moody has been famous as a story-teller," she wrote. "He has never been too busy to stop and listen to a joke, and retaliates in kind, no matter where . . . at his favorite work in the garden, or driving his road wagon to the schools with some of its produce. It was on one of these latter occasions, when he stopped to tell a joke, that a camera snapped and a picture was taken by [his] nephew [Ambert]."[7]

This was entirely in keeping with who Moody was in his final years. That battered old road wagon was perhaps the best place of all to glimpse his faith then. He'd known kings and presidents—but cherished hauling produce to his schools, greeting "his girls" and "his boys," as he called them—and seeing something of their lives in the schools God had given him. The schools, as Emma Moody had said, were "the dearest hope of his life."

⚬⚬⚬

Lavinia Hart's article about D. L. and Emma Moody was dated Sunday, December 18. Will Moody, their eldest son, wrote of the days that followed. "It is doubtful if Father ever had a severer trial than that of the last month. After sixty-two years of an unusually active life . . . to be suddenly laid aside to wait patiently, and in extreme weakness for God's will, was indeed a severe test."[8]

Until now, Moody's recovery was hoped for, but by December 20, it seemed a fast-fading hope. Till that time, despite his worry over Northfield and Mount Hermon, there were some happier moments, when he showed flashes of his old fire and curiosity. Emma may have issued an edict against "news from the outside world," but somehow or other, he got someone to smuggle in newspapers. When he felt up to it, he would sit in his bedroom chair, wearing what Victorians called "a dressing gown," or robe, and read.

The Boer War was then in its early days, and Moody followed reports with "keen interest." As his second son, Paul, remembered: "He and my brother were pro-Boer, and I was not, and we had endless arguments."[9]

Remarkably, one of those exchanges about the Boer War has survived (likely recorded by Paul). It seemingly came out of nowhere. Moody had been resting quietly, with closed eyes, when suddenly, he spoke up about President Kruger, the leader of the Boers:

"I know," he said, "what I would do if I were old Kruger."

Thinking he had been dreaming, his son asked if he'd had a good rest.

"I wasn't asleep," he replied; "I was thinking of that horrible war."

"Well, what would you do if you were Kruger, Father?"

"Oh, I would just send a message to Lord Salisbury, and state that there had been so many hundreds killed on the Boer side, and so many on the English side. And I would say that, as an old man, I should soon have to stand before God, and that I didn't want to go before Him with all this blood on my conscience, and I would tell England to make her own terms of peace."

Here, his son suggested that "possibly England herself was not entirely innocent."

"That's quite so; but if Kruger placed himself in that position, after showing the fight he has, England would have to make the best of terms, or answer for it to the best element in her own land, as well as the entire civilized world."[10]

On Thursday, December 21, it was decided that Paul Moody would travel to New York City to consult with a specialist who had already seen his father. The family also wished to arrange for a new nurse, as the one Moody had was "an efficient but doleful creature he could not abide."[11]

However, something intervened that Paul later would consider providential. He was not awakened early enough and missed the train he was scheduled to take. "Otherwise," he later wrote, "I should have been away when Father died."

The day before, Wednesday, Paul had "been alone with him when he had had an alarming fainting spell." Once he regained consciousness, Paul remembered, "He seemed more concerned with my concern, about which he rallied me, than he did about himself, and joked about the unwisdom *for my sake* of leaving me in the room alone with him."[12]

It was courage in the face of dire news. "Early that morning," the doctor told Paul and the rest of the family that Moody "would not last the day out." Paul later wrote: "He was restless in bed and more comfortable in one particular chair, but he was fully aware of everything, especially our alarm, and submitted for a time to the heart stimulants."[13]

At three in the morning on Friday, December 22, Will Moody went to his father's sickroom, to take a turn watching over him. "For several hours," he wrote, "Father was restless, and unable to sleep. About six o'clock, he quieted down, and soon fell into a natural sleep, from which he awoke in about an hour."

Then suddenly, Will remembered, "I heard him speaking in slow and measured words . . . he was saying, 'Earth recedes; heaven opens before me.'" Will's first impulse "was to try to arouse him from what appeared to be a dream.

"'No, this is no dream, Will,' he replied. 'It is beautiful . . . If this is death, it is sweet. There is no valley here. God is calling me, and I must go.'"[14]

Meantime, the nurse summoned the rest of Moody's family, and his physician, who had spent the night in the house. Moody continued to talk quietly and "seemed to speak from another world his last message." He was remarkably lucid.

"I have always been an ambitious man," he said—"ambitious to leave no wealth or possessions, but to leave lots of work for you to do." He then spoke to Will, saying, "you will carry on Mount Hermon. Paul will take up the Seminary, when he's older. Fitt will look after the Institute, and Ambert [Moody's nephew] will help you in the business details."[15]

Next, he seemed for a time to see beyond the veil—for he suddenly brightened and said: "This is my triumph; this is my coronation day! I have been looking forward to it for years."[16]

Then, a great mercy came.

Moody's final years had been saddened by the deaths of two grandchildren he'd loved dearly—Will's children, a little boy, Dwight, and a little girl, Irene. Now, so close to the end, his face lit up, and he spoke in words of quiet joy: "Dwight! Irene!—I see the children's faces."

After this, he grew suddenly weak and began to slowly lose consciousness. "Give my love to them all," he said. Then his beloved Emma came into the room. "Mamma," he said, "you have been a good wife to me . . ." and with that, he became unconscious.[17]

"It seemed to us all," Will wrote, "that he would never come back again, and for a time, we thought that he was passing rapidly away." One half hour later, however, he revived under the effect of heart stimulants. Raising himself on an elbow, he asked: "What does all this mean? What are you all doing here?"

Gently, he was told he hadn't been well, and then, he remembered. He said: "This is a strange thing. I have been beyond the gates of death, to the very portals of Heaven, and here I am back again. It is very strange."

Moments later, a new thought came to him. With surprising strength, he said: "I'm not at all sure but that God may perform a miracle, and raise me up. I'm going to get up. If God wants to heal me by a miracle that way, all right; and if not, I can meet death in my chair as well as here." Then, he said he was determined on getting up, and could not be dissuaded. He walked across the room to an easy chair, where he sat down.[18]

However, a second "sinking turn" left him exhausted, and he was persuaded to return to bed. There he remained, quietly waiting the end, for an hour.

To the last, he thought of those around him. Turning to Emma, he said: "This is rough on you all, and I'm sorry to distress you . . . It is hard to be kept in such worry."

Once more, the doctor thought to give a hypodermic injection of nitroglycerin. Moody looked at him in a questioning way and said: "Doctor, I don't know about this. Do you think it best? It is only keeping the family in anxiety."[19]

A few moments later, another sinking turn came. He never awakened.

"Father," Will Moody wrote, "fell on sleep quietly and peacefully, and it was not hard to imagine his reception in that other world, among the hosts of loved ones awaiting his coming."

Three days later, a friend sent a telegram with this beautifully wrought sentence: "Mr. Moody's love for music is at last satisfied this Christmas morning."[20]

A year or two before, Moody had been walking one evening to the Northfield Auditorium with a friend. He sat down on the grass of Round Top to rest. From that high hill, he looked out over the beautiful summer landscape, gilded with the westering sun, and said:

"I should like to be here when Christ comes back!"[21]

His family remembered this, and, to honor his wish, he was laid to rest on Round Top—borne on a funeral bier carried by boys from Mount Hermon.

Generations have walked to the crest of that hill. Prayers are offered there. Some stand simply, in silence. It is a hallowed place.

To watch a sunset there is to glimpse colors let down from the tapestry of hope that shaped so many lives. It is worth going to see.

In the weeks following Moody's death, two letters arrived that must have done much to solace the grief of his family. The first came within days and was from President William McKinley.[22]

Emma Moody with her family in 1901. Back row: Mrs. Moody with Constance and Will Moody. Front Row: A. P. and Emma Moody Fitt, Emma IV; Mary, May Whittle Moody, Paul Moody

The Executive Mansion,
Washington, D.C., Dec. 26th, 1899

Dear Mrs. Moody,
I have been grieved to learn of the death of your husband, whose many years of unselfish work for the good of others won for him so high a place in the public regard.

The effect of Mr. Moody's great services to mankind will long endure as a fitting monument to his noble character and purposes.

Please accept the sincere sympathy of Mrs. McKinley and myself in your bereavement, and believe me,

Very truly yours,
William McKinley

The second letter was written a few weeks later, in February. It was a hand-written letter from the president of Yale, Timothy Dwight. Dr. Dwight was a descendant of Jonathan Edwards, herald of the Great Awakening in the 1700s.

D. L. Moody had been the great herald of heaven's hope for the 1800s. Thus, Dr. Dwight's letter was more than a deeply thoughtful letter of condolence—

it was, in its way, a symbol, or emblem, of the bright renewal of faith that marked the lives and legacies of Edwards and Moody.

The graves of D. L. Moody and Emma Revell Moody at Round Top, overlooking the Pioneer Valley

Dr. Dwight's letter was addressed to Emma Moody.[23]

New Haven, Feb. 8th, 1900

Dear Madam,

I give myself the privilege, I hope, with your allowance, of offering you and your children the expression of my sympathy in the bereavement which has come upon you and of my high estimate of the Christian service of your husband during his long and most honorable career. He was, indeed, a true man—full of love, of faithfulness, of consecration, of cheerful hope, of earnestness to help and to save, of the genuine Christian spirit. He has passed, and as we cannot doubt, to a blessèd reward.

The men, young and old, here at Yale University always welcomed your husband as he came among us, and his coming was always an inspiration to many hearts. I think he liked the spirit here, and I am sure that the young men of the successive classes liked his spirit. They believed in him, and trusted him. To many among them, he gave new and nobler impulses for all their future life. To all, he spoke as one who had no desire but the desire to do good, to be a helpful friend in the things pertaining to the highest and deepest life. Our university, I am sure, will bear him in appreciation and grateful remembrance in the years to come.

You have been, and are receiving daily, rich testimonies of the regard and gratitude from many who were in the intimacy of friendship with your husband, and from many, many more who bear him in their thought as connected with the beginning and growth of their Christian lives. It is pleasant to think of the feeling that is cherished toward a man who gave himself so fully to the work of saving others. The inheritance which belongs to his children is a rich inheritance.

May the blessing of God, and the comfort that is in Christ—the blessèd hope of the gospel, and the peace that endures—always be with you and yours, until the end of the earthly life comes, and the gate of the heavenly city opens to you.

With great respect,
I am sincerely yours,
Timothy Dwight

—— ⌀ ——

And what of the fatherless boy who first knew the touch of grace on those hills in Northfield?

Somewhere along the way, D. L. Moody, the boy who once seemed anything but a poet, became something like one. "Earth," he used to say, "is the little isle; eternity the ocean round it."[24] And he grew fond of quoting the greatest poet of his age: Alfred Lord Tennyson. He wove words Tennyson had written into one of his oft-repeated stories:

"The poet Tennyson once asked an old Christian woman if there was any news.

"'Why, Mr. Tennyson,' she said, 'there's only one piece of news that I know, and that is—Christ died for all men.'

"At this, Tennyson gave a reply that was one with the message Moody had been telling all his life. Tennyson told the agèd saint:

"'That is old news, and good news, and new news.'"[25]

Never was the gospel better expressed, nor did the nineteenth century ever see a more faithful herald of its message, than D. L. Moody. Streams he set in motion are flowing still.

WITH THE TALENTS
GOD HAD GIVEN

A lamp in the night, a song in time of sorrow,
A great glad hope, which faith can ever borrow.[1]

—Major D. W. Whittle

In November 1927, *The New York Times* published its review of *A Worker in Souls*, Gamaliel Bradford's just-published biography of D. L. Moody. The *Times* reviewer took the measure of Bradford's book, and its subject, then offered this telling conclusion: "Society will have reason to be grateful if there arises a revivalist so sound in himself, so true to his faith, so human in his contacts . . . as D. L. Moody."[2]

Few heralds of the gospel have been given as fine a tribute as this. But Moody himself would have been quick to point to something else—saying he would have been nothing were it not for the message it had been his to tell.

Two keepsakes capture the essence of that message—the timeless message that had transformed his and so many other lives. The first keepsake was but one-sentence long, yet rich in truth. "Love," Moody said, "is the lever with which Christ lifts the world."[3]

On another occasion, Moody had reflected on the great search for meaning in life so many have known—that he had once known. So it was that he said: "You know the world is after peace—that's the cry of the world. That is what the world wants. Probe the human heart, and you'll find down in its depths a want, a cry for rest. Where can rest be found? Here it is, right here. Put your trust in the living God, with all your heart, mind, soul, and strength, and you'll have peace."[4]

D. L. Moody knew what it was to find the place of peace. His life, and the many good works God gave him to do, radiated from it.

Notes

Frontispiece

1. George Adam Smith, *The Life of Henry Drummond* (New York: McClure, Phillips & Co., 1901), 89, 147.

Preface: McKinley, T. R., and Wilson

1. "Dwight L. Moody Was a Really Great Man," *The New York Times*, 6 November 1927; http://query.nytimes.com/mem/archive/pdf?res=F70D1EF63C5D16793C4A9178AD 95F438285F9

2. A. P. Fitt, *Moody Still Lives* (New York: F. H. Revell, 1936), 149.

3. Emma Moody Powell, *Heavenly Destiny* (Chicago: Moody, 1943), 230.

4. *The Congregationalist and Christian World*, 12 November 1914, 624.

Chapter 1: From Home to Boston

1. Quoted in W. H. Daniels, *D. L. Moody and His Work* (American ed., Hartford, CT: American Publishing, 1875), 36. For brevity, I've condensed this epigraph citation. NOTE: In 1875, the same year Daniels's memoir of Moody was published, the American Publishing Co. released *Mark Twain's Sketches New and Old*, which contained "The Notorious Jumping Frog of Calaveras County," among other famous stories. That Moody and Twain shared the same publisher at this time was a measure of Moody's wide celebrity following his return to America from his celebrated mission to Great Britain (1873–1875).

2. William R. Moody, *The Life of Dwight L. Moody* (London: Morgan & Scott, 1900), 17.

3. Moody's kinship with these distinguished Americans is described in John C. Pollock, *Moody* (New York: Macmillan, 1963), 4.

4. Ibid., 5.

5. Ibid., 4. See also Lyle W. Dorsett, *A Passion for Souls* (Chicago: Moody, 1997), 28–29. Both authors describe Edwin Moody's traits and financial struggles.

6. Paul D. Moody and Arthur Percy Fitt, *The Shorter Life of D. L. Moody*, vol. 1 (Chicago: Bible Institute Colportage Assoc., 1900), 10.

7. Daniels, *D. L. Moody and His Work*, 3–4.

8. D. L. Moody and Charles Goss, *Echoes from the Pulpit* (Hartford, CT: Worthington & Co., 1900), 490–91.

9. Moody, *The Life of Dwight L. Moody*, 20.

10. Ibid.

11. Ibid., 21.

12. Moody and Fitt, *The Shorter Life of D. L. Moody*, 10.

13. Moody and Goss, *Echoes from the Pulpit*, 491.

14. Pollock, *Moody*, 4–5.

15. Daniels, *D. L. Moody and His Work*, 4–5.

16. Ibid.

17. Ibid., 5.

18. Pollock, *Moody*, 5. See also Moody, *The Life of Dwight L. Moody*, 21.

19. Moody, *The Life of Dwight L. Moody*, 28.

20. Daniels, *D. L. Moody and His Work*, 12–13.

21. Moody, *The Life of Dwight L. Moody*, 30.

22. Ibid., 29.

23. Ibid., 32.

24. As quoted in Moody, *The Life of Dwight L. Moody*, 32–33.

25. A. W. Williams, *The Life and Work of Dwight L. Moody* (Philadelphia: Ziegler & Co., 1900), 26.

26. Pollock, *Moody*, 5.

27. Daniels, *D. L. Moody and His Work*, 13.

28. Moody and Goss, *Echoes from the Pulpit*, 601.

29. Ibid.

30. Daniels, *D. L. Moody and His Work*, 11.

31. T. J. Shanks, *D. L. Moody at Home* (Chicago: F. H. Revell, 1886), 64.

32. J. W. Chapman, *The Life and Work of Dwight L. Moody* (Toronto: Bradley-Garretson, 1900), 52. See also Pollock, *Moody*, 5.

33. Daniels, *D. L. Moody and His Work*, 13.

34. Chapman, *The Life and Work of Dwight L. Moody*, 52–53.

35. Daniels, *D. L. Moody and His Work*, 15.

36. Pollock, *Moody*, 28.

37. Daniels, *D. L. Moody and His Work*, 14.

38. Moody, *The Life of Dwight L. Moody*, 33.

39. Ibid.

40. Ibid., 33–34.

Chapter 2: Young Man About Town

1. D. L. Moody and Charles Goss, *Echoes from the Pulpit* (Hartford, CT: Worthington & Co., 1900), 172.

2. W. A. Newman and W. E. Holton, *Boston's Back Bay* (Lebanon, NH: University Press of New England, 2006), 44.

3. A longtime Moody family friend writes that "at seventeen years [Moody's] kinsman, Mr. Holton of Boston, accepted [him] as a clerk in his shoe store, corner of Court Street and Brattle Street, or Cornhill, where I purchased shoes of Dwight." See the *Christian Register*, 25 January 1900, 91. For an 1857 image of Holton's Boot and Shoe Store, see *Ballou's Pictorial*, 7 November 1857, 289.

4. John C. Pollock, *Moody* (New York: Macmillan, 1963), 7.

5. William Moody, "Memories of Moody," *The Saturday Evening Post*, 7 April 1900, 915.

6. Ibid.

7. H. D. Northrop, *The Life and Labors of Dwight L. Moody* (Philadelphia: Premier Publishing Co., 1899), 57.

8. Elias Nason, *The Lives of the Eminent American Evangelists* (Boston: B. B. Russell, 1877), 42.

9. Ibid., 43.

10. Moody, "Memories of Moody," *The Saturday Evening Post*, 915.

11. Nason, *The Lives of the Eminent American Evangelists*, 43.

12. Moody, "Memories of Moody," *The Saturday Evening Post*, 915.

13. Nason, *The Lives of the Eminent American Evangelists*, 43.

14. Moody, "Memories of Moody," *The Saturday Evening Post*, 915.

15. Nason, *The Lives of the Eminent American Evangelists*, 43.

16. Letters between Samuel Holton and D. L. Moody, see Pollock, *Moody*, 8.

17. Ibid., 9.

18. Ibid.

19. Paul D. Moody and Arthur Percy Fitt, *The Shorter Life of D. L. Moody*, vol. 1 (Chicago: Bible Institute Colportage Assoc., 1900), 19.

20. Pollock, *Moody*, 9–10.

21. Ibid., 10.

22. Ibid.

23. Ibid.

24. Ibid., 11. See also Lyle W. Dorsett, *A Passion for Souls* (Chicago: Moody, 1997), 45.

25. Pollock, *Moody*, 11.

26. Dorsett, *A Passion for Souls*, 45.

27. Pollock, *Moody*, 12.

28. Ibid., 11.

29. Dwight L. Moody, *The Way Home* (Chicago: Bible Institute Colportage Assoc., 1904).

30. Dorsett, *A Passion for Souls*, 45–46.

31. Ibid., 46.

32. Ibid.

33. Moody and Goss, *Echoes from the Pulpit*, 520–21.

34. J. W. Chapman, *The Life and Work of Dwight L. Moody* (Toronto: Bradley-Garretson Co., 1900), 74–75.

35. William R. Moody, *The Life of Dwight L. Moody* (London: Morgan & Scott, 1900), 38.

36. Pollock, *Moody*, 12.

37. Ibid., 13.

38. Ibid.

39. Chapman, *The Life and Work of Dwight L. Moody*, 75.

40. Ibid.

41. Ibid., 76.

42. Ibid.

43. Ibid.

44. Moody and Goss, *Echoes from the Pulpit*, 156.

45. Robert and Samuel Wilberforce, *The Life of William Wilberforce*, vol. 1 (London: John Murray, 1838), 75.

Chapter 3: West to the Windy City

1. "Moody's Ready Wit Saves Him," *The New York Times*, 3 November 3, 1889. This article is archived online at: http://query.nytimes.com/mem/archive-free/ pdf?res=F00613FE3 C5F15738DDDAA0894D9415B8984F0D3.

2. William R. Moody, *The Life of Dwight L. Moody* (London: Morgan & Scott, 1900), 61.

3. John C. Pollock, *Moody* (New York: Macmillan, 1963), 16–17.

4. Moody, *The Life of Dwight L. Moody*, 43.

5. Pollock, *Moody*, 16. See also Moody, *The Life of Dwight L. Moody*, 44.

6. Ibid., 16–17.

7. J. F. Stover, *A History of the Illinois Central Railroad* (New York: Macmillan, 1975), 5.

8. Information about Cyrus McCormick in the article, "Cyrus McCormick (1809–1884)," posted online by the Massachusetts Institute of Technology (MIT) at: http://web.mit. edu/invent/iow/mccormick.html.

9. The information in this paragraph is taken from the dust jacket copy and page 23 of Axel Madsen, *The Marshall Fields: The Evolution of an American Business Dynasty* (Hoboken, NJ: J. Wiley, 2002).

10. Information provided in the article, "Farwell (John V.) & Co.," posted online by the *Encyclopedia of Chicago* at: http://www.encyclopedia.chicagohistory.org/pages/2660.html.

11. D. L. Moody, *Power from on High* (London: Morgan & Scott, 1882), 71.

12. Pollock, *Moody*, 17.

13. Lyle W. Dorsett, *A Passion for Souls* (Chicago: Moody, 1997), 55.

14. Pollock, *Moody*, 17.

15. Moody, *The Life of Dwight L. Moody*, 45.

16. Ibid.

17. Ibid.

18. Ibid.

19. Pollock, *Moody*, 19.

20. Moody, *The Life of Dwight L. Moody*, 46.

21. Ibid., 47.

22. Pollock, *Moody*, 18.

23. Ibid., 20.

24. Ibid., 21.

25. Moody, *The Life of Dwight L. Moody*, 69. Moody, describing his early days in competition with other aspiring businessmen, recalled: "There was only one of them but what I felt I could equal, and that was Marshall Field." See also Pollock, *Moody*, 21.

26. Moody, *The Life of Dwight L. Moody*, 49.

27. Biographical information archived online via the historic site, The Inn at Ormsby Hill, at: http://www.ormsbyhill.com/history.html.

28. Norman Williams' June 20, 1899 obituary is archived online at *The New York Times*; see http://query.nytimes.com/mem/archive-free/ pdf?res=F50C15FC355D11738DDDA 90A94DE405B8985F0D3.

29. Biographical information archived online via the New Hampshire Division of Historical Resources; see http://www.nh.gov/nhdhr/publications/ warheroes/thompsonj.html.

30. Paul D. Moody and Arthur Percy Fitt, *The Shorter Life of D. L. Moody* (Chicago: Bible Institute Colportage Assoc., 1900), 25.

31. W. H. Daniels, *D. L. Moody and His Work* (Hartford, CT: American Publishing Co., 1876), 34.

32. Pollock, *Moody*, 25–26.

Chapter 4: A Sunday School Drummer

1. Paul D. Moody and Arthur Percy Fitt, *The Shorter Life of D. L. Moody*, vol. 1 (Chicago: Bible Institute Colportage Assoc., 1900), 27.

2. John C. Pollock, *Moody* (New York: Macmillan, 1963), 23.

3. Sexton's recollections are cited in Ibid., 23–24.

4. J. V. Farwell, *Early Recollections of Dwight L. Moody* (Chicago: Winona Publishing Co., 1907), 11–12.

5. Ibid., 8.

6. Ibid., 7.

7. Ibid., 8.

8. Ibid., 9.

Chapter 5: Camps and Battlefields

1. D. L. Moody, *Twelve Select Sermons* (Chicago: F. H. Revell, 1884), 60–61.

2. William R. Moody, *The Life of Dwight L. Moody* (London: Morgan & Scott, 1900), 75.

3. Ibid, 76.

4. Ibid.

5. Ibid.

6. Ibid., 77.

7. D. L. Moody to Betsy Moody, as quoted in John C. Pollock, *Moody* (New York: Macmillan, 1963), 44.

8. The dialogue among Hawley, Moody, the head guard, and the captain that follows appears in Moody, *The Life of Dwight L. Moody*, 77–79, and the narrative is adapted from page 77.

9. Pollock, *Moody*, 44.

10. Insights offered in Ibid.

11. As quoted in Ibid.

12. Ibid., 44–45.

13. As cited in Ibid., 45.

14. Ibid.

15. Ibid.

16. Moody, *The Life of Dwight L. Moody*, 81–82. See also Pollock, *Moody*, 49.

17. Emma Moody is the source of this story. See Pollock, *Moody*, 49.

18. George Whitefield, *Sermons on Important Subjects* (London: Henry Fisher, 1828), 447.

19. As quoted in Moody, *The Life of Dwight L. Moody*, 84–85.

20. Ibid., 85.

21. W. C. Harris, *Lincoln's Last Months* (Cambridge: Harvard University Press, 2004), 62.

22. J. V. Farwell, *Early Recollections of Dwight L. Moody* (Chicago: Winona Publishing Co., 1907), 47–48. See also Harris, *Lincoln's Last Months*, 62.

23. D. L. Moody, *Latest Sermons* (Chicago: Bible Institute Colportage Assoc., 1900), 73.

24. Moody, *Twelve Select Sermons*, 35–36.

Chapter 6: Emma

1. Emma Moody Powell, *Heavenly Destiny* (Chicago: Moody, 1943), 6.

2. Ibid., 33, 41.

3. Ibid., 40.

4. Ibid., 23. Here it is stated: "[A] young brother wrote, 'We all knew Sister Emma was our father's favorite.'"

5. Ibid., 35.

6. Ibid.

7. Fleming Revell Jr., as quoted in John C. Pollock, *Moody* (New York: Macmillan, 1963), 27. See also Powell, *Heavenly Destiny*, 35.

8. Powell, *Heavenly Destiny*, 37.

9. William R. Moody, *The Life of Dwight L. Moody* (London: Morgan & Scott, 1900), 44.

10. Ibid., 59.

11. Fleming Revell's statement of Moody's earnings appears in Pollock, *Moody*, 37.

12. These figures have been calculated using the website, Measuring Worth; see: http://www.measuringworth.com/uscompare/.

13. Moody, *The Life of Dwight L. Moody*, 58.

14. Ibid., 59–60.

15. Ibid., 60.

16. Ibid.

17. Ibid.

18. Ibid., 60–61.

19. Ibid., 61–62.

20. Ibid., 61.

21. Ibid.

22. Pollock, *Moody*, 47.

23. Ibid., 46.

24. Moody, *The Life of Dwight L. Moody*, 366. As of 1900, when Will Moody wrote *The Life of Dwight L. Moody*, "more than $1,125,000 [alone] was received from royalties" on *The Moody Sankey Hymn Books*. In today's dollars, that sum would equal approximately $26 million dollars.

25. Definitions provided by the Merriam-Webster Online Dictionary at: http://www. merriam-webster.com/dictionary/pluck.

26. Powell, *Heavenly Destiny*, 48.

27. Ibid., 49–50.

28. Ibid.

29. Moody, *The Life of Dwight L. Moody*, 76.

30. Ibid., 105.

31. Ibid.

32. Ibid., 105–7.

33. Ibid., 107.

34. Will Moody, as quoted in Powell, *Heavenly Destiny*, 7–8.

Chapter 7: The Pickpocket's Gift

1. Edward Pell, *Dwight L. Moody* (Richmond, VA: B. F. Johnson Publishing, 1900), 562.

2. Emma Moody Powell, *Heavenly Destiny* (Chicago: Moody, 1943), 48.

3. Paul D. Moody and Arthur Percy Fitt, *The Shorter Life of D. L. Moody*, vol. 1 (Chicago: Bible Institute Colportage Assoc., 1900), 54–58. Here, the story of Moody's early activities on his arrival in England in 1867 is given, along with the story of his first meeting with Harry Moorhouse.

4. Powell, *Heavenly Destiny*, 61–62.

5. Moody and Fitt, *The Shorter Life of D. L. Moody*, 55–56.

6. Ibid., 57.

7. Ibid., 58.

8. Ibid.

Chapter 8: The Chicago Fire

1. J. B. McClure, ed., *Anecdotes and Illustrations* (Chicago: Rhodes & McClure, 1877), 100.

2. Emma Moody Powell, *Heavenly Destiny* (Chicago: Moody, 1943), 69.

3. William R. Moody, *The Life of Dwight L. Moody* (London: Morgan & Scott, 1900), 133.

4. McClure, ed., *Anecdotes and Illustrations*, 84.

5. Moody, *The Life of Dwight L. Moody*, 107.

6. Ibid.

7. Paul D. Moody and Arthur P. Fitt, *The Shorter Life of D. L. Moody*, vol. 1 (Chicago: Bible Institute Colportage Assoc., 1900), 65.

8. Ira D. Sankey, *My Life and the Story of the Gospel Hymns* (Philadelphia: Sunday School Times Co., 1907), 27.

9. Ibid., 27–28.

10. Ibid., 28.

11. Powell, *Heavenly Destiny*, 65.

12. Ibid., 66.

13. Ibid., 67.

14. Ibid.

15. Moody and Fitt, *The Shorter Life of D. L. Moody*, 66.

16. Moody, *The Life of Dwight L. Moody*, 126.

17. Moody and Fitt, *The Shorter Life of D. L. Moody*, 66.

18. Ibid., 66–67.

19. Moody, *The Life of Dwight L. Moody*, 134–35.

20. Ibid., 135.

21. A. W. Williams, *The Life and Work of D. L. Moody* (Philadelphia: Ziegler & Co., 1900), 146.

22. Moody, *The Life of Dwight L. Moody*, 135.

23. John C. Pollock, *Moody* (New York: Macmillan, 1963), 90.

24. D. L. Moody, *Glad Tidings: Sermons at the New York Hippodrome* (New York: E. B. Treat, 1876), 471. The subtitle of this book shows how trustworthy the transcriptions of Moody's sermons here are. It reads: "from the stenographic reports, taken *verbatim*, expressly for *The New York Daily Tribune*."

25. Pollock, *Moody*, 91.

Chapter 9: The Mission to Great Britain

1. As quoted in Charles Raikes, "Moody and Sankey," *Mission Life*, ed. Rev. J. J. Halcombe (London: Wells Gardner, 1875), 359–66. Earl Shaftesbury's tribute to Moody is given on page 360. Charles Raikes was a distinguished author, identified as "C.S.I., Lay Member of the Committee on Special Missions, Salisbury Diocesan Synod." Another source for this tribute from Shaftesbury is the untitled press notice given in *Sunday Magazine* (London: Daldy, Isbister, & Co., 1875), 642.

2. The sobriquet "the poor man's Earl" was applied to Lord Shaftesbury in the June 13, 1868 issue of *The Athenæum: Journal of English and Foreign Literature, Science, and the Fine Arts*, no. 2120, 830.

3. See D. W. Bebbington, "Moody, Dwight Lyman (1837–1899)," *Oxford Dictionary of National Biography* (Oxford: Oxford University Press, 2004); http://www.oxforddnb.com/view/article/53843.

4. The precise dates for the start and close of Moody's mission to Britain are: June 17, 1873 to July 21, 1875. See Bebbington, "Moody, Dwight Lyman (1837–1899)."

5. Paul D. Moody and Arthur Percy Fitt, *The Shorter Life of D. L. Moody*, vol. 1 (Chicago: Bible Institute Colportage Assoc., 1900), 68–78. Here, the story of Moody's life, from the period just after the great Chicago Fire, through his great preaching tour of the British Isles, is given.

6. Ibid., 69.

7. Ibid.

8. John C. Pollock, *Moody* (New York: Macmillan, 1963), 99.

9. Ibid.

10. As cited in Moody and Fitt, *The Shorter Life of D. L. Moody*, 72.

11. Ibid.

12. Ibid., 73.

13. William R. Moody, *The Life of Dwight L. Moody* (London: Morgan & Scott, 1900), 150.

14. Moody and Fitt, *The Shorter Life of D. L. Moody*, 73.

15. Ibid., 73–74.

16. As cited in Ibid., 74.

17. Ibid., 74–75.

18. Ibid., 75.

19. Ibid.

20. Edwin Hodder, *The Life and Work of the 7th Earl of Shaftesbury* (London: Cassell & Co., 1887), 688–89.

21. Moody and Fitt, *The Shorter Life of D. L. Moody*, 76.

22. Ibid.

23. Moody, *The Life of Dwight L. Moody*, 236.

24. Moody and Fitt, *The Shorter Life of D. L. Moody*, 77–78.

25. See the untitled, unattributed death notice for D. L. Moody given in the January 5, 1900 issue of *The Literary World*, (London: James Clarke & Co., 1900), 12.

Chapter 10: Golden Days

1. G. B. Cutten, *The Psychological Phenomena of Christianity* (New York: Scribner's Sons, 1908), 183.

2. Great biographical information about G. B. Cutten is given on page 141 of *The Phi Gamma Delta* (1922). See also "Colgate's Cutten," *Time*, Monday, 2 February 1942, archived online at: http://www.time.com/time/magazine/article/ 0,9171,849752,00.html.

3. Cutten, *The Psychological Phenomena of Christianity*, 183–84.

4. Ibid., 183.

5. William R. Moody, *The Life of Dwight L. Moody* (London: Morgan & Scott, 1900), 235.

6. Ibid.

7. Ibid.

8. *The Brooklyn Daily Eagle Almanac*, comp. William Herries (New York: Press of the Brooklyn Eagle, 1886), 87.

9. Moody, *The Life of Dwight L. Moody*, 236.

10. *New York Tribune*, 6 November 1875, 4, quoted in Moody, *The Life of Dwight L. Moody*, 236.

11. Ibid.

12. Ibid.

13. Ibid.

14. Ibid., 236–37.

15. W. A. Candler, *Great Revivals and the Great Republic* (Nashville: Publishing House of the Methodist Episcopal Church, 1904), 232. Candler held two advanced degrees, the D.D. and L.D.

16. Ibid., 233.

17. See *The Papers of Ulysses S. Grant*, vol. 26, 1875, ed. J. Y. Simon (Carbondale, IL: Southern Illinois University Press, 2003), 558. See also B. J. Evensen, *God's Man for the Gilded Age* (New York: Oxford University Press, 2003), 76.

18. It is fascinating to note that Moody's life had connections to eight American presidents: Abraham Lincoln, U. S. Grant, Rutherford B. Hayes, James Garfield, William McKinley, Theodore Roosevelt, and Woodrow Wilson. Moody was related to Franklin D. Roosevelt.

19. This newspaper article from *The New York Daily Tribune* is archived online at: http://fultonhistory.com/Newspapers%206/New%20York%20NY%20Tribune/New%20York%20NY%20Tribune%201875%20Oct%20-%20Dec%20Grayscale/New%20York%20NY%20Tribune%201875%20Oct%20-%20Dec%20Grayscale%20-%200620.pdf.

20. Lyle W. Dorsett, *A Passion for Souls* (Chicago: Moody, 1997), 236.

21. Ibid.

22. Moody, *The Life of Dwight L. Moody*, 243.

23. Ibid.

24. Coleman's prose portrait, "They Saw Abraham Lincoln in Life," appeared in the February 6, 1913 issue of *Interior* magazine.

25. Moody, *The Life of Dwight L. Moody*, 245.

25. Ibid.

26. Ibid.

27. Ibid.

28. Ibid., 245–46.

29. Ibid., 246.

30. Ibid.

31. Ibid.

32. D. L. Moody, *Bible Characters* (Chicago: F. H. Revell, 1888), 91, 93.

33. Ibid., 96–97.

34. Ibid., 104.

35. Ibid., 106.

36. Coleman, as cited in Moody, *The Life of Dwight L. Moody*, 247.

37. Ibid., 248.

38. The proof could be found in the numbers: by 1900 *The Moody Sankey Hymn Book* had run to "five million copies, and twenty different translations." Ibid, 250.

39. Ibid., 248.

40. "Safe in the Arms of Jesus," from *Echoes from the Heart*, comp. Emma Moody (London: Sampson Low, Marston, Searle & Rivington, 1876), 61. These lines are from the hymn, "Safe in the Arms of Jesus." In public domain.

41. The hymn "How Can I Keep from Singing" is featured on the music soundtrack for the landmark PBS documentary film *Mark Twain* created by filmmaker Ken Burns.

42. Moody, *The Life of Dwight L. Moody*, 248.

43. Ibid.

44. Ibid., 250.

45. Quoted in Ibid., 251–52.

46. See B. J. Evensen, *God's Man for the Gilded Age* (New York: Oxford University Press, 2003).

47. Moody, *The Life of Dwight L. Moody*, 252–53.

48. Donn Piatt, *Memories of the Men Who Saved the Union* (New York: Belford, Clarke & Co., 1887), 141, 146, 152.

49. Moody, *The Life of Dwight L. Moody*, 253.

50. *The New York Times*, as quoted in Ibid., 253.

Chapter 11: Northfield

1. James Stalker, "Mr. D. L. Moody," *Living Age*, 17 March 1900, 691.

2. See William R. Moody, "The Origin and Growth of the Northfield Work, Part 1," *Record of Christian Work*, February 1904, 83.

3. Ibid.

4. Ibid.

5. Most of the stories told from here forward of the early history of Northfield Seminary can be found in H. W. Rankin, *The Handbook of the Northfield Seminary and the Mt. Hermon School* (New York: F. H. Revell, 1889), 13–42.

6. Ibid., 14.

7. Janet Mabie, *The Years Beyond* (East Northfield, MA: Northfield Bookstore, 1960), 67.

8. Rankin, *The Handbook of the Northfield Seminary*, 15.

9. Mabie, *The Years Beyond*, 68.

10. William R. Moody, *The Life of Dwight L. Moody* (London: Morgan & Scott, 1900), 207.

11. T. J. Shanks, ed., *The Home Work of D. L. Moody* (Chicago: F. H. Revell, 1886), 14.

12. R. S. Rhodes, ed., *Dwight Lyman Moody's Life* (Chicago: Rhodes & McClure Pub. Co., 1907), xxx.

13. Burnham Carter, *So Much to Learn* (East Northfield, MA: Northfield Mount Hermon School, 1976), 263.

14. Paul D. Moody and Arthur Percy Fitt, *The Shorter Life of D. L. Moody*, vol. 2 (Chicago: Bible Institute Colportage Assoc., 1900), 24.

15. *Record of Christian Work*, vol. 40, no. 8, 581.

16. H. D. Northrop, ed., *The Life and Labors of Dwight L. Moody* (New Brunswick: R. A. H. Morrow, 1899), 163.

17. "Moody's Educational Scheme," *The New York Times*, 22 August 22 1879, archived online at http://query.nytimes.com/mem/archive-freepdf?res=F00D12F6385A127B93C0AB 1783D85F4D8784F9.

18. Ibid.

19. Ibid.

20. Rankin, *The Handbook of the Northfield Seminary and the Mt. Hermon School*, 24.

21. Ibid.

22. Ibid., 26.

23. Ibid., 29–30.

24. W. C. Covert, "The Life and Work of D. L. Moody," *Christian Workers Magazine*, February 1918, 458.

Chapter 12: Mount Hermon

1. See the August 1906 issue of *The Record of Christian Work*, vol. 25, no. 8 (East Northfield, MA: W. R. Moody, 1906), 549.

2. The story given here of John McDowell's early life has been gleaned from several sources: John McDowell, "Three Typical Incidents," *The Congregationalist*, 12 November 1914, 628; obituary, *Princeton Alumni Weekly*, 10 December 1937, 288; John McDowell, "The Life of a Coal Miner," *World's Work*, October 1902, 2659–60; and "Reverend John McDowell, '94," *Daily Princetonian*, 27 February 1908, 1.

3. John McDowell, "The Life of a Coal Miner," *World's Work*, October 1902, 2659.

4. Thomas Coyle, ed., *The Story of Mount Hermon* (Mount Hermon, MA: Mount Hermon Alumni Assoc., 1906), 7.

5. See William R. Moody, "The Origin and Growth of the Northfield Work," *Record of Christian Work*, March 1904, 159.

6. Ibid.

7. Ibid.

8. Coyle, ed., *The Story of Mount Hermon*, 14. See also Moody, "The Origin and Growth of the Northfield Work," 159.

9. Coyle, ed., *The Story of Mount Hermon*, 12.

10. Ibid., 11. See also L. W. Dorsett, *A Passion for Souls* (Chicago: Moody, 1997), 29.

11. Coyle, ed., *The Story of Mount Hermon* 11.

12. Ibid., 7–8.

13. As cited in Ibid., 8–9.

14. Ibid., 17.

15. Ibid., 22–23.

16. McDowell, "Three Typical Incidents," 628.

17. "John McDowell," obituary, *Princeton Alumni Weekly*, 288. McDowell received doctor of divinity degrees from both Princeton, his alma mater, and the College of Wooster. In 1932 he received a doctor of laws from Occidental College in Los Angeles.

18. *New York Times*, 14 November 1937, and archived online at: http://query.nytimes.com/mem/archive/pdf?res=F20A13FB3F581A7A93C6A8178AD95F438385F9.

19. John McDowell, *Dwight L. Moody: The Discoverer of Men and the Maker of Movements* (New York: F. H. Revell, 1915), 34.

20. As quoted in Moody, August 1906, 548.

21. As quoted in *The Congregationalist and Christian World*, 12 November 1914, 628.

Chapter 13: A School and Publisher for Chicago

1. *The Institute Tie*, December 1901, 115.

2. T. J. Shanks, ed., *A College of Colleges* (Chicago: F. H. Revell, 1887), 212.

3. Paul D. Moody and Arthur Percy Fitt, *The Shorter Life of D. L. Moody*, vol. 2 (Chicago: Bible Institute Colportage Assoc., 1900), 13.

4. *Record of Christian Work*, February 1886, 5–6; cf. *Chicago Tribune*, 23 January 1886, 3; as cited in James Vincent, *The MBI Story* (Chicago: Moody, 2011), 32.

5. Moody and Fitt, *The Shorter Life of D. L. Moody*, 14.

6. Ibid.

7. For a discussion of the arguments for the 1886 founding date, see Vincent, *The MBI Story*, 34–35.

8. Lyle W. Dorsett, *A Passion for Souls* (Chicago: Moody, 1997), 166.

9. Ibid.

10. Ibid.

11. Ibid.

12. Ibid.

13. Ibid., 168. Under Emma Dryer's guidance and supervision, 673 cottage prayer meetings were held, 479 visits to the sick were undertaken, and an astonishing 10,628 tracts and religious papers were distributed.

14. General background information posted online by the Moody Bible Institute, see http://www.moodyministries.net/crp_MainPage.aspx?id=62.

15. Ibid.

16. W. H. Houghton and C. T. Cook, *Tell Me About Moody* (Chicago: Bible Institute Colportage Assoc., 1937), 64.

17. Moody and Fitt, *The Shorter Life of D. L. Moody*, 66.

18. Ibid.

19. Vincent, *The MBI Story*, 35–36.

20. See the unattributed article, "Schools for Christian Workers," *Outlook*, 31 December 1898, 1075.

21. Bernard R. DeRemer, *Moody Bible Institute* (Chicago: Moody 1960), 31; as cited in Vincent, *The MBI Story*, 100.

22. Vincent, *The MBI Story*, 101.

23. D. L. Moody, *Secret Power* (Chicago: F. H. Revell, 1881), 23.

24. Unattributed article, "Reminiscences of D. L. Moody," *Institute Tie*, January 1905, 232. This article was likely written by A. P. Fitt, then editor of *Institute Tie*.

25. As cited in Jim Vincent, "The Man Who Learned to Stick," *Moody Monthly*, June 1985, 44.

26. Ibid. The Great Doctrines of the Bible, released in 1912, is available in hardcover from Moody Publishers.

27. Moody and Fitt, *The Shorter Life of D. L. Moody*, 71.

28. Ibid.

29. Ibid., 72.

30. Ibid., 73.

31. Vincent, *The MBI Story*, 193.

32. *Record of Christian Work*, September 1895, 339.

33. Ibid.

34. Ibid.

35. Moody and Fitt, *The Shorter Life of D. L. Moody*, 97.

36. Ibid. Lifetime sales of Moody's classic *The Way to God* would exceed 775,000 by the year 2000.

37. BICA was renamed Moody Press in 1941, and the publisher celebrated its 100th anniversary in 1994. In 2002 Moody Press became Moody Publishers. For more information, see "About Moody Bible Institute" on pages 301–303.

38. Moody and Fitt, *The Shorter Life of D. L. Moody*, 97.

39. Ibid., 103.

40. Henry Drummond, "Mr. Moody: Some Impressions and Facts," *McClure's Magazine*, 1895, 188–89.

41. Ibid., 189.

42. Ibid.

43. All quotations in this section are from Drummond, "Mr. Moody: Some Impressions and Facts," 189.

44. Dorsett, *A Passion for Souls*, 301.

Chapter 14: The Lands of Faith

1. William R. Moody, *The Life of Dwight L. Moody* (London: Morgan & Scott, 1900), 333.

2. *Anecdotes & Illustrations of D. L. Moody*, comp. J. B. McClure (Chicago: McClure & Rhodes, 1878), 30.

3. Moody, *The Life of Dwight L. Moody*, 329–30.

4. Ibid., 330–31.

5. Moody, *The Life of Dwight L. Moody*, 331.

6. Ibid., 332.

7. Ibid.

8. Ibid., 333.

9. Ibid., 333–34.

10. Ibid., 334.

11. Ibid.

12. Ibid.

13. Ibid.

14. Ibid., 335.

15. Ibid.

16. Ibid.

17. Ibid. 336.

18. Ibid., 337.

19. Ibid., 337–38.

20. Ibid., 338.

21. Ibid.

22. Ibid., 339.

23. Ibid., 340.

24. Ibid.

Chapter 15: Deliverance at Sea

1. "The Spree's Great Peril," *New York Times*, 4 December 1892; archived online at: http://query.nytimes.com/gst/abstract.html?res=9405E3DF1731E033A25757C0A949D94639ED7CF.

2. Paul D. Moody and Arthur Percy Fitt, *The Shorter Life of D. L. Moody*, vol. 1 (Chicago: Bible Institute Colportage Assoc., 1900), 99–100.

3. Ibid., 100.

4. Ibid.

5. Ibid., 100–101.

6. Ibid., 101.

7. Ibid.

8. Ibid., 101–2.

9. Ibid., 102.

10. Ibid.

11. Ibid.

12. Ibid., 102.

13. Ibid., 102–3.

14. Ibid.

15. O. O. Howard, *The Autobiography of Oliver Otis Howard*, vol. 2 (New York: Baker & Taylor, 1908), 560.

16. Ibid., 559–64.

Chapter 16: Moody at the World's Fair

1. Henry Drummond, "D. L. Moody—The Man and the Evangelist," *Literary Digest*, 22 December 1894, 19.

2. William R. Moody, *The Life of Dwight L. Moody* (London: Morgan & Scott, 1900), 355.

3. Ibid., 357.

4. As quoted in H. B. Hartzler, *Moody in Chicago: of The World's Fair Gospel Campaign* (Chicago: F. H. Revell, 1894), 70–71.

5. Moody, *The Life of Dwight L. Moody*, 357–58.

6. Hartzler, *Moody in Chicago*, 24.

7. Paul D. Moody and Arthur P. Fitt, *The Shorter Life of D. L. Moody*, vol. 1 (Chicago: Bible Institute Colportage Assoc., 1900), 87.

8. Numbers provided by *Chicago Tribune* in the article, "World Columbian Exposition (1893)," posted online at: http://www.chicagotribune.com/topic/science-technology/technology/world-columbian-exposition-(1893)-EVHST000087.topic.

9. Moody and Fitt, *The Shorter Life of D. L. Moody*, 87.

10. Cf. Nehemiah 8:10.

11. Moody and Fitt, *The Shorter Life of D. L. Moody*, 87.

12. Ibid., 87–88.

13. Ibid., 88.

14. Ibid.

15. Kevin Belmonte, *D. L. Moody* (Nashville: Thomas Nelson, 2010), 153.

16. Moody and Fitt, *The Shorter Life of D. L. Moody*, 88.

17. H. B. Hartzler, *Moody in Chicago* (Chicago: F. H. Revell, 1894), 64.

18. Moody and Fitt, *The Shorter Life of D. L. Moody*, 87.

19. As quoted in Ibid., 89.

20. Hartzler, *Moody in Chicago*, 119. See also Moody, *The Life of Dwight L. Moody*, 361.

21. Moody, *The Life of Dwight L. Moody*, 361.

22. Moody, *The Life of Dwight L. Moody*, 361–62.

23. Ibid., 362.

24. Moody and Fitt, *The Shorter Life of D. L. Moody*, 93.

25. Ibid.

26. Ibid.

27. Quoted in Moody and Fitt Ibid., 94.

28. John C. Pollock, *Moody* (New York: Macmillan, 1963), 283.

29. Quoted in Moody, *The Life of Dwight L. Moody*, 364.

30. Ibid., 362–63.

Chapter 17: The Place of Character

1. E. V. Lucas, *The Life of Charles Lamb*, vol. 1 (London: Methuen & Co., 1905), 238.

2. Charles Inglis, "Reminiscences of D. L. Moody," *The Christian Workers Magazine*, February 1919, 391. Here, Inglis states: "It was my privilege to meet Mr. Moody in 1867, in London."

3. Ibid., 393.

4. Ibid., 391.

5. Ibid.

6. Ibid.

7. Ibid., 392.

8. Ibid., 393.

9. Ibid., 393–94.

10. Stanley Gundry, ed., *The Wit and Wisdom of D. L. Moody* (Chicago: Moody, 1974), 38.

11. As quoted in William R. Moody, *D. L. Moody* (New York: Macmillan, 1930), 503.

12. *The Congregationalist and Christian World*, 12 November 1914, 624.

13. Ibid., 623.

14. Ibid., 619.

15. Ibid., 620.

16. D. L. Moody and Charles Goss, *Echoes from the Pulpit and Platform* (Hartford, CT: Worthington and Co., 1900), 42.

17. *The Congregationalist and Christian World*, 12 November 1914, 620.

18. As cited in *The Congregationalist and Christian World*, 12 November 1914, 624.

19. Ibid.

20. Henry Franklin Cutler, "Mr. Moody's Appreciation of Education," *The Congregationalist and Christian World*, 12 November 1914, 626.

21. Ibid.

22. Sir J. Kynaston Studd, "Mr. Moody at Oxford and Cambridge," *The Congregationalist and Christian World*, 12 November 1914, 644.

23. Ibid.

24. Ibid.

25. J. R. Mott's Nobel Prize biographical essay is archived online at: http://www.nobelprize.org/nobel_prizes/peace/laureates/1946/mott-bio.html.

26. John R Mott, "Moody's Power with College Men," *The Congregationalist and Christian World*, November 12, 1914, 645.

27. Ibid.

28. Ibid.

29. Ibid.

30. Ibid.

31. William James, *Essays in Philosophy*, eds. Fredson Bowers and Frederick Burkhardt (Cambridge: Harvard University Press, 1978), 199.

32. William James, *The Varieties of Religious Experience* (New York: Longmans, Green and Co., 1902), 487.

Chapter 18: The Banner of Heaven

1. See the unattributed article, "Mighty Moody," in the January 16, 1928 issue of *Time* magazine, 31. This article is archived online at: http://www.time.com/time/magazine/article/0,9171,731388,00.html.

2. D. L. Moody and Charles Goss, *Echoes from the Pulpit and Platform* (Hartford, CT: Worthington and Co., 1900), 555.

3. D. L. Moody, *Twelve Select Sermons* (Chicago: F. H. Revell, 1881), 123–24.

4. D. L. Moody, as quoted in J. W. Hanson, *The Wonderful Life and Works of Dwight L. Moody* (Chicago: W. B. Conkey Company, 1900), 152.

5. Moody and Goss, *Echoes from the Pulpit and Platform*, 319.

6. *Catholic World*, July 1900, 570.

7. D. L. Moody, *To the Work!* (Chicago: F. H. Revell, 1884), 24–25. See also *Catholic World*, October 1867, 139.

8. D. L. Moody, *Heaven* (Chicago: F. H. Revell, 1884), 19–20.

9. D. L. Moody, *The Overcoming Life* (New York: F. H. Revell, 1896), 86.

10. Moody, *To the Work!*, 8.

11. D. L. Moody, *New Sermons* (New York: Goodspeed & Co., 1877), 29.

12. Moody, *Twelve Select Sermons*, 31.

13. D. L. Moody, *Glad Tidings* (New York: E. B. Treat, 1876), 439.

14. Cf. 2 Corinthians 3:2.

15. Moody, *To the Work!*, 141.

16. From a newspaper clipping of Moody's 1897 meetings in the Auditorium Theater, Chicago. This clipping is housed in the Moodyana Collection at the Moody Bible Institute library archives.

17. D. L. Moody, *Latest Sermons* (Chicago: Bible Institute Colportage Assoc., 1900), 31.

18. Moody, *Glad Tidings*, 453.

19. Stanley Gundry, ed., *The Wit and Wisdom of D. L. Moody* (Chicago: Moody, 1974), 39.

20. Moody, *To the Work!*, 131–32.

21. W. H. Daniels, *D. L. Moody and His Work* (Hartford, CT: American Publishing Co., 1875), 392.

22. Moody, *The Overcoming Life*, 54, 57, 58–59. For narrative flow, I have slightly rearranged the original sections of this citation.

23. D. L. Moody, *The Way Home* (Chicago: Bible Institute Colportage Assoc., 1904), 10.

24. Moody and Goss, *Echoes from the Pulpit and Platform*, 420.

25. Ibid.

26. Ibid., 442.

27. Robert P. T. Coffin, "A Review of Paul D. Moody's *My Father: An Intimate Portrait of Dwight Moody*," in Book Talk: A Review of New England Books, a column in the May 1938 issue of *Yankee*, May 1938, 36.

28. Ibid.

29. Paul D. Moody and Arthur Percy Fitt, *The Shorter Life of D. L. Moody*, vol. 1 (Chicago: Bible Institute Colportage Assoc., 1900), 46–47.

30. W. H. Daniels, *Moody: His Words, Work and Workers* (New York: Nelson & Phillips, 1879), 257.

31. John C. Pollock, *Moody* (New York: Macmillan, 1963), 64. Spurgeon's gift of a multivolume set of his writings to Moody is described on page 396 of Lyle W. Dorsett's *A Passion for Souls* (Chicago: Moody, 1997).

32. Daniels, *D. L. Moody and His Work* (Hartford, CT: American Publishing Co., 1876), 35. For narrative flow, I have compressed this citation and modified pronouns—KB

33. See *Record of Christian Work*, October 1898, 509.

Chapter 19: Yale and the Coming of Summer

1. W. G. Clark and W. A. Wright, eds., *The Complete Dramatic and Poetical Works of William Shakespeare* (Philadelphia: Claxton and Co., 1881), 416. These are lines spoken by the king in Act II, scene 1 of *Henry VI, part second*.

2. John C. Pollock, *Moody* (New York: Macmillan, 1963), 308.

3. See the unattributed article, "Mr. Moody Defends Yale," *New York Times*, 14 February 1898 edition. This article is archived online at: http://query.nytimes.com/mem/archive-free/pdf?res=F20D11F6395811738DDDAD0994DA405B8885F0D3.

4. Ibid.

5. Ibid.

6. Ibid.

7. J. B. Reynolds, S. H. Fisher, and H. B. Wright, eds., *Two Centuries of Christian Activity at Yale* (New York: Putnam's Sons, 1901), 242.

8. Ibid.

9. *Christian Workers Magazine*, February 1919, 393.

10. Ibid.

11. Reynolds, Fisher, and Wright, eds., *Two Centuries of Christian Activity at Yale*, 242.

12. Ibid.

13. Ibid, 242–43.

14. Ibid., 243.

15. Ibid.

16. Ibid., 243–44.

17. Ibid., 244.

18. Ibid., 244–45.

19. Ibid., 245.

20. Ibid., 246.

21. Ibid., 246–47.

22. Ibid., 247.

23. Reynolds, Fisher, and Wright, eds., *Two Centuries of Christian Activity at Yale*, 248.

24. Ibid., 248–49.

25. Ibid., 249.

26. Ibid., 250.

27. Ibid., 251.

Chapter 20: No Place Like Home

1. Robert and Samuel Wilberforce, *The Life of William Wilberforce*, vol. 5 (London: John Murray, 1839), 218.

2. A description of Moses given in Deuteronomy 34:7.

3. Moody's preaching itinerary for late 1898 through early 1899 is given in the January, February, and March issues of *Record of Christian Work* (New York: F. H. Revell, 1899).

4. A story given in W. R. Moody, *The Life of Dwight L. Moody* (London: Morgan & Scott, 1900), 439–40.

5. Lyle W. Dorsett, *A Passion for Souls: A Life of D. L. Moody* (Chicago: Moody, 1997), 26.

6. D. L. Moody, *Latest Sermons* (Chicago: F. H. Revell, 1900), 43.

7. *Record of Christian Work*, May 1899, 225.

8. Moody, *The Life of Dwight L. Moody*, 285.

9. Ibid., 288.

10. *Record of Christian Work*, February 1904, 85.

11. *Record of Christian Work*, May 1899, 225.

12. Ibid.

13. Moody, *The Life of Dwight L. Moody*, 325.

14. Ibid., 506–7.

15. Ibid., 508.

16. Paul D. Moody and Arthur Percy Fitt, *The Shorter Life of D. L. Moody*, vol. 1 (Chicago: Bible Institute Colportage Assoc., 1900), 96.

17. J. W. Chapman, *The Life and Work of Dwight Lyman Moody* (London: James Nisbet & Co., 1900), 195.

18. Henry Drummond, *Dwight L. Moody* (New York: McClure, Phillips & Co., 1900).

19. "Prof. Henry Drummond, F.R.S.," *Harvard Crimson*, October 6, 1887. This article is archived online at: http://www.thecrimson.com/article/1887/10/6prof-henry-drummond-f-r-s/.

20. Drummond, *Dwight L. Moody*, 42.

21. James McConaughy, as quoted in *Christian Work*, 2 August 1900, 158.

22. McConaughy, "Mr. Moody with His Boys and Girls," *Youth's Companion*, 199.

23. Ibid.

24. McConaughy, as quoted in *Christian Work*, 2 August 1900, 158.

25. Dorsett, *A Passion for Souls*, 259.

26. Moody, *The Life of D. L. Moody*, 275.

27. John C. Pollock, *Moody* (New York: Macmillan, 1963), 222.

28. Emma Moody Powell, *Heavenly Destiny* (Chicago: Moody, 1943), 137.

29. E. A. McAlpin, "Genuineness Verses Refinement," an article in the January 15, 1920 issue of *The Continent*, vol. 51, no. 3 (Chicago: McCormick Pub. Co., 1920), 73.

30. See S. H. Hadley, "How I Came to Know D. L. Moody," *Institute Tie*, September 1904, 12–13; and Moody, *The Life of Dwight L. Moody*, 499.

31. Moody and Fitt, *The Shorter Life of D. L. Moody*, 108.

32. Ibid., 109.

33. Ibid.

34. Ibid., 109–10.

Chapter 21: The Last Campaign

1. These lines from the hymn "Ivory Palaces," by Harry Barraclough, appear in the October 11, 1920 issue of *Sabbath Recorder*, vol. 89, no. 15 (Plainfield, NJ: American Sabbath Tract Society, 1920).

2. Paul D. Moody and Arthur Percy Fitt, *The Shorter Life of D. L. Moody*, vol. 1 (Chicago: Bible Institute Colportage Assoc., 1900), 113.

3. William R. Moody, *The Life of Dwight L. Moody* (London: Morgan & Scott, 1900), 467.

4. J. W. Chapman, *The Life and Work of D. L. Moody* (Toronto: Bradley-Garretson Co., 1900), 259–64.

5. Ibid., 259–60.

6. Ibid., 262–63.

7. G. T. B. Davis, *Dwight L. Moody: The Man and His Mission* (Chicago: K.T. Boland, 1900), 175.

8. As quoted in George Thompson Brown Davis, *Dwight L. Moody: The Man and His Mission* (Chicago: Boland, 1900), 178.

9. Ibid.

10. Moody, *The Life of D. L. Moody*, 252–53.

Chapter 22: To the Westering Sun

1. An unattributed news bulletin given on page 49 of the January 1900 issue of *Record of Christian Work* (East Northfield, MA.: W. R. Moody, 1900).

2. William R. Moody, "Dwight L. Moody's 'Coronation Day,'" *Record of Christian Work,* February 1900, 81.

3. Lavinia Hart, "Pen Picture of the Life of D. L. Moody, Now Closing," *New York World,* December 18, 1899.

4. Ibid.

5. Ibid.

6. Ibid.

7. Ibid.

8. Moody, "Dwight L. Moody's 'Coronation Day,'" 81.

9. Paul Moody, *My Father: An Intimate Portrait of Dwight Moody* (Boston: Little, Brown and Co., 1938), 173.

10. Story cited in William R. Moody, *The Life of Dwight L. Moody* (London: Morgan & Scott, 1900), 471.

11. Moody, *My Father,* 173.

12. Ibid., 174.

13. Ibid.

14. Ibid., 82.

15. Moody, "Dwight L. Moody's 'Coronation Day,'" 82.

16. Ibid.

17. Ibid.

18. Ibid., 83.

19. Ibid.

20. Ibid.

21. Paul D. Moody and Arthur P. Fitt, *The Shorter Life of D. L. Moody,* 1 (Chicago: Bible Institute Colportage Assoc., 1900), 125.

22. Emma Moody Powell, *Heavenly Destiny* (Chicago: Moody, 1943), 304.

23. Ibid., 304–5.

24. D. L. Moody, *Heaven* (Chicago: F. H. Revell, 1884), 87.

25. D. L. Moody, *Moody's Stories* (New York: F. H. Revell, 1899), 98. In 1839, Tennyson wrote to his future wife, telling her that he was staying with "an old friend" at Mablethorpe. "He and his wife," Tennyson said, "are two perfectly honest Methodists. When I came, I asked her after news, and she replied, 'Why, Mr. Tennyson, there is only one piece of news that I know, that Christ died for all men.' And I said to her, 'That is old news and good news and new news.'" See A. C. Benson, *Tennyson* (London: Methuen & Co., 1906), 110; *The Life and Works of Alfred, Lord Tennyson,* vol. 1 (New York: Macmillan, 1899), 208.

Afterword: With the Talents God Had Given

1. William R. Moody, *The Life of Dwight L. Moody* (London: Morgan & Scott, 1900), 477.

2. See the unattributed review, "Dwight L. Moody Was a Really Great Man," *The New York*

Times, 6 November 1927. This article may be viewed online at: http://query.nytimes.com/mem/archive/pdf?res=F70D1EF63C5D167A93C4A9178AD95F438285F9.

3. E. L. Pell, *Dwight L. Moody* (Richmond, VA: Johnson Publishing, 1900), 562.

4. D. L. Moody, *Eleven Sermons Never Before Published* (New York: Christian Herald, 1911), 138.

Appendix: Paul Moody's Tribute to His Father

1. *Saturday Review,* vol. 40, 1957, 33.

2. Paul Dwight Moody, "A Son's Tribute," *Congregationalist and Christian World Magazine,* 12 November 1914, 625–26.

About Moody Bible Institute and Moody Church

1. *Celebrating the Joy of Changed Lives* (Chicago: The Moody Church, 2014), 20.

2. Ibid.

3. "A Brief History of the Moody Church," www.moodychurch.org/150th-anniversary/brief-history-moody-church/

4. *Celebrating the Joy,* 101, 79.

Appendix

PAUL MOODY'S
TRIBUTE TO HIS FATHER

Paul Dwight Moody, born in 1879, was a distinguished educator, just as his father, D. L. Moody, was. President of Middlebury College from 1921–1947, Paul Moody was also, to quote *The Saturday Review*, the "benign and understanding godfather" of the famous Bread Loaf Writers Conference.[1] In 1941, he posed for a picture with the poet Robert Frost, my distant cousin. On a personal level, I'm fond of that image. But it's a symbol as well of Paul Moody's legacy as a patron of the writer's craft.

Paul Moody was an author himself and wrote a book with a distinguished pedigree. It was a memoir called *My Father: An Intimate Portrait of Dwight Moody*, published in 1938 by Little, Brown and Company. I'm privileged to own a copy.

Prior to writing his book, however, Paul Moody wrote a brief and poignant tribute to his father. To see D. L. Moody there is to discover more of the legacy he left as a father.

It was a goodly heritage. Paul Moody was still an undergraduate at Yale when his father died. But the life lessons he'd already received were things he carried with him ever after. Those life lessons shine in the tribute Paul Moody wrote. Artfully, movingly rendered, it is only fitting that it closes this book.

"A Son's Tribute"[2]

If one whose life had been spent on the slopes of some great mountain—the streams of which had watered his fields, even as the shoulders and ridges protected him from the winds—should awake one morning to find that in the night the whole mountain had been removed—his sensation, I imagine, would not be altogether dissimilar to ours that December morning when we tried to realize that the Past had suddenly stepped forward and claimed the Present. For some of us life has never been quite the same, nor can it ever be.

But this is an impression, and recollections are more to the point.

When I was a small boy, I was on one occasion quite unintentionally disobedient in respect to going to bed. Father spoke with unwonted abruptness and severity, and I sought my bed, crying. I was hardly there, before he was kneeling by my side, sobbing like a child and imploring my pardon for his impatience and harshness. The strength which enabled him to humble himself to his little boy combined with such tenderness . . . seemed then and now both wonderful and Christ-like. I believe I owe more to the memory of this incident than anything else in my life.

I once saw him run and throw his arms about an old man, and with tears of joy running down his face, mutually embrace and kiss with regular Gallic abandon—and this in broad daylight on the main street. Visitors in the old days will remember the face of the old man, Paul Dumonal, known by everyone as "Paul the Frenchman," or "Old Paul."

He was a veteran of the Franco-Prussian War and the war of Italian independence, and his grizzled face was seamed and scarred with wounds. He had turned up in Northfield in the early 1880s, no more than a tramp, and had found work on the roads. He had felt himself discriminated against in pay and appealed to Father, who did not wish to interfere, but solved the matter by hiring him to work in our garden, where he remained many years.

He had long been a slave to drink, and I wish I could tell at greater length the story of his liberation. It was difficult to talk to him, for he could not understand. He spoke the worst English I ever heard. My mother called it an Irish brogue with a French accent. So he was not talked to much.

But he was loved a great deal.

And he responded to the treatment. I think his reasoning was simple: "I like whisky. Mr. Moody don't. I like Mr. Moody more than whisky. So I must not drink."

It was a long and hard struggle. But the sprees were increasingly infrequent. Finally, he came to my mother with the request that she keep his wages for him.

One day, when his victory had been for some time complete, he announced his intention of returning to France for a visit. Over one thousand dollars stood to his credit in the bank. It seemed impossible that he could go away for long, and come back the same. The anxiety in our home had become hopelessness when a year had gone by without a word.

Then one day, as my father stood watching some work at the church, he saw a station wagon winding up the hill, and in it Old Paul in a suit of youthful gray and a resplendent red tie. The victory had been complete. He had not only come back, but come back as he had gone. It was then the two friends fell on each other's necks for the whole town to see.

Old Paul never [foreswore] the church of his fathers, but he always went to ours, and the pope for whom he fought, and the whole college of cardinals, could not have stopped him.

I can still see him sitting in his accustomed corner of the gallery, understanding nothing, but reverently worshiping the God of his best friend. Whenever he was questioned by me as to his faith he always declared it *"just same as Papa's."* Then came his invariable formula: *"Papa, he good man. Mamma, she good lady."*

The old Frenchman outlived [my Father] some eight years and remained with us, and nothing was more touching than his devotion to the grave on Round Top, where, early in the morning, he could sometimes be seen kneeling in prayer. Outside his family, I do not think there was anyone more loved by my father, or anyone who loved him more unselfishly and devotedly than Old Paul.

And of those whom my father has welcomed in "the house not made with hands," who are there by any effort of his to preach the gospel of Jesus Christ, there is none whose presence means more than the old Frenchman's who was converted not by preaching but by loving.

I was twenty when Father died, and I would rather not say more, for I know the tendency of the world to discount a son's estimate, especially over a lapse of years. Nothing I can say would satisfy my love and memory. Yet even while it dissatisfied me, it would seem to others, not privileged to know him as we did in the home, exaggerated and extreme.

He wrote me, the week he received the news of Henry Drummond's death, that he had never known a better or more Christ-like man.

Like attracts like.

It is characteristic of his humility, his tolerance of those who did not see eye to eye with him, that he could say this. A prophet is often without honor in his own family, as well as in his own country, and no man is a hero to his valet. But Carlyle well said that no man was less of hero, because his valet had the perception and outlook of a valet.

But in our home, we all felt that as a father [D. L. Moody] was even greater and better than in any other relationship. He was the humblest, gentlest, and most trustful and Christ-like man I have ever known. As a small boy, I thought God must be like my father.

ACKNOWLEDGMENTS

My debts to the friends of this book are many.

First, I wish to thank Moody Publishers for granting me the privilege of telling D. L. Moody's story. To tell a new generation of readers about "the Lion of Northfield," as I've come to think of Mr. Moody, has been a richly rewarding experience. I'm deeply grateful to have partnered with a publisher that has shown such a sterling commitment to excellence, across the board, in helping me follow the biographer's craft. To all at Moody Publishers who had a hand in producing this book—from the leadership team and the editorial staff, to the graphics design and marketing departments, and all those who proofread the book—my sincere thanks.

I am equally indebted, on many levels, to my literary agent, Rachelle Gardner, and Books & Such Literary Agency. I have so often benefited from the wise counsel and expertise that has resulted in this biography finding its best publishing home. Thank you, Rachelle, for your steadfast belief in this book. It has meant all the difference.

My friendship with Mr. Moody's great-grandson, Dave Powell, and his lovely wife, Lucia, has graced this project from start to finish. His commendation of my work, at a very early stage, inspired me to carry on with all the hard work it takes to bring a book across the finish line. Thank you, friends, for all the kindness, smiles, and laughter. Northfield is the more hallowed for me because you've been there.

My thanks to all who read this book early on, when its first chapters were being written. Every writer needs encouragement at such times, and I was given that. And to all those who took time to read the manuscript and send commendations, I am deeply grateful. Your words will go on with this book, like so many keepsakes. Indeed, that is what they are.

To Mr. Moody himself, I owe an immeasurable debt. I might have written and researched this book, but he has been my teacher. I have been very glad of his company.

Last, but never least, thank you, Kelly and Sam. I am grateful this book will be there for you—a small return, but a very heartfelt one, for all that you've given me. Bless you both for being my wife and son.

ABOUT MOODY BIBLE INSTITUTE AND MOODY CHURCH

Three months after D. L. Moody died, the board of trustees chose to rename the Chicago Bible Institute the Moody Bible Institute of Chicago. Now, more than 125 years after its founding, Moody Bible Institute remains, like its founder, intent on changing its world for Christ.

As a Bible institute, it continues to focus on preparing men and women for evangelism, using teaching and technologies of the twenty-first century. Once a two-year certificate granting institution, in 1966 MBI began granting college degrees in cooperation with other schools, and by 1988 it brought the four-year degree program in-house. The school is accredited by the Higher Learning Commission of the North Central Association of Colleges and Schools.

Students in Chicago can enroll in one of twenty-four majors to earn a bachelor of arts. Chicago's strong music program offers a B.A. in music or B. Mus. in music and worship (five years) to prepare graduates who will serve churches as instrumentalists, singers, and ministers of music.

MBI opened its first satellite campus in Spokane in 2006. Among its four-year degree programs are a bachelor of science in biblical studies or ministry leadership and a bachelor of arts in youth ministry. Its mission aviation program grants a bachelor of science in missionary aviation technology. Dating back to 1946 on the Chicago campus, the aviation program has sent an average of 50 percent of all missionary pilots into service in the past seventy years, aiding missionaries as they spread the gospel into remote regions of the world.

In all this learning, the focus for students has remained on personal ministry. In the early years students had practical Christian work assignments. Today, through practical Christian ministry assignments, students may serve in churches, youth clubs, visitation, hospitals, retirement or assisted-living facilities. They may be after-school tutors, mime or musical entertainers, even counselors or aides to immigrants settling in Spokane or Chicago neighborhoods.

Graduate-level training also is available. With campuses in Chicago and suburban Detroit, leaders at Moody Theological Seminary recognize that advanced education is often vital in the twenty-first century. MTS awards M.A. degrees in eight majors, as well as the M.Div. degree. In all their courses, practical ministry is the focal point. Academic Dean John Jelinek says, "Bound up with our emphasis on sound theological education is an emphasis on practical ministry skills for a variety of ministry settings."

Like their innovative founder, leaders at MBI use the latest technologies to extend training to those unable to attend classes on campus due to family or work commitments. Moody Distance Learning links professors and students via the Internet to earn course credits leading to an associate degree or a bachelor of science in biblical studies or ministry leadership. On the graduate level, MDL offers a master of arts in applied biblical studies completely online, with thorough interactions with professors and fellow students, as well as self-study.

Meanwhile Moody Publishers has extended D. L. Moody's vision for inexpensive books by adding e-books that can be read on Amazon's Kindle, Barnes & Noble's Nook, and many other electronic reading devices introduced in the twenty-first century. Audio books allow readers to listen on the road and, of course, traditional hardback and paperback books fill bookshelves. Its vision statement declares that Moody Publishers is committed to helping readers "know, love, and serve Jesus Christ."

In 1926, Moody Bible Institute, known for its education and publishing divisions, added broadcasting with radio station WMBI in Chicago. Today, the Moody Broadcasting Network, known simply as Moody Radio, has thirty-five owned-and-operated stations from coast-to-coast. It offers network-produced programming including *Midday Connection, In the Market with Janet Parshall,* and *Music Through the Night* that is broadcast via satellite to more than twelve hundred outlets. With audio streaming via the Internet, the programs have an international audience.

In 2007, round-the-clock broadcasting began with three audio channels heard wherever someone turns on a personal computer, electronic tablet, or smartphone and links to the Internet. *Proclaim!* offers inspiring messages from well-known communicators. *Majesty Radio* features classic hymns and sacred music. *Praise & Worship* reminds listeners of the greatness of God and His salvation offered to mankind.

And so the gospel message that Dwight L. Moody loved to proclaim in the United States and abroad continues through the teaching, publishing, and broadcasting ministries of Moody Bible Institute. The words of Moody in October 1899 remain true today. "I didn't realize we'd done that well!" he remarked upon reading an institute report. Those proclamation ministries reflect MBI's current vision: Biblical Mission, Global Vision.

In addition to founding Moody Bible Institute, the Bible Institute Colportage Association, Northfield Seminary for girls, Mount Hermon School for boys, and Northfield Bible Training School, D. L. Moody also established the 1,500 seat Illinois Street Church in 1864. From it would arise the Moody Church. Today that church, 150 years old, has retained and extended the evangelistic vision of its founder, D. L. Moody.

As one of the deacons of the Illinois Street Church, Moody helped secure its first pastor, J. H. Harwood. When the Great Chicago Fire, fed by wooden sidewalks, roared through the downtown October 8, 1871, both Moody's home and the church were among its victims. But weeks after the fire, the temporary North Side Tabernacle (1871–1876) rose. There worshipers attended on Sundays and during weekdays the church, "concerned with the practical aspects of the Gospel . . . provided food clothing, and comfort for the destitute."[1]

Two years after the fire, members began raising funds to build a solid brick church on the corner of Chicago Avenue and LaSalle Street. The entire congregation seemed to participate—children even donated their nickels to buy bricks—and so did Moody and his soloist and accompanist Ira Sankey, who donated $35,000 in royalties from their hymnbook, highly popular in the United Kingdom.[2] The Chicago Avenue Church, dedicated in June 1876, would include some outstanding pastors the next thirty-eight years years, including Wheaton College President Charles A. Blanchard (1891–1893) and Moody Bible Institute superintendent and later president, Reuben A. Torrey (1894–1906).

The church D. L. Moody founded outgrew its Chicago Avenue location and in 1914 temporarily occupied the 5,000 seat "Big Tabernacle" on the corner of North Avenue and Clark Street. There between the Sunday services, the tabernacle held evangelistic meetings most weekdays. Many of the new believers joined the church. Its heart for evangelism was apparent, and in 1916, amid the brutality of World War I, thirty-seven members were serving as missionaries around the world.[3]

The tabernacle was spacious, but the barnlike structure was strewn with sawdust on its floors and was in need of repairs. Within three years the church purchased the tabernacle lot and once again prepared to raise funds for another major building program. In 1924 the cornerstone was laid on the new building, initially called the Moody Memorial Church and today known as the Moody Church. A plaque near the entrance remains today, identical to a sign Mr. Moody had placed inside the original Illinois Street Church: "Ever welcome to this house of God are strangers and the poor." The welcome carpet was out to the community, young and old, well-off and destitute.

Moody Church today remains a beacon to the city. More than seventy countries are represented in the congregation, and "the church celebrates diversity rather than shies away from it." (It welcomed its first African-American members in 1962.)[4] Today its summer youth and sports (basketball and soccer) camps, eighty-four missionaries, women's care, and Hispanic ministry are among many ways the church reaches its community and the world. After 150 years, Moody Church remains a spiritual anchor for Chicago.

SELECT ANNOTATED BIBLIOGRAPHY

Any biographer of D. L. Moody is fortunate in the key sources that may be consulted. Here are nine sources that have been of great value to my research.

Dorsett, Lyle W. *A Passion for Souls: The Life of D. L. Moody.* Chicago: Moody, 1997.

Painstakingly researched, with full access to family papers from all major repositories, this biography reflects the skill and gifts of a trained historian and author, noted for his fine books about C. S. Lewis. This biography is lucid and reflective, while its pages are studded with source materials that bring Moody and his world to life.

Evensen, Bruce J. *God's Man for the Gilded Age: D. L. Moody and the Rise of Modern Mass Evangelism.* New York: Oxford University Press, 2003.

This is a magisterial account of D. L. Moody and his age, a fascinating and carefully documented account of how Moody became a unique figure: a man of vibrant faith and philanthropy—yet a man who was also a skilled administrator and innovator. In an era when the power of mass media was just beginning to be felt, Moody was truly a man made for his times.

Fitt, Arthur Percy. *Moody Still Lives: Word Pictures of D. L. Moody.* Chicago: F. H. Revell, 1936.

Written by Moody's Irish-born son-in-law, A. P. Fitt, this book presents a near view of D. L. Moody through the lens of his home life and habits of the heart. It also explores all aspects of his life and work, even as it considers their relevance and power in 1936, the eve of the 100th anniversary of Moody's birth.

George, Timothy, ed. *Mr. Moody and the Evangelical Tradition.* London: T & T Clark International, 2005.

This collection of essays reflects the best of academic thinking about the entire landscape of Moody's life and legacy. It is rigorous in scholarship, while compelling in content. Reflections on Moody's theology, cultural impact, and enduring legacy are hallmarks of this book.

Goss, Charles, and D. L. Moody. *Echoes from the Pulpit and Platform*. Hartford, CT: Worthington & Co., 1900.

Charles Goss's well-considered brief memoir of Moody opens this stout volume, and its remaining pages are devoted to presenting a veritable trove of D. L. Moody's sermons, all recorded verbatim by one of the finest stenographers of the late 1890s. If one wishes to experience Moody's sermon craft and pulpit presence, this is the best source to consult.

Moody, Paul D., *My Father: An Intimate Portrait of D. L. Moody*. Boston: Little, Brown and Company, 1938.

Written by D. L. Moody's youngest son, Paul, this book remains an authoritative text about the philanthropist, preacher, and educator. Paul Moody was a distinguished preacher in his own right, and later president of Middlebury College. This book was published under the auspices of the Atlantic Monthly Press, and it received a fulsome review from the Pulitzer Prize–winning poet Robert P. Tristram Coffin.

Moody, William R. *The Life of Dwight L. Moody*. London: Morgan and Scott, 1900.

Written by D. L. Moody's eldest son, this book remains an authoritative life story, rich in its citations of primary source materials. Chief among these are D. L. Moody's letters, other family papers, and the many lengthy and revealing recollections written specifically for this book by D. L. Moody's surviving friends. Assisted by John Bancroft Devins, the well-known editor of the *New York Observer*, Will Moody crafted a lengthy and compelling book of just over five hundred pages.

Pollock, John Charles. *Moody*. New York: Macmillan, 1963.

Written in close cooperation with the Moody family, with full access to papers then privately held, and drawing on extensive interviews with D. L. Moody's only surviving daughter-in-law, May Whittle Moody, this book represents the best type of narrative history. Carefully researched and crafted, it mingles both a sense of immediacy and authority. D. L. Moody emerges from its pages as a compelling, vibrant figure.

Vincent, James. *The MBI Story: The Vision and Worldwide Impact of Moody Bible Institute*. Chicago: Moody, 2011.

Comprehensive in scope, rich in documentation from archival sources, *The MBI Story* traces the history of Moody Bible Institute from the days of its founder and namesake, D. L. Moody, to its 125th anniversary. Scholars and general readers alike, indeed anyone who seeks to thoroughly explore all facets of MBI's storied legacy, would do well to begin here.

SUBJECT INDEX

Page numbers in *italics* denote illustrations.

PERSONS INDEX

Page numbers in *italics* denote illustrations.

ISBN-10: 0-8024-5181-0
ISBN-13: 978-0-8024-5181-1

The world has yet to see what God can do with a man fully consecrated to Him. These words, spoken to D.L. Moody by a fellow evangelist, fired his imagination and gave him a vision for living all out to the glory of God. "By God's help, I aim to be that man," Moody said.

Lyle Dorsett's lucid, thoughtful prose reveals the heart of this great evangelist, recounting his life and realistically probing his strengths, weaknesses, virtues, faults, triumphs, struggles, and motivations to find a man after God's own heart.

"I thoroughly enjoyed each chapter and gladly recommend it. Chapter four alone, on Moody and the Civil War, is worth the price of the book."

–George Sweeting,
Chancellor Emeritus, Moody Bible Institute

by Author Lyle Dorsett
Find it now at your favorite local or online bookstore.

www.MoodyPublishers.com

From the Word to Life

Moody Radio produces and delivers compelling programs filled with biblical insights and creative expressions of faith that help you take the next step in your relationship with Christ.

You can hear Moody Radio on 36 stations and more than 1,500 radio outlets across the U.S. and Canada. Or listen on your smartphone with the Moody Radio app!

www.moodyradio.org